3|09

D1236200

WITHDRAWN

Down in Orburndale

Down in

Orburndale

A Songwriter's Youth in Old Florida

Bobby Braddock

LOUISIANA STATE UNIVERSITY PRESS ✦ BATON ROUGE

Published by Louisiana State University Press
Copyright © 2007 by Bobby Braddock
All rights reserved
Manufactured in the United States of America
FIRST PRINTING

DESIGNER: *Amanda McDonald Scallan*
TYPEFACES: *Whitman, Swing, and Haettenweiler*
PRINTER AND BINDER: *Edwards Brothers, Inc.*

Library of Congress Cataloging-in-Publication Data

Braddock, Bobby.
Down in Orburndale : a songwriter's youth in old Florida /
Bobby Braddock.
    p. cm.
ISBN-13: 978-0-8071-3222-7 (cloth : alk. paper)
1. Braddock, Bobby. 2. Composers—United States—
Biography. 3. Singers—United States—Biography. I. Title.
ML410.B7787A3 2007
782.421642092—dc22
[B]
                                    2006022148

Photograph on p. 98 courtesy Special Collections Department,
Georgia State University Library. Background image on
p. 150 from U.S. Department of Defense archives. Photograph
on p. 178 courtesy Carl E. Chambers. Photographs on p. 206
courtesy Ken Ashburn. All other images from author's personal
collection.

The paper in this book meets the guidelines for permanence
and durability of the Committee on Production Guidelines for
Book Longevity of the Council on Library Resources. ∞

I dedicate this book to the
memory of my parents,
Paul and Lavonia Braddock

The South moves north, the North moves south
A star is born, a star burns out
The only thing that stays the same
Is everything changes, everything changes

"Time Marches On," Bobby Braddock
©Sony/ATV 1996

CONTENTS

ACKNOWLEDGMENTS

When I first got it in my head that I was going to write a book about things I did and people I knew, long ago and far away, I was a babe all over again, and I would still be wandering around naked and lost if not for my friend John Egerton, the renowned Southern writer who has served as my instructor, mentor, critic, line editor, advocate-in-chief, and, whether he likes it or not, agent.

As I trudged along, learning *how* to write a book *as I wrote it,* I was indeed fortunate to have friends who believed in me enough to support me or liked me enough to indulge me, in either case eliciting my undying gratitude. There are four people who let me burden them with my book, chapter by chapter—bound together by Kinko's coil spring—and often page by page and phrase by phrase, delivered over the phone or by e-mail: author and journalist Michael Kosser, my songwriting friend Kathy Locke, my book-loving friend Chari Pirtle, and my much loved only child, Lauren Braddock Havey.

The long and probably incomplete list of first readers who tackled my complete manuscript in various incarnations include Lep Andrews, Tami Andrews, Carmen Beecher, David Bellamy, Howard Bellamy, Matraca Berg, Woody Bomar, JoAnn Braddock, Paul Braddock Jr., Walter Campbell, Marshall Chapman, Don Cook, Stanley Cox, Lynn Franklin, Dixie Gamble, Stephanie Gibbs-Walker, James M. Havey, James M. Havey Jr., Karen Hellard, Maggy Hurchalla, Lee Hutchinson, Tammy Jacobs, Arlene Kortright, Shannon McCombs, Don Pace, Lois Pace, Ed Petterson, Alice Randall, Sparky Reed, Janet Reno, Bob Robison, Ed Seay, Troy Tomlinson, Ron Watson, and Paul Worley.

And there are those who helped me out when long-term memory, reference books, and the Internet failed, including Wayne Aman, Ken Ashburn, Red Cannon, Herman Hess, Tony Purvis, Dot Taylor, Jay Taylor, and Jimmy Watford.

I must give a special tip of the hat to Carmen Beecher for the wonderful maps she drew for this book and to Dennis Carney, the great photographer and computer genius who assisted me in the production of the chapter pictures.

Last but not least is my acknowledgment of LSU Press executive editor John Easterly, who has so kindly and graciously welcomed me and made me feel so much at home in this new world of words without music.

To all of the above I give a big, hearty *thank you*. I have truly had a lot of wonderful help in re-creating a young Southern life and writing a book called *Down in Orburndale*.

Although this story is entirely true, many names—and in some cases addresses or hometowns—have been changed to preserve the privacy of unwitting book characters. The author has used real names of immediate family, most other relatives, and most close male friends.

ORBURNDALE

On a hot July night in 1884, Major Louis McClain sat in his tent, reading his mail in the flickering light of a kerosene lantern. Major McClain, a civil engineer, had written a journalist friend in Boston, telling him that he was laying out the streets for a brand new rail-road village on the Central Florida frontier. He had described the many beautiful lakes in the vicinity. On this night, he lit his pipe as he read the response from his friend, who wrote, "My wife tells me that your description of that region down there reminds her of the town where she spent her childhood, Auburndale, Massachusetts." The major liked the sound of that and decided to name this new town Auburndale.

In the coming decades, the area was settled by people who came to find work in what would become the leading citrus-producing county in America. Most of the settlers were from small farms in North Florida, Georgia, and Alabama, and the pronunciation of Auburndale became "Orburndale." Not everyone called it that, but enough did that it sort of stuck and became a second name.

I grew up in "Orburndale" long after it was a new town in the wilderness but long before it became a part of the Tampa-Orlando urban sprawl. The comedy and tragedy and true romance that un-folds in these pages takes place around the middle of the twentieth century in an area and an era now gone: rural and small-town Cen-tral Florida before Disney World. Little balls of gold covered the sur-rounding countryside like weeds and wildflowers, as far as the eye could see. This was the land that shaped me and set me in motion on a crazy uncharted course that became a magical, musical journey. And this is a chronicle of that long-ago journey and the unforgettable characters I met along the way. This is the story of another place and another time.

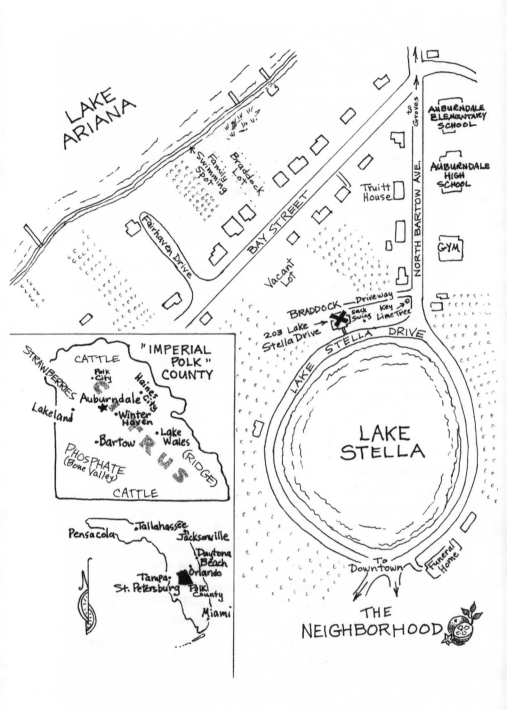

LAKE ARIANA

Family Swimming Spot

Braddock Lot

Fairhaven Drive

BAY STREET

Truitt House

to Groves

NORTH BARTON AVE.

AUBURNDALE ELEMENTARY SCHOOL

AUBURNDALE HIGH SCHOOL

GYM

Vacant Lot

BRADDOCK — Driveway
203 Lake Stella Drive → ✗ sack swing   Key Lime Tree

LAKE STELLA DRIVE

LAKE STELLA

"IMPERIAL POLK" COUNTY

STRAWBERRIES

CATTLE

Polk City

Haines City

Auburndale

Lakeland

Winter Haven

Bartow

Lake Wales

CITRUS

(RIDGE)

PHOSPHATE (Bone Valley)

CATTLE

Tallahassee

Pensacola

Jacksonville

Daytona Beach

Tampa
St. Petersburg

Orlando

Polk County

Miami

To Downtown

Funeral Home

THE NEIGHBORHOOD

Down in Orburndale

CHAPTER ONE

Poggy Boy and Boney Girl

P.E. SENT A telegram to his sister that read, "The doctor seems to think Lavonia will be all right, but the baby will probably not make it." That was me he was referring to, and when your baby's positioned to come out feet first, as I was—with his destiny in the hands of an octogenarian obstetrician in a small Southern city in 1940—you might view the outcome with some pessimism.

Earlier that day, in the August morning heat, Paul Edward Braddock Senior, the mayor/city manager/municipal judge of Auburndale, Florida, had gently squeezed the hand of his plumpish but attractive wife, Lavonia—at thirty-three, nearly a quarter of a century his junior—then pushed the ignition button and started the family car, a Dodge sedan. P.E., as he was known thereabouts, looked back over his shoulder, wide eyed and making loud sucking sounds, as he always did when backing the car out of the attached garage. From the car window, Lavonia waved good-bye to their small son Paulie, who stood on the walkway with her sister Ruth, as P.E. backed past the banyan tree to the turn-around spot in the backyard, then shifted into low gear as he headed out the private dirt road to North Bartow Avenue. He turned right at the key lime tree, slowly rounded the curve where the street became Lake Stella Drive, and drove past the front of the Braddock house and around Lake Stella (believed by some to be bottomless).

On the other side of the little lake, they crossed the Atlantic Coast Line railroad tracks and went past the city park and through the small downtown area to the south side of town where they turned right on Highway 92 for the ten-mile trip to the hospital in Lakeland (LAY-klun).

Calmly P.E. reassured his wife, sounding something like a deep-voiced W. C. Fields with a Southern accent, as they drove past orange groves and cow pastures and the steamy snake-infested waters of a large swamp called Saddle Creek, past the stench of a cowhide tannery, into the Lakeland city limits and onto the long boulevard that circled Lake Parker. The gray Dodge turned right onto the Dade City highway, then right again into the large parking lot at Morrell Memorial Hospital, a clay-colored three-story stucco building. My time on this earth was about to begin.

This branch of the Braddocks had come to northeastern Florida from a plantation near Savannah, Georgia, in the 1790s. P.E., the son of an older man—just as I would someday be the son of an older man—was the son of Joseph Decatur Braddock, who had enlisted in the Confederate Army while in his teens, making me one of the youngest people in America to have a grandfather in the Civil War. (As a divorced single man, I would learn that "my grandfather was in the Civil War" was not a good line to use at singles bars.)

After Joseph Decatur Braddock and his two brothers returned home from the war, they engaged in a shoot-out with the three Turner brothers in what would come to be known as the Braddock-Turner Feud. The Turner brothers, though Georgia born, had given aid and comfort to the Yankees during the war. The dead included two Turners and one Braddock. Joseph carried a bullet in his belly for the rest of his life.

Joseph married Louisa Bright in 1868. They raised a large family on a farm near the village of Seville (pronounced SEE-ville). Louisa and two of the eight children died in a typhoid fever outbreak. Joseph went broke a few years later when the Great Freeze destroyed his entire citrus crop. He couldn't afford to send my father, his youngest child, to college, as he had the older children. So Paul Edward Braddock learned a trade: telegraphy.

In the early part of the twentieth century, P.E. went to work for the railroad as a telegraph agent and followed his work down to the central part of the Florida peninsula in Polk County. Called Imperial Polk by local boosters, it was nearly twice the size of Rhode Island

and almost as large as Delaware. Polk had become Florida's premier citrus-growing county. Scattered among the hundreds of lakes were the thriving communities of Lakeland and Bartow and several smaller but fast-growing towns like Winter Haven, Haines City, Frostproof, Lake Wales, Mulberry, Fort Meade, and Auburndale. P.E. settled in Auburndale.

P.E. married a Florida-born girl named Bessie Hill. She gave him two daughters, Louise and Lucille, who would remember him as an affectionate but tyrannical father. He built a two-story house in the center of the little town and bought land in the country where he planted citrus groves. Whenever he could afford it, he bought more land and planted more groves, riding out daily from town on his bicycle to tend and oversee his orange and grapefruit trees. ("They're the prettiest ahhran-ges in Polk County, Flahrr-da," he often said.)

He soon began to expand his horizons, growing and shipping watermelons and tomatoes, selling real estate, becoming an officer at the local bank, and opening up a couple of drugstores. By the 1920s, P. E. Braddock was a wealthy man. Bessie Braddock was a jealous woman and had reason to be. So the Braddocks got a divorce, an anomaly in a small Southern town in 1922.

Eunice Lavonia Valentine was a slender, good-looking Georgia girl, with a sharp-featured face that betrayed the mingling of the English and the Scots-Irish with the Native Americans. It was said that Lavonia smiled from ear to ear, and she smiled just as big with her deep green eyes. She had an innate sweetness and kindness, and even her little barbs of criticism were preceded by a nervous laugh and followed by a big smile as she changed the subject.

This daughter of an itinerant farmer was part of a large family that lived in a little house on Pine Street. When they moved to Auburndale, it was 1923, and Lavonia was sweet sixteen. The town had a population of about one thousand, and a lot of poor people from the farms of Georgia and Alabama, like the Valentines, were moving down to this place called "Orburndale" to work in the citrus industry, either picking fruit or packing it.

The day she moved to town, Lavonia heard about the Braddocks, the *divorced* Braddocks. One Sunday afternoon, at the weekly concert in the city park, her next-door neighbor girlfriend nudged her and said, *"That's him, Lavonia, that's him!"* P.E. was wearing a vanilla ice cream–colored suit, and had a young redhead hanging on his arm. He was a handsome older man, despite the alcoholic bags under his intense blue eyes.

In such a small town, everyone knew everyone else in their own age group, so Lavonia became friends with the two Braddock girls, Louise and Lucille. They often went to Pebwah Drugstore ("Peb" for P. E. Braddock and "wah" for W. A. Hobby, the pharmacist half of the partnership). P.E., who had tried unsuccessfully several times to get a foot-traveling Lavonia to accept a lift in his Cadillac roadster, would serve free ice cream treats to his daughters and their girlfriends, and sometimes took them for a joy ride in his car. Eventually, Lavonia ended up sitting next to P.E.

She was drawn to his old-fashioned courtliness and his never-ending play-on-words sense of humor. She accepted his offer of a job at People's Bank of Auburndale, where he was vice-president. Because he didn't like to eat alone, she would join him for lunch at the little café down the street. When her mother hemorrhaged to death after delivering a stillborn child, the poor girl and the middle-aged "mover and shaker" became closer. By 1926, when she was nineteen and he was forty-three, they had become a major item.

Louise and Lucille didn't mind their friend dating their father because, after all, he had dated a lot of young women. But they weren't too pleased when they realized their Dad was madly in love and talking marriage. Though P.E. was head over heels, Lavonia was slower to come around. There were a lot of Auburndale boys who were crazy about her—they didn't like this old guy alienating her affections by sending her flowers and buying her candy and little gifts.

And P.E. was one hell of a Sunday date. There would be a forty-mile trip to Tampa for dinner at a Spanish restaurant where he would tip the orchestra to play what he had decided was *their* song, "Always." Next he would take her to a vaudeville show. Then on the journey back to Auburndale, they would stop off in Lakeland, at a drugstore he owned, where he would fix them ice cream sodas.

He wrote her a lot of letters on business trips he took to Tennessee or North Carolina or Rhode Island, or when she was out of town, visiting her cousins in Georgia. Constantly, he would ask, "Are you being true to me?" or he would write, "I hope you're being true." In his beautifully elegant and elaborate handwriting, he told her, "I haven't even looked at another girl or woman since I left you," and he probably meant it. P.E. had it bad. When it seemed that he might be losing her, he nobly and pitifully declared, "Dear, it will not be long 'til *he* comes again, and it would hardly seem right for me to go 'round with you and then take a backseat when he comes, as I did before, so I think it is best for you, dear, and best for me that we don't see each other again." But as soon as he had written it, his pen cried out in despair, "Oh! My God! How am I to live away from *you, my only love, my life?*"

She stuck with this dramatic, badly smitten man. Before the big depression hit, Florida had its own depression, when the state's real estate boom went bust. P.E. didn't lose everything, but he lost his wealth, and though he would always remain comfortable from the income of two hundred acres of citrus groves plus scattered rental properties around town, he would never again be a rich man.

P.E. had loaned out a lot of money that he never got back. One day, as he and Lavonia were driving through Auburndale, he saw a familiar figure climbing out of a red Model-A coupe at the Ford Garage, a man who owed him several thousand dollars but hadn't paid him back a cent. P.E. slammed on the brakes, jumped out of his car, and, gritting his teeth from the side of his mouth like Popeye, yelled, "You dirty skunk!" and started strangling the man. Luckily, a local policeman happened along and pulled him off, and the insolvent debtor managed to get away.

The farmer-businessman and the sharecropper's daughter shared many adventures, like the bank robbery which resulted in them both being tied up after P.E. tried to take the gun away from the robber, then somehow—with both hands tied behind him—managed to toss the key *into* the vault. When the escaping bandit was gunned down in his getaway car in front of the bank, a lady screamed, "Get a *doctor!*"

"Doctor, hell-l-l," P.E. declared in his W. C. Fields-talks-Southern voice, "if he's not *dead*, shoot him *againnnn!*"

Lavonia was at P. E's side while he was recovering from a near-fatal car wreck he had been involved in with a drinking buddy. When her mother passed away, she felt an obligation to raise her little brothers, and Lavonia kept postponing marriage. But she and Paul got closer and closer, and her letters had become as mushy as his. She called him "Poggy Boy," and he called her "Boney Girl."

The Braddocks and the Valentines had been fellow travelers for two centuries, taking the same journey from the British Isles to South Carolina, where P.E.'s wealthy ancestors fought for independence and Lavonia's poor ancestors fought for the king, moving on down across land and time to Georgia and then to Florida. They finally united in marriage at the Polk County courthouse in Bartow in August of 1933.

Paul Edward Braddock Jr. was born December 15, 1936, at Morrell Memorial Hospital in Lakeland, at a time when most Auburndale babies were born at home. P.E. was proud, at a late age, to finally have a son.

On August 5, 1940, Lavonia hoped to get a daughter, but it wasn't to be. A second son *almost* wasn't to be. Things didn't look so good on this hot afternoon. Lavonia, always slender, had gained over fifty pounds during her pregnancy, the doctor was in his eighties, and the eleven-pound baby was trying to come out feet first.

MAYOR SAYS IT'S A BOY!

Mayor and Mrs. Paul Braddock are the proud parents of an eleven pound baby boy, named Robert Valentine Braddock. He was born August 5 at Morrell Memorial Hospital in Lakeland. Mayor Braddock reports both mother and baby are doing well. Robert has an older brother, Paul Jr., who will be four in December. The Braddocks reside at 203 Lake Stella Drive.

CHAPTER TWO

Lake Stella Stories

I T WAS A FEELING of terror beyond words. The dream was always the same: a feeling of impending disaster, followed by a deadly impact that touched off a gigantic fiery explosion. My top-of-my-lungs scream awakened the entire household. Why would a little tiny boy have such a big horrible dream? Again and again?

Forty-something years later, in a hypnotic "regression" session, I would tell a New Age practitioner that the nightmare was about my past life as a German named Herman who was blown up in an airplane during the invasion of Poland. Was nineteen-year-old Herman one of the very few in the Luftwaffe to be shot down by the Polish Air Force? And if there is such a thing as reincarnation, why did I come back so quickly, eleven months after my death?

Let it be said here that this is not one of those mystical books about past lives or conversations with God. It is a story of *this* life. But I can't possibly recount the earlier years without touching on it. Those who do believe in reincarnation hold that small children, in all their innocence, still carry some past life residue. They point to some toddler, who, having learned only a few words in his native tongue, suddenly speaks flawless ancient Portuguese. Or how about the American man who, throughout his life, spoke German in his sleep? That man would be me. I can only say that it happens, but I can't tell you why.

In September of 1942, a hit song blaring from America's radios was urging the country's young women, "Don't Sit Under the Apple Tree" with anyone else but their sweethearts who would someday come marching home from the war. My mother had four brothers serving in the military. Her baby brother Junior was a twenty-one-year-old marine, jumping into foxholes as Japanese planes opened fire over Guadalcanal, an island in the South Pacific. Her fun-loving, guitar-playing brother Elton was in the U.S. Army and had come home on leave to be married in our house. Though I was only two, I clearly recall sitting on my mother's lap as my uncle, wearing his uniform, stood facing his bride in front of the candlelit mantel.

My earliest recurring memory is of me lying in my dark bedroom, listening through my open window to the dissonant harmonies of the crickets and rain frogs and alligators down by Lake Stella. I could barely hear the radio playing in the living room (which we called the front room), and there was a muted conversation between my parents and my older brother Paulie, who got to stay up later than I did. I was comforted by the sound of a train rolling into Auburndale, just across the little lake and up one street, reassured to know there was somebody out there. There would be the occasional sound of a car hitting the bump on Bay Street, which ran between the parklike lot behind our house and big Lake Ariana. And every once in a while, there was the distant laughter and piano playing of some grown-ups having a party, though I never knew who or where they were.

I have no memories of a drinking father. Daddy became a *reformed* alcoholic when I was two. Mother was the reformer. Polk County was the most heavily populated "dry" county in Florida. Family man that he was, Daddy did his drinking at home, though local legend had it that he once took part of the garage with him as he drove downtown. The final straw was when a well-to-do family friend, a matronly, wid-owed, winter resident from Ohio named Mrs. Tidball, came to our house and saw Daddy passed out on the floor, just inside the door—in his underwear. That did it for Mother! She started pouring syrup of ipecac, which induces vomiting, into his whiskey bottles. One day he drawled, "I just cannn't keep that stuff on my *stomach* anymooore." He became a teetotaler. Until his dying day, he never knew it was Mother's sweet manipulation that slew the mighty beast alcohol.

Years later, in my teens, I would begin to call my parents Mom and Dad, and my brother would insist on being called Paul, instead of

Paulie, which he disliked. But in these early years, they were Mother and Daddy and Paulie.

The house at 203 Lake Stella Drive looms larger in my memory than it was in fact. But it was large enough, a pretty white stucco house with a red roof. Company would come in from North Bartow Avenue on the long dirt driveway to the right of the house, but a salesman or someone asking directions would pull up in front of the house on Lake Stella Drive. There were royal palms (and oaks, before the big hurricane of 1944) in the front yard, which was lush with shrubbery and ablaze with azaleas and poinsettias, a tribute to my green-thumbed parents. A red sidewalk led up the hill (a hill only by flatland standards) to the red steps that had huge planters on each side. Tropical foliage was everywhere. The big screened front porch was surrounded by a red awning, monogrammed with a large "B." I once saw an aggressive lizard biting the neck and riding the back of another lizard on the outside of the front porch screen. "Mother, come look at the *lizards! What* are they *doing?*" Mother swatted the screen with a broom from the inside, sending the lizards flying into the front yard, Mrs. Lizard feeling the earth move under her feet in a moment of passion.

I associate the age of three with fear. Just after turning three, I saw the remains of a little military plane about an hour after it had crashed in my Uncle Monte's backyard, near Haines City—an incident that, along with my fireball nightmares, solidified a gigantic flying phobia. I was afraid of the fire truck, a relic from the 1920s nicknamed "Old Lizzie." I was afraid of the noisy old garbage truck (I would scream every time I heard it coming up our long dirt-road driveway) until Daddy arranged for the garbage men to take us for a ride in it around Lake Stella, to show me it was okay.

At the time of the Civil War, when most of its population was in the northern part of the state, Florida was among the deepest of the Deep South, and was the third state—after South Carolina and Mississippi—to secede from the union. In the twentieth century, the state's warm climate had begun to attract large numbers of people from the cold North, at first to the lower east coast, next to the west coast. Gradually, the Yankee invasion moved inward then upward, quietly but deliberately changing the landscape like a tsunami, and today Florida has become the least "Southern" of the Southern states.

From the time of my birth to the time of this writing, Auburndale's population has quadrupled—many of the more recent arrivals coming from the Northeast, the Midwest, and below the border—but in the 1940s, it was a small country town, and *very* Southern; it was *Orburndale*. The people who worked at the packing houses and citrus processing plants lived in little frame or concrete block houses in town. The black agricultural workers lived in the southeast part of town known as "the quarters." The white grove workers and fruit pickers tended to live out in the "flatwoods" or near the groves. The nicer homes, town or country, were usually on or close to the many lakes in the area.

Every Saturday afternoon, multitudes from miles around came to the middle of town to buy groceries, or shop at the drugstore or dime store or feed store. There was a vacant lot in the middle of the city where street evangelists preached to anyone who would listen, and where Mr. Hancock collected money from subscribers to the *Tampa Tribune*.

There were four blue stars on a white banner on our front door, one for each of my mother's brothers in the military. There was a big billboard across from the city park that listed all the Auburndale boys who were in the service, with a gold star next to the names of those who had given their lives. One local lady heard her absent son call out her name, and later learned that it had been at that exact moment that he was killed in action. In an almost total unanimity not seen before or since, millions of young men were joining forces with those of fifty other nations in an attempt to stop despots who intended to literally take over the world; our boys were out there saving America.

America had its beginnings as a racist, slavery-condoning society.

Even the Great Emancipator, Abraham Lincoln, had views that may sound segregationist and bigoted in this more enlightened age. America's mores changed over time, but in the 1940s the South had not caught up with the rest of the nation and was still deeply rooted in its past.

My parents didn't use the word *nigger.* They used either the universally accepted designation *colored,* which African Americans then called themselves, or the typical Southern mispronunciation of *Negro* in that era, *nigra.* I never heard them say an unkind word to a black person or call an African American man *boy.* Their philosophy was one of paternalism, like the O'Hara family's attitude toward Mammy in *Gone with the Wind.* What it amounted to was a polite way of maintaining racial superiority. I think white Southerners were naïve enough to believe that blacks really liked things the way they were. It took a great uprising in the 1950s and 1960s to show us otherwise. But to pretend that things in those days were not the way they were, or to pretend that my neighbors and my family and I were not a part of it, would be to disguise the truth.

A lot of people in our neighborhood had "maids." It was a Southern tradition for African American domestic workers to ride in the backseat of the white folks' car, enter the white folks' house from the back door, and eat their midday meal there at a separate table with their designated utensils. I wondered why our housekeeper at the time, whether it was Queen Esther or Josephine or Retha, was forbidden to ride next to my father in our Lincoln Zephyr sedan, but it was okay for her to ride next to him in the Plymouth coupe, which had no backseat. If it was okay to sit next to the driver in the Plymouth, then why not in the Lincoln Zephyr also? I never challenged it, but I wondered.

I also wondered about the black children who bought ice cream cones at Taylor's Rexall Drugs. They had to buy theirs at the side door and take it outside, while we white kids got to sit on the big red stools at the counter. I never challenged it, but I wondered.

Daddy was the consummate Southern gentleman. The former mayor (he chose not to run for reelection) would drive through town tipping his hat to every lady he saw, whether they were walking or driving, greeting them, not loud enough for anyone but me to hear, with a "How *do?*" or sometimes just "*do.*"

He called me his pal and enjoyed taking me along to the orange groves, where he would let me examine the fruit with his magnifying glass, to see if there were any *rust mites*. In the groves (only a Yankee would call them orchards), he wore combat boots, khaki shirt and pants, and a sort of African safari helmet or pith helmet, which he called a cooter shell hat.

He was a very affectionate and loving man, but also a very strict disciplinarian. In the old Southern tradition, he kissed his children on the mouth, his little boys as well as his grown daughters. I never knew whether I was going to get a juicy kiss or the hell beat out of me (often with multiple belts). Mother's spankings, or even switchings, were gentle by comparison.

One day as Paulie and I rode with him through downtown Auburndale, he remarked, "Now there's a cah-h-h just like *our* cah-h-h."

"Well, I'll be doggoned," I replied.

He abruptly pulled the car over to the side of the road, adjacent to the city park. "*What* did you say?" he asked. gritting his teeth from the side of his mouth like Popeye.

Meekly, haltingly, "Well . . . I'll be . . . dog . . . goned?"

Like a cobra with its hood up, his arm stood erect with the hand postured in slap position. He scowled and growled, "Don't . . . you . . . *ever* . . . use that word again." I didn't in his presence. But when I learned to *really* cuss, I did a lot of it under my breath.

Though I loved and respected my father, I was especially close to my mother. She made all my favorite pies: mincemeat, key lime, butterscotch, and pecan. She was the queen of sweet things, making such delicacies as orange marmalade, guava jelly, kumquat preserves, and my favorite, watermelon rind preserves. She took me to the grand old ornate Polk Theatre in Lakeland (with twinkling stars on the ceiling), patient with me as I constantly asked, "When's the funny part?" meaning the cartoon, usually Popeye—the character who inspired me to eat lots of spinach, which I thought would someday enable me to lift the refrigerator off the floor. At night, Mother sang me tender lullabies, such as "That Little Boy of Mine" and "Little Man, You've Had a Busy Day."

When Paulie and I were toddlers, our mother toilet trained us with the words "*beeble-beeble-beeble*"—as she ran the bathtub water to get us to "number one"—and "*grunt! GRUNT! GRUNT!*" for "number two." To us, *beeble* and *grunt* registered as nouns as well as verbs. ("Uh-oh, Paulie got some beeble on the floor.") The male appendage came to be known as "the beeble place," and the rear end was "the grunt-grunt place." In 1979, I would record an album that included a song I wrote titled "Everybody's Got a Grunt-Grunt Place," bringing my mother great mortification; she was afraid she would go down in history as the mom who made up nicknames for body parts.

Every summer or two, the Braddocks vacationed at Daytona Beach, about a hundred miles northeast of Auburndale. I could smell the salt in the air long before we crossed the Halifax River to the beach side of Daytona. As we turned right on South Atlantic Avenue, I became excited at the sight of the endless blue-green ocean with its large white-capped waves. Our destination was Membrey's Ocean Front Cottages, owned by some family friends who charged us thirty-five dollars for the week.

If I had a horrible past life experience in the air, I must have had a wonderful one at sea. I liked the ocean breeze and couldn't wait to get my feet in the water. At Daytona, the sand was so hard that people were allowed to drive on the beach at speeds not exceeding ten miles an hour. There were hot dog stands and sun-browned people in little thatched huts who rented out beach umbrellas and inflatable rafts. Daddy liked to float around on an air-filled pillowcase, until the time he got caught up in the undertow and floated out to sea. I knew Africa was on the other side of the ocean and was afraid Daddy would float away to the dark continent, but he managed to get back to the shore, to the relief of my hysterical mother.

In the summer of 1944, Uncle Junior was seeing action on another South Pacific island, Guam. The war followed us from Auburndale to Daytona Beach. In Auburndale, there were air raid drills (why would anyone want to bomb *Auburndale?*), and Daddy was an air raid warden. His job was to go around the neighborhood to make sure everyone had turned off their lights. In Daytona, it was mandatory to pull the blackout shades down over our windows at night, just in case there were any German submarines offshore. At Daytona's boardwalk amusement park arcade, there was a little apparatus that afforded me the opportunity—for the cost of ten cents—to shoot toy bullets at the likeness of Hitler or Tojo or Mussolini.

"Do they have policemen in Germany and Japan?" I asked my mother.

"I suppose they do," she said with good-natured detachment.

"Well," I queried, " if they're bad countries, then how do they know who to put in jail?"

Mother had a way of adding to her big smile a slight look of frustration as she said, "I don't *kno-w.*"

We walked out of the arcade facing the ocean. The breeze from the mighty Atlantic tempered the warmth of the July sun as the foamy waves roared in. Whenever it was within the scope of my vision, all I could see was the sea—I couldn't keep my eyes off it. Even at three or four years old, I was having a love affair with the Atlantic Ocean. The look and the scent had something to do with it, but more than anything else, it was the sound: awesome and fearsome, friendly and lonely, immediate and timeless, and beautifully haunting. On the nights we were at the beach, I would lie there in bed, comforted by something old and familiar, lulled to peaceful sleep by the moaning and sighing of an old friend.

Corporal punishment made Paulie repentant, but it made me angry and defiant, and I received more than my share of spankings. When I walked up to a lady visitor on my hands and knees, barking like a dog, Mother spanked me. When I looked up under a manikin's dress at Tecoy's Dress Shop—and sweet old Tecoy (TEE-koy) Mims said, "Oh, he only wants to see what makes it stand up" and I said, "Oh no, *that's* not what *I* wanna see"—Mother spanked me. And if she had known that I was jumping from chair to couch to chair to couch to the Latin rhythms playing on a Tampa radio station, while she was out in the kitchen, Mother would have seriously spanked me.

But Daddy's spankings, *whippings* actually, were truly something to be feared, administered in anger without restraint. I had been warned not to "run" Patsy, the family bird dog. Apparently, Daddy wasn't aware that exercise was good for a dog; he probably thought all her energy should be saved up for the hunting trips. One day he saw me "running" the dog; that is, I was running and Patsy was running after me.

"*I told you not to run the dog!*" he shouted as he came after me, pulling off his wide clear plastic belt. I managed to get inside the house and outrun my sixty-one-year-old father, locking myself in the bathroom, refusing to come out.

After what seemed like an eternity, Paulie came to the door and told me, "Daddy said if you come out, you won't get a whippin'." I came out. My father had spurts of violence, but he was a man of his word.

Though my parents administered the firm hand of justice, they also encouraged me in my creative endeavors. They bought yellow second sheets, coarser and less expensive than typing paper, for me to draw my cartoons on. I made up stories, quickly and furiously cartooning the pictures, one scene per page. I liked to draw the adventures of God and Jesus, God being an older version of Jesus. I honestly thought God's last name was Almighty because Daddy always referred to him that way. I thought God's main job was taking care of the weather because Daddy usually talked about God Almighty when there was a drought or a freeze or a storm.

On October 17, 1944, a major hurricane was in the Gulf of Mexico and seemed to be headed our way. Daddy had gotten out his hurricane maps and was listening to the radio announcer on WLAK in Lakeland, who was giving updates of the latitude and longitude location of the storm. My dad had his huge Bible in his lap and told us, "God Al-mighty will dooo as HE seeees fit."

The hurricane had hit the Florida Gulf coast about fifty miles southwest of us, and by morning it was raging across Polk County.

The electricity was off, but in the flickering kerosene lamplight, Daddy was reading the Bible through his bifocal lens and still talking about a higher power. He was, of course, worried sick about the storm destroying his citrus crop, as it was about two months before harvest time.

I knew I wasn't supposed to show it, but I was having the time of my life. The large cushions from our front porch glider had been removed to the living room, and Paulie and I used them to make a little hut. I loved hearing the loud roar of the wind and watching the horizontal sheets of heavy rain. The palm trees in the front yard were bending sideways. A little tornado had come in just ahead of the hurricane, uprooting our oak trees and damaging the front porch roof and awning.

Daddy was worried about the awning flapping around wildly in the wind and felt he needed to tie it down. Mother begged him not to go out in the severe weather, but my thin father put a couple of bricks in each pants pocket, as though they would make the difference between whether or not he blew away, and braved the vicious storm as he rolled up the awning and tied it down.

Like most Southerners in 1944, my parents were "yellow dog Democrats"—that is, they would vote for a yellow dog before they would vote for a Republican. Later in their lives, following the Southern trend, they would start voting Republican in presidential races. Mother always voted the way Daddy voted because he told her, "If we don't vote the saaame wa-ay, we cancel each other out."

Daddy thought that Franklin Roosevelt, whose Democratic coalition of Northern liberals and Southern conservatives made him unbeatable, absolutely hung the moon. He was convinced that Roosevelt's "bank holiday" in 1933 had saved America from financial ruin, and he also enjoyed the famous fireside chats on the radio. If FDR did something too liberal, Daddy blamed it on Mrs. Roosevelt. Once, when a local businessman criticized the president, my father's response was, "Noo-o-o, that was Eleanor's fault."

My four-year-old take on the election of 1944 was that a man named Dewey went to the White House in an attempt to get Roosevelt's job but was kicked out and landed on the White House lawn. I thought about it every time I heard this bird in our banyan tree screaming, "Dewey, Dewey, Dewey!"

Next to the long dirt driveway was the giant banyan tree, which we called the rubber tree. Over the next several years, it would attract kids from all over town because it was very easy to climb, considering its size. Probably a hundred names and hearts were carved on that big tree. It offered such nice shade that Daddy, who was inclined to exaggerate, would say, "You know, after raking up the leeeaves on a hot summuh day, I can sit down under that treee, and it gets so coooool that I have to go inside and get a *sweater.*"

Our house fronted on deep little Lake Stella, and behind us, on the other side of the parklike vacant lot and across Bay Street, was Lake Ariana, which has a circumference of about five miles. At night, the alligators crawled through our yard, going from one lake to the other. Paulie was becoming a good fisherman and would sometimes catch a baby gator, which he always returned to the water.

Living directly behind us on Bay Street was a good old man named P. V. Hall, who seemed to have a knack for being beholden to the Braddock family. He owed Daddy so much money during the Depression that he paid him back over the years with milk from his dairy. And when he built his lakefront house, on a lot next to a Braddock lot, about two inches of his house went over the property line onto our side. So he gave us permanent recreational privileges in his backyard on Lake Ariana. That was our official swimming place—alligators, water moccasins, and all.

"Darling, would you like to go to the groves with Daddy?" my father would often ask me, much to my delight.

So it was into the Plymouth coupe and down the long dirt driveway. Instead of turning right at the key lime tree, toward town, we turned left onto North Bartow Avenue, which became Ariana Boulevard and circled the big lake, taking us north of town and into the country. The nicest homes in Auburndale were on Lake Ariana, some owned by well-to-do citrus growers, some owned by wealthy people who had retired to Florida from other states, such as the former mayor of Dayton, Ohio, or the cigarette-smoking old woman from Oklahoma who had done prison time for income tax evasion.

Except for twenty acres way across the county near Eagle Lake, the family groves were out in the country from Auburndale. There was "the eighty" (acres) just outside of town, and "the old forty" and "the young forty" a few miles farther out. Turning off Berkley Road onto Braddock Road, the clay road that led to the old forty and the young forty, we sometimes stopped off at Mrs. Johnson's house. Whether it was a beautiful twenty year old or an elderly widow woman like Mrs. Johnson, my father's approach to a female was always the same. He would remove his hat, get out of the car as he gently ran a comb through his full head of silver hair, then hum "Red River Valley" as he walked up to her. "Get any *rain* last night? Yess-s-s, I brought little Bobby along today. Nooo-o-o, Paulie's in school."

We sometimes dropped in on a small grower named Eli Jones, a real Cracker. My dad's definition of a Cracker was anyone, like himself, who was born in Florida. Eli fit the more universal definition of that term, an isolated native of the Florida backwoods.

"Oh, Mister Braddick, I shore woosh hit would rain. Oh lordy, my pore wife was so sick last night, but there warn't nothin' I could do to holp her out. She started a-vomuckin' and a-vomuckin,' and jes vomucked all night long."

When somebody badly fractured the English language, Daddy, who was proud of his own large vocabulary (which he sometimes overused), would get a tiny smile on his face. When we got back home, Mother smiled really big when he told her about Eli Jones's wife vomuckin'. My mother's smile was *very* big but not toothy. It was a big line that smiled on up into her face as far as it would go, and where the mouth left off, the eyes took over and smiled as well.

One day Mother and I rode by the fairgrounds in Winter Haven (WINNER-havun), where the annual Orange Festival was held. The area had been turned into a big prison camp, surrounded by barbed wire. "Look at all the German prisoners," she said. The men had their shirts off and were tanned; I remember that many of them were blond. "They make 'em work in the orange groves and packing houses," she continued.

When one of the German prisoners managed to escape, Daddy spent a little more time on his nightly rounds through the house. He peered cautiously from the breezeway door, opening it just enough to shine his flashlight on the adjoining patio and surrounding yard, his hand firmly grasping the snub-nosed revolver in his bathrobe pocket.

There was a glass-paned door that opened from our dining room onto the breezeway that led to the kitchen. One day in early 1945, I was pushing on the door, trying to keep Paulie from coming into the dining room, when my hands went through the glass, deeply cutting my arms and wrists.

Our pediatrician was in Lakeland, but there were two doctors in Auburndale. We usually used old Dr. Simmons, whose trail of house calls could be identified by the smell of his cigars. Apparently, Dr. Simmons couldn't be located that day. For the first and only time, we used Dr. Dougan, reputed to be an abortion doctor (abortions then were illegal) and a "dope addict." Tales of Dr. Dougan speeding through downtown late at night were legendary. Instead of taking me to Dr. Dougan's office, we went to his house; perhaps it was on a weekend. Mrs. Dougan was his nurse. As the doctor stitched my wounds, his wife said, "*Tough* little brat, isn't he?"

I was steaming. "*I'll have you know that I don't allow anybody to call me a brat!*"

I hope nobody will think little four-year-old Bobby had telekinetic powers, but that night we heard the mournful siren atop the city water tower three blocks away, beckoning the local volunteer fire department. Daddy, Paulie, and I saw a bright orange glow across Lake Ariana and drove to the blaze. Dr. Dougan's two-story house, where I had been stitched up just a few hours earlier, was burning to the ground.

Several months into 1945, I had an even more serious accident. Paulie and I were playing hide and seek. Daddy was washing the Plymouth coupe to the side of the house at the top of the hill. As Paulie slowly counted to ten underneath the rubber tree, I ran around to the front of the car and wrapped my little body around the grill, thinking I'd found a good hiding place. Apparently, the emergency brake wasn't on, because the car started rolling down the hill through our front yard, with me clinging to the front of it. The Plymouth picked up speed, with no place to go but a telephone pole or "bottomless" Lake Stella, neither one a good destination. I don't know if I jumped or fell off, but I landed on the grass just before the car hit the telephone pole. It ran over my legs, but soft little bones were protected by cushiony grass, and all I got were tire prints. However, my head was pretty badly cut up by whatever was underneath the car. I remember my family running toward me, with a look of absolute horror on their faces.

"Bobby! Bobby!" my father exclaimed, running ahead of my speechless, frightened mother.

"Are we still gonna get to go to the beach?" I asked as I sat there rubbing my bloody head.

We did indeed get to go to the beach and were there when a man on the radio said something about Japan surrendering. My father shouted, "The wah is OVER!"

When I turned five years old, my age seemed to have a real value rather than just being some number I had been taught to say. I associate age five with sitting on the front porch steps in the evening, getting a sweet whiff of orange blossoms from the surrounding countryside, or the orange juice aroma permeating the nighttime air when the juice plants were in full production. Though these two events were unlikely to occur simultaneously, in my memories they join together to ride the soft wind on a moonlit night, as the palm fronds wave in slow motion and the crickets and the night birds play their strange haunting symphony.

One might not want to let a five year-old boy venture a block away from home by himself in twenty-first-century suburbia, but it seemed perfectly safe in Auburndale for me to walk through the park-like lot behind our house, with cabbage palms and tall royal palms all around—being careful not to step barefoot on any sand spurs—then cross Bay Street and walk down a hill to the big home of the Short family on the shores of Lake Ariana. Susannah Short's father was a prominent man in town and a political friend of my father's. Mother would always tell the story of me running home one day, saying I was never going to Susannah's house anymore because she wanted to play "doctor." But Mother didn't get the whole story; I distinctly remember Susannah saying, "Let me see your *peter!*"

So if I had my first (frightening!) encounter with sexuality at age five, I also wrote my first song then. It was about Mrs. Tidball, the well-to-do widow from Ohio who spent winters in Auburndale. Paulie and I—not to her face, of course—called her Tidball. Whenever Mother left Paulie and me in the car while she made a quick run into the drugstore or the dime store, I would jump up onto the steering wheel, gripping the wheel tightly as I sat in it. Steering the wheel back and forth with my body, I would sing, to the tune of "For He's a Jolly Good Fellow," an original composition titled—for reasons long forgotten—"Tidball Sittin' Down On the Table." This was the beginning of what would become a normal part of my childhood routine: making up my own words for popular songs.

During my early years, the only regular car vacations were to Daytona Beach, or to see my half-sister and family—two counties south of Polk—because with a war going on, gas had been rationed. We once took a train trip to see my mother's sister, Aunt Ruth, in North Georgia, but it wasn't until the summer of 1946 that I went on my first long trip.

We drove to New Jersey to visit my dad's oldest sister Louise. She and another sister, Victoria, had left Florida around 1900 and had become dress designers at Macy's Department Store in New York, earning about $200 each per week, a significant salary for that time. They had both married and settled down in northern New Jersey. When Victoria had passed away earlier in 1946, Daddy had promised Louise that he would bring the family up for a visit in the summer.

In those days, there were no motels as we know them today. In the towns and cities, there were hotels, and there were houses that had florescent signs advertising guest rooms. Out on the highways were what they called tourist cabins or motor courts. In the Carolina twilight, we enjoyed the scent of pine needles and fresh cut grass as we sat in lawn chairs in front of a motor court. Daddy, who never met a stranger, was talking to the proprietor about the prettiest ahhranges in Polk County Flahrr-da. The owner, a ruddy-faced man, was wearing a pistol in a holster, explaining that there had been a rash of robberies in the area lately.

"Don't blame you for carrying a gun, I'd do the saaame thing," P. E. Braddock declared, then proceeded to tell the man about the great bank robbery of 1927.

As the Lincoln Zephyr headed up the eastern seaboard, Daddy and Mother sang "Let Me Call You Sweetheart" and "Always" and "Let the Rest of the World Go By." We headed northward through the little cities and towns, a hot and sticky ride averaging no more than forty miles an hour in those days before air-conditioned cars or four-lane interstate highways.

At a filling station, Daddy told Mother, "I'd give just about *anything* for a good cup of coffee right now."

"Here honey, drink this coke, it has caffeine in it."

"GOD all-*MIGHTY*"—was there a hurricane coming?—"I don't know how people *drink* this stuff! It buhhrrns all the way down."

Red Bank, New Jersey, is about twenty miles from New York City as the bird flies, but twice that distance by car or rail. Aunt Louise and Uncle Charley lived there in a nice little house with a large backyard that went down to the banks of the Navesink River.

My aunts' forty-five years in the Northeast had resulted in two generations of Yankee-born relatives. The daughter of my recently departed Aunt Victoria thought it was hilarious, me saying, "I've never seen a lady smoke a *cigaREET.*"

On July 4, Daddy took Paulie and me to a street fair in Red Bank. The bright red gas balloon he bought me escaped my hands, becoming smaller and smaller until it disappeared into the summer sky. I was so upset that he said, "It's all right, darling, let's go buy another one."

The New Jersey kin had planned a picnic outing at a nearby beach the next day. I woke up sick at my stomach, so I stayed with Aunt Louise and Uncle Charley while everyone else went to the gathering.

Aunt Louise, a sweet lady who looked like my father with a wig, had bought a Walt Disney comic book to read to me. She was surprised to learn that I already knew how to read (my mother had taught me by reading me the funny papers). On the cover of the comic book was a picture of Donald Duck watching TV.

"What's *that*, Aunt Louise," I asked, pointing to the thing.

"They call it *television*," Uncle Charley said gruffly, his cigar bobbing up and down as he spoke.

"Tele-vision," I repeated slowly.

"Radio with a picture," he added. "Radio with a picture."

The next day, my stomach was bloated, and I was in terrible pain. They took me to a doctor who said it was my appendix and that it had to come out immediately. Uncle Charley said, in his gravelly New York–like Newark accent, "The man's an *alarmist,* go to another doctor first," which we did. The other doctor gave me some awful-tasting green medicine. We had planned to visit my aunt and uncle in Maine, but because of my delicate stomach condition, we went home instead.

I played out the summer being a cowboy in our yard. When Daddy played cowboy with me, he would yell, "BANG BANG!"

I thought, "That's silly, real guns don't go BANG BANG."

I also loved playing with Brownie, the liver-and-white pointer bird dog Daddy had gotten the year before for quail hunting. Whenever we yelled, "gonna get Brownie somethin' to eat," she would vigorously bang her tail against the breezeway door with a knock-knock-knocking sound. When we hid from Brownie, she would search and search, and when she found us, she would throw back her head and howl, "*a-roo a-roo a-roo,*" as though she were laughing.

"Why, that dog's almost *human*," Daddy would proudly say.

As I played around the shrubbery with the human dog and Fluffy, the white Persian cat, my big brother fished on the shore of Lake Stella, in front of the house. With his dark hair and big pleading eyes, Paulie would throughout childhood be the "handsome" one, and I, with my goofy expressions and unmanageable blond-turning-brown hair, would be the "cute" one.

At summer's end, my sweet, smiley-faced, thirty-nine-year-old mother took me a block away to Auburndale Elementary School, grades one through six, to register me for my first year. (There was no kindergarten in Auburndale.) I was wearing a checkered shirt and dorky-looking riding pants. The summer heat had given its first hint of retreat, and I noticed a scent of burning leaves in the air. When Mother and I got home, Paulie and Daddy were sitting at the card table in the living room. The phonograph was playing Dinah Shore's "Doin' What Comes Naturally," from the Irving Berlin musical, "Annie Get Your Gun." *Hey,* I thought—as I strutted through the room—*I'm a schoolboy now.*

CHAPTER THREE

School Daze

A UBURNDALE ELEMENTARY SCHOOL was a two-story brick building built in 1915. It fronted on North Bartow Avenue, half a block north of the entrance to our long driveway. There were giant mossy oak trees in the school's spacious front yard, and out back were tall Australian pines with long dark green needles that whistled in the wind. From the second floor, you could look to the left and see the roof of our house and little Lake Stella, then look to the right and see big Lake Ariana.

I was assigned to the class of Mrs. Edna Adams, a frowning woman, whom I called—not to her face of course—Miz Atom Bomb. She was not one to express outrage nor joy, and her sentences were short and snappy. One day, when a boy shoved me, I knocked him down, and Miz Atom Bomb said, "Good for you!" I already knew how to read and write and color, and I had a pretty good window to the world with our *Compton's Pictured Encyclopedias* at home, so first grade didn't seem difficult. We group sang songs like:

> I wanna wake up in the mornin'
> Where the orange blossoms grow.

I learned some countrified pronunciations from some of my classmates. *Once* was *wunst, desk* was *dest,* and when we were old enough for tests, they were called *testes.*

After the first semester, all first graders were moved about a mile away to a new facility made up of three army barracks next to a citrus grove. On one unseasonably warm winter day, during recess, I removed my shoes (envying the country kids who came to school barefooted) and, while playing tag, managed to stub my toe pretty badly on the protruding root of a grapefruit tree. "You shouldn't be taking off your shoes," Mrs. Adams quietly scolded in her munchkin voice. "You should be thankful that you *have* shoes."

My parents were *constantly* telling us we should be thankful. Whether it was breakfast, dinner (Southern for *lunch*), or supper (Southern for *dinner*), we never ate a meal at home without first expressing our gratitude to the Lord for our grits and eggs and fresh-squeezed orange juice or our fried chicken or baked ham with mashed potatoes, cow peas, okra with tomatoes, key lime pie and glass after glass of iced tea. We took turns, so I had to "say the blessin' " every fourth meal. Paul and I would express quickly mumbled perfunctory thanks, Mother would sweetly recite her standard seventeen-word prayer, and Daddy would offer up a long heartfelt benediction in his deep, resonant voice.

My mom was a member of the Church of Christ, a noncharismatic group of ultra-fundamentalists who held that there must be a "thus sayeth the Lord" for everything connected to the church. Because there was no scriptural example of it, instrumental music was not used in worship services, so the congregational singing was a cappella (and usually very good). The congregants considered themselves to be the restoration of the original church—they were fond of proclaiming "Church of Christ, founded 33 A.D."—and only those who jumped aboard that train could ride into the Kingdom of Heaven. All others would burn in Hell. Not only would the Buddhists, Hindus, Muslims, and Jews be lost, so would all other Christians besides themselves, from Mother Teresa to Billy Graham.

My mother was broad-minded enough to think that God would probably let some Baptists into Heaven too. Daddy was a Baptist, and though he rarely entered God's house, he always honored the Lord on His day by wearing a tie.

In the summer of 1947, we took a trip to Macon, Georgia, to see my mother's Uncle Jim and Aunt Claudie. Their son-in-law, with whom the old couple lived, was the jailer of the Bibb County jail. Their residence was there in the tall prison building. Apparently no white people in Macon ever broke the law in 1947 because all the inmates were black.

Then we went to Mother's nearby hometown, Gordon. Though I didn't know him, my fifth cousin Jim Williams, who would find posthumous fame as the alleged murderer of his houseboy/lover in the 1994 book *Midnight in the Garden of Good and Evil*, was born and raised in Gordon. We went there to attend the Hawthorne family reunion. Mother's first cousin, called Cousin Ben by all, was the patriarch of the Hawthorne clan.

Cousin Ben, a suspender-wearing septuagenarian, rocked on his front porch in the stifling Georgia heat and patted his brow with a handkerchief. Suddenly, Daddy started scratching himself frantically—his back, his neck, his arms and his legs.

"Whatsa mattuh, P.E.?"

"Cousin Ben, they just keeeep stickin' in me."

"Godamighty, P.E., *what's* stickin' in yuh?"

"All these *Hawthornes!*"

The next day we went to see my mother's aunt—her father's much older sister. The ancient woman gave us a vivid account of General Sherman's Yankee troops marching through Georgia when she was a young child, stealing her family's livestock and burning down their barn. As we departed, my father heading our silver blue Lincoln-Zephyr south toward Florida, I couldn't get the Yankee soldiers off my mind.

"Why did *Americans* do that to *Americans?*" I asked my mother.

She smiled her big smile, looked straight ahead, and said, " I don't *kno-w.*"

When I was seven, my parents started me on piano lessons, six years of little old ladies trying to teach me to read music when my inclination was to play by ear. It would be several years before I discovered that I could learn more piano by listening carefully to our records than from the conventional, by-the-book music teachers.

Piano lessons, in fact, turned out to be a contributing factor to one of the worst arguments my parents ever had. I recall only two major fights between my father and mother, but those incidents were violent and crazy, and I remember them vividly and powerfully. Both of them took place in the latter half of 1947.

Once Mother tried to intervene in a spanking that Daddy was about to give my brother. It was just a few minutes before Paulie was to go for his piano lesson, and she didn't want him to go there upset. My father went berserk and started choking her. When he realized what he was doing, he stopped abruptly, then bolted out of the house, and tore off down the dirt road in his Plymouth coupe. He dropped by later, long enough to leave a note on the door, implying that he was going to kill himself and informing us that we could find his car in the eighty acre grove; it was signed "The D.F. (meaning *damned fool*) that everybody hates." Around dusk he was back home. He sheepishly eased through the breezeway door and pulled me aside and whispered, "Darling, has Mother got supper ready yet?"

In retrospect, the other fight was pretty funny. I don't remember what they were angry about, but I remember them standing in their bedroom, arguing back and forth.

"Shut up!" Mother snapped.

"Don't tell *me* to shut up, *you* shut up!" Daddy roared. Mother slapped him across the face.

"DON'T YOU SLAP MY FACE!" he thundered and slapped her right back.

"DON'T YOU SLAP MY FACE!" she screamed, and on and on they went, standing there slapping each other across the face like two of the Three Stooges. This was during the hurricane of 1947, so Daddy wasn't able to get in the Plymouth coupe and drive away. Instead, he chose to lie down in the corner of the bedroom in a fetal position.

But those times were exceptions. I would describe their relationship as a loving one. She quoted him, voted like him, laughed at all his jokes and puns, and was very protective of him. He doted on her, and though she seemed to feel that he was a bit parsimonious, he would give her a Whitman's Sampler on birthdays and holidays (guess who ate most of the candy) and the biggest, laciest card he could find—inscribed with his own romantic prose and with a hundred dollar bill enclosed.

They never addressed each other by first name, except when we had company. Once engaged in conversation, they sometimes called each other *honey*, but to initiate a conversation, it was always "Hey." If they were not in the same room, they would whistle for each other, as one would call a dog.

To be dog-called by P. E. Braddock was not necessarily a sign of disrespect, because he loved his liver-and-white pointer, Brownie, only a little less than he loved the humans in his family. Some men would say Brownie wasn't worth a damn as a hunting dog because she wouldn't go into the water to retrieve a bird, but Daddy didn't seem to think it really mattered. Come fall, he usually returned from an afternoon in the woods with his hunting bag filled to the limit. That meant a wonderful meal of quail with Mother's delicious gravy. After hunting season, when Daddy brought home the quail, came the holiday season, when Daddy brought home the Christmas tree (a constantly shedding little Florida longleaf pine). Childhood memories are filed away under holidays and seasons. Or climate and weather. Like a song or a scent, they can bring back a time and a place.

It was in the late spring's warmth of 1948, while I was still seven, that I discovered my sexuality. The first girls I was attracted to were cartoon characters, such as Daisy Mae and Wolf Gal in the *Lil' Abner* comic strip. Then there were the movie stars; I was particularly hot for Yvonne DeCarlo, long before she was a Munster. I had reached an age at which the thing I was most aware of was awareness.

There is a time in one's life that evangelical Christians refer to as the Age of Accountability. I clearly recall when I reached mine; I know it now, and I knew it then. I had been given a red Schwinn bicycle for my eighth birthday; Daddy and Paulie taught me how to ride it on the playground behind the school. The first time I rode the bike around little Lake Stella, I had a feeling of freedom that I had never known before.

I turned to the right, out of our driveway—past the key lime tree—and glided down the hill, with Lake Stella on my left and our large vacant lot on the right. As I passed our house, there were Mother and Daddy, standing proudly in the front yard. Beyond the house was an orange grove belonging to the family of future U.S. senator and Florida governor Lawton Chiles. The palm fronds along the shoreline moved slightly in the summer breeze as a couple of ga-tors lay loglike in the lake. I passed a small clearing where the Baines family's house sat, then approached the fork that went downtown on the right and around the lake on the left. I continued around Lake Stella, where a couple of boys were fishing from the shore. The old Baynard mansion—soon to be Kersey Funeral Home—sat atop the hill on the right as I approached then glided by another orange grove. Having circled the lake, I rode downhill on Lake Stella Drive for the last leg of my journey. Looking straight ahead to the west, I saw the sun hovering over the treetops. It appeared to be a giant yellow-or-ange ball, an exaggerated cartoon sun, and I felt that I was pedaling right into it, entering into the knowledge and the understanding that I would need to get through life. I would never view things quite the same from that point on.

Now that I had a bicycle, I was allowed to ride it to the Auburn Theatre matinees (every time the marquee changed) instead of hav-ing my mother drop me off and pick me up. My relationship with my mom was sometimes a bit rocky once I reached adolescence, but in the first decade or so of my life she was the one thing on this earth that I knew I dearly loved. If she happened to be a little late getting home from shopping, I would be frantic, pacing the floor. Around the time I was eight years old, I didn't even call her "Mother," I called her "Angel."

Something had been eating away at me, though. I went through grades one and two without a single spanking or paddling, but I had a third-grade teacher, Mrs. Hall, a very attractive and impish young newlywed just out of college, who paddled me a lot. She paddled most of the boys; go figure. The rule at our house had always been if you got a spanking at school, then you'd get another one at home. If a teacher had killed me at school, would my parents have tried to kill me again at home? I guess it had something to do with not bringing dishonor on your family. Anyway, I had been given several paddlings but had failed to tell my parents about it, which was to me about the same as lying. I would learn to lie to my parents with no twinge of conscience when I became a wild teenager, but at eight years old, it was getting to me that I had been deceiving my Angel. I was in the front yard walking around a royal palm tree—the one with Daddy's old real estate broker sign on it. Around and around and around the tree I walked, trying to muster up the courage to tell her. I finally went to the kitchen, where she was starting to prepare supper.

"Angel, Miss Hall's given me a bunch of whippin's at school. I'm sorry. Does that mean I have to get a bunch of whippin's at home now?"

She put her arms around me and drew me close to her, and said, "No, honey."

"Are you going to tell Daddy?"

"No, honey."

The neighborhood gathering place was a screened porch on North Bartow Avenue, directly across the street from the high school. Mrs. Truitt, the mother of Paulie's best friend, Jere, held court there every day. Everyone who went there—usually teenagers—had a fine time because she was not only a good listener but very funny and a great gossip. Mrs. Truitt, who had been a college beauty queen named Helen Peek, had grown quite chubby by middle age and rarely left her cushy chair. She spoke in the accent of the old Georgia aristocracy, pronouncing road as "roared" and porch as "po-wich." Especially fun was Mrs. Truitt's commentary on the neighborhood people as they drove by—complete with her own nicknames—such as, "There goes ol' Pusseltary, he doesn't have enough sense to diiiiie." She referred to my father, not to his face of course, as "Ho," because when Daddy sneezed—it was so loud, you could hear it a block away on Mrs. Truitt's front po-wich—it sounded like he was shouting "ME HO!" Her take on Daddy combing his hair and humming as he approached a female was, "Oh look, Ho's gettin' dum-de-dummed fo' a dame."

Paulie and Jere had been best buddies for years and had fished together in every one of the dozen or so lakes around Auburndale, many times over. One Saturday summer morning, Mother was standing by the window between the record player and the telephone, looking out at our vacant lot where Daddy had hung a "sack swing"—a crocus sack filled with Spanish moss—to the big oak tree. "Hey," she called to my dad, "Jere Truitt's swingin' on the sack swing with a colored boy." I don't remember if they were doing it together or taking turns, but I do remember the controversy it caused. The Truitts were just as segregationist as my parents, but Southerners drew the lines in different places on different occasions. This young man was the son of one of Mr. Truitt's sawmill hands; their family also had a full time African American housekeeper. I think the Truitts viewed it as the plantation owner's son (Jere) playing with one of the slave children. Daddy handled it diplomatically and condescendingly.

"Jerrr-y," he called out as he walked across the lot and approached the boys.

"Oh, hey, Mr. Braddock," Jere replied.

"Listen," he said in his W.C./Foghorn voice, "You know-w-w, you boys can't dooo this, you're gonna have to run along now. Go get some ice creeeeam or a nice cold milkshake." He gave each of the boys a quarter, as if he were paying a small fine for being prejudiced.

Later that afternoon, while Daddy was headed out the long dirt driveway, Jere's sister Jean Ann, who was about my brother's age, stood alongside the road as he passed by and stuck out her tongue. Like the proverbial elephant, P. E. Braddock never forgot. Years later, when Jean Ann Truitt was crowned Miss Auburndale, Mother was *ooh*-ing and *aww*-ing about how beautiful Jean Ann looked and how glad she was that she'd won. Daddy shook his head in dismay and said, "She stuck her tongue out at me." You would have thought she had done it just that night from the stage, as they crowned her and handed her the roses.

Daytona Beach continued to be the family vacation spot. Daddy would never agree to any other kind of vacation unless it was to visit relatives. He was born in that county on a farm about thirty-five miles to the northwest, as the crow flies, when Daytona was just a newly founded village, so to him it was sort of like going home. There was talk of going out West to visit his brother, my Uncle Bright, who, as a young man, had settled in Montana and become a prosperous wheat farmer—but we never went. Mother started working on Daddy a couple of months in advance about vacation because his initial response would always be, "I'm just so-o-o busy, don't think I can manage to get awaa-ay."

As soon as we had put our luggage in the cottage, we were all on the beach. Paulie was at the water's edge with his rod and reel, I was riding the waves on a rented float, Daddy was sculpting a big sand castle—or an alligator—and Mother was sunbathing.

On one rare day when Paulie joined me in swimming, we let the current carry us down the beach two or three hundred feet. As we walked back to the area in front of Membrey's Oceanfront Cottages, I saw Mother with her hands to her face, sobbing uncontrollably and shaking all over. Way out in the ocean were two boys in trouble, and the lifeguards were trying to rescue them. She thought it was my brother and me. When I yelled "Mother," she ran to us and cried, "Oh, thank God!" I thought, "Boy, she really *does* love us, doesn't she!"

Later that afternoon, a summer storm came in from the west. As my dad and I hurried up the steps from the beach to the cottages, a bolt of lightning exploded the trunk of a cabbage palm tree just a few feet away from us. The central part of Florida has more lightning than anywhere else in America, so this wasn't our first close call; lightning had once hit the pavement between my mother and me as we crossed a street in Auburndale, and one night it had come through the crack in our front door and shot through the house like a thousand white crackling snakes. One of my father's brothers, Spicer, had been killed by lightning in 1907.

Soon after we returned home from our summer vacation, I started fourth grade back in the old building on North Bartow Avenue, in my own neighborhood.

One stormy day, Daddy came to pick me up after school so I wouldn't have to walk home in the rain. I was embarrassed when one boy said, "Hey Bobby, your gran'daddy's out there lookin' for you."

The last few months of the 1940s now play out like little movies in my mind: an alligator eating our neighbor's small dog . . . a local policeman, in front of our house, charging not only a driver but also his three passengers with speeding . . . myself, opening presents underneath the tree on a rainy yuletide day as my father sang quite seriously in his booming baritone, "I'mmmm streeeeaming from a *wet* Chris-maaaasssss." I watched in wonderment my first heralding of a new decade and pondered the various things that had been predicted for the 1950s, such as flying cars, men from Mars, and the coming of the Lord.

In 1950, Auburndale had a population of 3,763, a figure I remember to this day, and an increase of 1,000 over 1940. The population of Polk County was approximately 120,000. The biggest news in Florida was the tremendous number of people migrating from other places in the five years following World War II. The biggest news in America was the cold war, most people assuming there would eventually be a *hot* war, a nuclear one, with Russia and the world of communism. Almost every literate family subscribed to a newspaper in 1950, and most large cities had at least one morning and one afternoon paper. Most people's connection to the news in real time was the radio, though about seventy of America's largest cities had TV stations. Jack Benny still ruled radio, and Milton Berle ruled the new *small* screen. The biggest movie stars were Humphrey Bogart, Katherine Hepburn, John Wayne, James Stewart, and many others who would remain superstars to TV, video, and DVD viewers for many decades to come. While the hottest pop vocalists were people with now-forgotten names like Vaughn Monroe, Frankie Laine, and Teresa Brewer, the hottest "hillbilly" singer had a name that resonates and mystifies to this day: Hank Williams.

On a cold night in early 1950, I was a very bad boy. Daddy's nightly tub bath was a ritual that began with him washing his full head of silver hair with Packer's Tar Soap (a product he had been using since the nineteenth century) and ended with him raising his body up out of the water, bent over with his butt sticking out, as he cupped water in his hands to rinse off his face. It was an old 1920s style bathtub that was not built into the side of the wall, so one could enter the bathroom from just off the living room area and see the back of the tub and—a perfect target—Daddy's rear end. Paulie dared me to barge into the bathroom as Daddy was finishing his bath and squirt him in the butt with a water gun filled with ice water. So I went to the kitchen and filled the plastic pistol, then stood outside the bathroom door until I heard the splashing sound. That was my signal. I threw open the door and there it was, my father's skinny butt hovering just above the foot of the tub. I took careful aim, and BULLSEYE! Ice water right on the spot. He hollered and turned around—gritting his teeth on the side of his mouth like Popeye—as he swung his arm in a wide arc in an attempt to slap me. He barely missed, and his body came tumbling back down into the tub where he cracked two ribs. Mother gave me a major spanking but Paul, who masterminded the ass-squirting, got off scot-free.

Mother became more and more involved in civic organizations, which appeared to be very highfalutin to many of the everyday folk of "Orburndale." One of my classmates, a boy named James, refused to believe that my mother was even from the South. Practically all of the working people around Auburndale were Southerners, but quite a few of the rich folks—retired couples and winter residents whom we called snowbirds—were from the North; and some of the wealthiest citrus growers, like the Adamses and the Stambaughs, had Northern roots. After seeing Mother preside over a veterans dedication program in the city park, James said, "I ain't never seen nobody from *Georgy* put on airs like *that!*"

That summer we went to visit my Uncle Elton and Aunt Charlotte in Maine. Their wedding in our living room was my first memory on planet Earth. Uncle Elton had met Aunt Charlotte while stationed in Maine during the war, and settled down with her there to raise a family. On our first day there, I heard my cousin Barry, who was six, screaming at the top of his lungs. He was screaming with joy and excitement. Standing in the front yard of their Cape Cod house, he had spotted a jet, high in the sky, in a time when there were not many jets to be seen anywhere. It had taken off from a military base in nearby New Hampshire. Barry's fascination with jets would lead to a very interesting career in aeronautics and a stint as the acting head of the Federal Aviation Administration (FAA) in the Clinton years.

There was a very bad day there in Maine. Paul, Cousin Barry, and I were roughhousing on their veranda. Paul was holding my head down under a pillow, and I was kicking and clawing to get up. In a rage, Daddy pulled off his belt and gave my brother and me a severe whipping. Then he spent the rest of the day with a seriously dark cloud over his head, a gloom and depression that permeated the house and affected everyone in it. Back then, I thought he was depressed at times like that because of what *we* had done, but looking back, I think it was because of what *he* had done.

When we got back to Florida, we celebrated my tenth birthday and invited some of my friends to a weenie roast. I had many friends but no best friend. Bert Killebrew lived in town; Ranny Hughes, Allen Broxton, and Jimmy Blake lived in the country. The neighborhood kids I played with were Chuck Brown, who would one day become a state judge, and Buddy Baker, who lived in a small house behind the school, and whose father had read "gird thy loins" in the Bible, so wore a girdle every day.

As sweltering summer turned into balmy autumn, the local PTA was meeting one night at the school auditorium, about a block from our house. They passed around secret ballots to the parents and teachers for the election of new PTA officers. The two nominees for president were Mother and her best friend Lou Davidson. The Davidsons had a chicken farm out on Highway 92. When the results were announced, Mother had lost by just one vote. Afterwards, on the walk back to our house, Daddy confessed that he had voted for Mrs. Davidson. "You're already president of the wom-mannn's club and the garrr-den club," he said. "I just thought it would be tooooo much on you." As we walked past the key lime tree onto the long dirt driveway, Mother just shrugged her shoulders and smiled her big smile.

My parents always made it their business to invite our schoolteachers to dinner some night early in the new school year. I wondered why my fifth grade teacher wasn't issued an invitation. I already knew that my father didn't like her, because he typically mispronounced the names of people he didn't like, and "Mrs. DuBois"—pronounced Doo-BWA—contemptuously rolled off my father's tongue as "Mrs. DOE-BO." I later heard that Mrs. DOE-BO had been having an affair with my father's close friend, a fellow citrus grower.

Citrus was so bountiful around Auburndale that it covered not only the rural landscape but parts of the town itself. Our backyard chicken pen bordered on a ten-acre orange grove. The land was purchased by a young, bespectacled businessman named Grantland Corker, who discovered that his newly acquired property included a tiny sliver of land in front of our house, where the lawn met the street. So the *front* of our front yard actually belonged to Grantland Corker. He asked an exorbitant amount for the property; I don't remember his price, but I know it was many times the value of the land. My father refused to pay. One afternoon, Mr. Corker and an employee drove up in a pickup truck and erected an ugly wire fence across our entire front yard, along his property line. We stood there and watched them put it up.

"Grantland, you should be ashamed of yourself," said my mother, her hands on her hips.

"Your husband thinks more of his money than he does his family," Mr. Corker muttered, barely looking up.

With that, Daddy pulled out his pocket knife and called Corker a "dirty skunk." When Daddy hissed and growled "dirty skunk," it sounded even more contemptuous than "rotten sonofabitch." He opened up his pocketknife and started cleaning his fingernails as the men climbed into the truck and drove away.

The editor of the weekly *Auburndale Press*, C. S. Lecky, wrote a front-page editorial that began, "There is a house on Lake Stella Drive where an American flag flies on every national holiday." He went on to praise Daddy and Mother's service to the community, then told about "an ugly wire fence" and recalled from his own boyhood what they used to call "spite fences." He ended his editorial with, "Grantland Corker built that fence. Drive around and take a look at it." I think one of Polk County's dailies, either the *Lakeland Ledger* or the *Winter-Haven News Chief*, picked up the story, because by Sunday afternoon there was a steady stream of traffic on Lake Stella Drive. It seemed that everybody in the county was driving by our house to look at the fence.

Grantland Corker was a devout Methodist. The Methodist minister, the Rev. Elliott Rich—who everyone called "Preacher Rich"—was a very large and very jolly man who was quite popular in Auburndale. He gladly played opposite the also rotund Baptist preacher in local donkey baseball games, he was the loudest voice from the bleachers at the high school football games, and he was also my father's favorite quail-hunting buddy, so quite naturally the role of arbitrator fell on Preacher Rich. The three met at the preacher's study one afternoon, and a compromise price was agreed upon. Grantland Corker took down the fence. Daddy told us the matter was settled and that we were to never talk about it again. Sorry, Dad, but I just had to tell it.

My sixth-grade teacher was a man named Beverly Anderson. Whenever I want to take my pulse but can't find a watch, all I have to do is close my eyes and visualize the second hand on the electric clock that was on the wall over Mr. Anderson's desk. Mr. Anderson had his pluses: he let me put out a weekly class newspaper, and he let us bring records to play on Tuesdays. But he would drone on and on in his upper Midwestern accent, telling all these sons and daughters of working-class Southerners that their parents' Democratic party was evil and that the end of the world was just around the corner.

One day during recess, he kept looking up at a girl who was wearing a starched skirt and sitting on the limb of an oak tree; when she came down, I heard him softly ask her, "Have you ever heard the poem 'I See Under'?" Apparently an equal opportunity pedophile, one day Mr. Anderson asked me to stay after class, then told me he'd noticed that I'd been scratching a lot and he wanted to check me out to see if I had "crabs." He took me to the cloak room, asked me to pull down my pants and shorts, then proceeded to examine every square centimeter of my genitalia. It never occurred to me that this was something I should tell my parents about.

It was about this time that Paul and I went to see an Abbott and Costello movie at the Auburn Theater. A stranger sat down next to Paul, though there were many empty seats available. The stranger was short, probably in his mid-thirties, and appeared to have no neck. He said his name was Fred Fry. When he found out that Paul was interested in fishing, he told him he had a new boat and a Johnson outboard motor. Paul, fourteen and naïve, thought Fred was just a congenial guy who was into boats, and told Mother and Daddy that Fred had asked him to go fishing. After meeting him they reluctantly agreed but changed their minds within a couple of days. Mother had found out from a relative in Lakeland that Fred had gone hunting with her son, but it wasn't for quail, and that he had been barred from all movie theaters in that city.

One evening, shortly after supper, Fred pulled his blue Chevrolet up in front of the house, and Paul and I were standing around talking to him. He had just thrown a trivia question at us and said, "Come on, quiz kids" when I heard Daddy's voice from the front porch.

"Paulll, Bobbb-by, come on in the house, I want to talllk to Mister Fryyyyyy." He looked stately and regal in his fine bathrobe and pajamas as he walked down the sidewalk—carrying a shotgun.

"Daddy, don't *shoot* him," I gulped. Fred Fry started his car and peeled rubber for about fifty feet as he tore out of there, tires squealing all the way around Lake Stella. We never saw him again.

Paul was more athletic and outdoorsy than I was, much more rugged. In my teen years, I would make a concerted effort to be a tough guy, but at age eleven, I was still a bit of a candy ass. My year in the Boy Scouts could have been a sitcom. I stayed up all night on my first camping trip, resulting in my falling asleep at the Saturday cowboy movie the next afternoon. My parents had to guide my sleepwalking body out of the Auburn Theater after the manager, Miss Agnes Shearouse, called them up and said, "I think y'all need to come down here and get Bobby, he's havin' nightmares."

One of my favorite places to be was the soda fountain at Taylor's Rexall Drugs, sitting atop a red swivel stool drinking a cherry smash or cherry Coke, or maybe a chocolate ice cream soda with a big vanilla scoop topped with whipped cream and a maraschino cherry. I also loved the malted milkshakes; they gave you a big ice-cold aluminum blender tumbler that held an additional frothing glassful.

One hot afternoon, I finished slurping my malt then walked out the side door of Taylor's. There was a crowd gathered on both sides of Lake Avenue. Across the street, in front of Tecoy's Dress Shop, two policemen and an ambulance driver were draping a sheet over a blood-covered young woman who lay lifeless on the sidewalk. Her estranged husband had chased her from the insurance office where she worked, on the second floor of the Auburndale Hotel. After firing a pistol into her face and chest, he had run into the dress store. Poor old Tecoy Mims had stood ashen-faced and expecting to meet her maker, but the young man had run past her into one of the dressing rooms, where he shot himself in the head. All of this happened while I was drinking my malt. I rode my bicycle home and told my parents what had happened. Crimes of passion weren't unusual around Auburndale, but this was my first encounter with one.

As the summer of 1952 drew to an end, I was preparing to enter seventh grade. Daddy, as always, spent a lot of time in his groves. Like a proud father-to-be, observing the stages of his wife's gestation, he loved to watch the little green oranges grow bigger by the day.

With most of her friends back from vacations, it was time for Mother to resume her Bridge Club activities. Out came the card table that she and Daddy used for their nighttime Canasta games. After a lunch of congealed salad, red velvet cake, and iced tea, four middle-aged ladies in print dresses laughed and talked and played their game to the hum of electric fans. On one such afternoon, Daddy came in from his orange groves, speeding up the driveway into the yard, making a mad dash for the house and the john, a result of the mineral oil that he had taken the night before. The urgent and violent purgative effects of this thick, greasy laxative could bring down a rain of brown terror. BAM went the door behind him as he raced through the house. The female foursome were sitting at the card table in the living room, shuffling cards, gossiping and sipping iced tea. P.E. hurriedly tipped his hat to the ladies, then ran into the bathroom and slammed the door behind him. The bathroom adjoined a hallway that divided the living room from the dining room. It was a mere twenty feet away from the bridge game. Then came the sound and the fury. Mother started talking fast and loud, hoping to cover up the revolting noises. Imagine the sound of an elephant passing gas in a fish pond (Mother talked faster and louder), or the sound of two warships fully engaged in battle in quadraphonic sound at a huge theater (*all* the ladies started talking faster and louder). Paul and I were rolling around laughing on the dining room floor. Later that week, workmen arrived to construct a new bathroom in the *back* of our house.

In that fall of 1952, most Americans were focused on the presidential race. Election night at our house meant Daddy sitting by the radio writing down the latest election returns on his Gulf Fertilizer notepad. He had an intense interest in politics and often made his decision on who to vote for based on which candidate had the most "determined look" in the picture that ran in the *Tampa Tribune*.

Daddy's most influential acquaintance, besides Auburndale-raised General James A. Van Fleet, was probably U.S. Senator Spessard L. Holland, a Polk County native. He was a white-haired gentleman of my father's generation and a former governor. In correspondence, he and Daddy saluted each other with "Dear sir and friend." Like many Southern Democrats of the 1950s, Senator Holland was more conservative than most Republicans. When he did not publicly endorse Adlai Stevenson, his party's presidential nominee in 1952, Daddy and Mother took the senator's cue and voted for the Republican nominee, World War II hero General Dwight D. Eisenhower, who swept the country and carried along four Southern states, including Florida.

Though seventh grade was officially junior high school, our class was in the elementary school building. My teacher was Mrs. Theo Edwards Waits, who had been my fourth-grade teacher. An eccentric but brilliant woman who came from an aristocratic Louisiana family, Mrs. Waits had had us fourth graders reading Charles Dickens and memorizing Longfellow and Poe, and, once again, she was teaching us way ahead of the curve.

A lot of the kids who went to Auburndale High, which was next door to the elementary school, didn't want to eat at the school lunchroom, so they went to Taylor's Drugstore for hamburgers and French fries. Many of the older ones drove cars. Paul, not old enough to drive a car without an adult, went to town on his Cushman motor scooter. Most of the younger high school students rode bicycles or walked, as it was less than half a mile to downtown. To get to Taylor's, you had to cross the Atlantic Coastline Railroad tracks, which ran through the city park. One day, a freight train was on the tracks. Lola Ridley, a pretty eighth-grade girl, was impatient and decided to crawl under the train. She was almost through to the other side when the railroad car suddenly lurched forward several feet, the huge iron wheel slicing off the bottom half of her leg. After school, a neighborhood friend Herman Becker and I rode our bikes to the scene of the mishap to look at the remaining little pieces of flesh. That night I didn't sleep very well. Students were thereafter forbidden to leave the school area during noontime.

For several years, it had been an Auburndale after-school ritual to turn on the radio in the afternoon and listen to *The Polk County Express* over WSIR in Winter Haven. "Blow that whistle, ring that bell, listen to that engine yell," went the theme song of this weekday show that played country music three days a week and pop music the other two. One thinks of a vacuum being created after something disappears, but there was a music vacuum *before* rock 'n' roll came along. We didn't know it then, but we were waiting for it to be born.

I was *raised* on radio. Radio was a huge playroom for a child's imagination, and it was almost as if there *were* a picture, because I saw all those people in my mind. Pre-television radio was a little like 1970s TV without a picture; the networks carried variety shows and news specials and sitcoms (although they didn't call them that). But from the first moment I ever heard of television (when I was five), I dreamed about us someday having it in our home. In the spring of 1953, we got our first TV set. The only stations reaching Auburndale were channel 4 in Jacksonville and channel 38 in St. Petersburg, and neither were reliable. There might be no reception at all or a crystal-clear picture—usually it was somewhere in between. Of course, television changed our lives. Every week, Paul's friends came over for the Wednesday Night Fights, then they'd get out in the yard and box afterwards. Mother peered over her reading glasses at *I Love Lucy*, and her woo-hoo-hoo laughs could be heard out in the yard. Daddy liked *Racket Squad* because the hero's name was Captain Braddock. I liked *Dragnet*. We all liked *Father Knows Best, The Ed Sullivan Show,* and *What's My Line.*

The only TV set I had seen in Auburndale prior to our buying one was in the home of our Church of Christ preacher Thurston Lee, who had come to Auburndale a year before, from Nashville. Thurston Lee was in his mid-forties, a tall, slightly overweight man with a swarthy complexion, dark eyes, slicked-back jet-black hair parted in the middle, and a thin mustache. He looked a bit like the man in the old silent movies who tied the girl on the railroad track. He was a very prudish and moralistic man who believed dancing was proper *only* for married couples, and then in the privacy of their homes. Swearing was sinful. Alcohol was absolutely taboo. Smoking, however, was quite another matter. Maybe it was because of the church's deep roots in the tobacco-growing state of Tennessee—that plus the fact that the Bible didn't condemn cigarettes because cigarettes hadn't been invented yet—but it was quite common and acceptable for Church of Christ men in those days to light up in the churchyard when services were over. Still, it was very unusual to see a *preacher* smoking. "Brother Lee" would walk out of his residence, next door to the church, wearing an olive green suit. With a big Bible under his arm, he would suck that last big draw off his cigarette as he strode swiftly into the yard of the church, then flick the hot weed onto the sidewalk. He looked not so much like a preacher as a don emerging from a meeting of the heads of the mob families.

In the summer of 1953, we drove up to Hammond, Indiana, a steel mill suburb of Chicago where my uncle and aunt lived. Paul drove the entire distance, with Daddy saying things like "Paul-l-l, watch that speedometer" and "Bobby, don't talk to your brother whiiile he's *driving.*" In Hammond, I got sick smoking cigars with my brother, watched TV with a neighbor lady who explained to me the virtues of Catholicism, and discovered *Mad* comics at a drugstore. On a Sunday afternoon, we all went to Chicago to a museum. For the rest of his life, Daddy would tell about going to a supermarket in Hammond, Indiana, and seeing some California oranges; always having a propensity for exaggeration (in this case, negative exaggeration), he would describe the fruit as being about the size of cherries.

We got back to Auburndale just before my thirteenth birthday. Mother would tell someone years later, "Enjoy your children up through age twelve, because after they hit their teens, it's nothing but heartaches."

CHAPTER FOUR

Mother's Heartaches

W HEN I TURNED THIRTEEN, the Korean War had just ended. Pat Benatar was a baby, and Albert Einstein was an old man. It was John F. Kennedy's first year in the U.S. Senate and Elvis Presley's last year at Humes High School in Memphis. My first wife was nine years old; my second one was two. It was the beginning of that awful limbo for me—that holding pattern between a boy and a young man.

I spent the rest of August 1953 riding my bicycle to various destinations like the recently completed new Auburndale High School, or Taylor's Rexall Drugs for a cherry coke, or the Auburn Theater to see *From Here to Eternity,* or the four-miles-distant packinghouse town of Lake Alfred, or to the city beach to swim in the snake-infested waters of Lake Ariana.

I'm no biologist, but I think it's pretty safe to say that on this continent, the farther south you go, the more snakes you'll find. I don't know what effect the decades of development since then have had on the snake population of Florida, but in the middle of the twentieth century, they were all over the place. There were green ones in the orange trees, brown ones in the oak trees, black ones in the sand, and striped ones in the grass. They coiled up in the shade on a hot sunny day, and they crawled all around at night. One managed to get inside the house and into my playpen when I was a toddler. My father killed copperheads and deadly little coral snakes in our backyard with a stick, and once shot a diamondback rattlesnake just as it was positioning itself to strike our dog. When swimming in the lakes, I feared the venomous cottonmouth moccasins more than I did the alligators. There were horror stories, like the one about the girl who was pulled screaming from a Polk County lake with a dozen deadly moccasins dangling from her dying body. My brother and I once started to launch a small fishing boat, quickly discovering that underneath the boat was the home of a huge water moccasin and her wriggling mass of babies. Snakes! Misunderstood creatures though these ancient examples of God's handiwork may be, snakes were in our yard, in our house, in my bed, and—to this day—in my dreams.

When school started in the fall, most of my eighth-grade classes were at the nearby former high school or in old barracks behind the main building. Brother Paul—now a junior—drove his souped-up 1951 Ford to the new Auburndale High School, about a block farther north of the old school, overlooking the shores of Lake Ariana.

Florida was experiencing unprecedented growth, with both coasts teeming with immigrants from the frozen North. Polk County was growing too, but a majority of its newcomers were Southerners. There were enough elderly retirees and winter residents from the North to justify a shuffleboard court in the city park, but they had no offspring in the schools, so we were not really affected by their culture. Auburndale's occasional new "Yankee" kid at school was typically from a small town or rural area in the Midwest, therefore not that different from the rest of us. To be accepted, a guy had to learn that short-sleeves on a shirt must be rolled up, preferably twice. With that came acceptance and assimilation.

Paul's best friend, Jere Truitt, was majoring in chemistry at Florida Southern College in Lakeland. Popular at school, Paul had three close buddies with whom he shared common interests—hunting, fishing, drag racing, and an occasional beer or cigarette. They used profanity among themselves and other guys but not in the presence of girls. When some boy, not in their crowd, used *damn* in mixed company at the Taylor's Drugstore soda fountain booths, Paul informed him, "You can't talk that way in front of the girls."

I had several friends in grammar school, then a new set of friends in high school, but in junior high I had no really close friends. I was in transition and wasn't quite sure who I was. Changing classes and having a different teacher for each subject made me feel more like a big guy, but I was lacking in self-confidence and had a tendency to live in my own little world.

I don't know where I got whatever musical talent I have. Both my parents loved to sing, just as most everybody loved to sing back then. Mother played the piano—everything in the key of C and with three chords. Playing "Stardust" with only three chords is like driving a truck in only one gear; it doesn't work. Daddy played some harmonica and could pick out "Jesus, Lover of My Soul" with one finger on the piano.

I didn't love the Eddie Fisher and Teresa Brewer records that a lot of kids liked to listen to on the radio, and, with the exception of Bill Monroe and his Bluegrass Boys, I *really* disliked the "hillbilly" music that my brother and his friends liked. I thought, "I could write that stuff myself," not knowing that in a couple of years I would start to fall in love with country music and never dreaming that someday I actually would write it for a living. At thirteen, I liked a lot of music that was really before my time: Louis Armstrong and Dixieland jazz, Sousa marches, and barbershop quartet singing. The closest I came to being in the Polk County musical mainstream was my enjoyment of white gospel quartet singing.

The previous year, my parents had bought me an alto sax, and I had signed up for the Auburndale High School Band. This year I was in the marching band and would get to go to all the out-of-town football games on the band bus. We had new uniforms, blue and gold, which were the school colors. I loved music, so of course I loved being in the band. But my favorite part was getting to be around the drum majorettes in their skimpy outfits.

At thirteen, I was thrilled and horrified by girls. I had fantasies about movie stars like Yvonne DeCarlo and Jane Russell. I had a crush on the girl who lived in a garage apartment next to the school but had no earthly idea how to act or interact around her. I wanted to escape from the little boy that I still was. When I hung out with one of the neighborhood kids, I didn't like my father referring to it as "playing." When I called the Auburn Theatre to ask what time the movie let out, I was fuming when the guy on the phone called me "ma'am." I began speaking so low in my yet-to-change voice that people had trouble understanding what I was saying.

As our little movie of life plays on, all of us are constantly growing and reinventing and metamorphosing. The only thing that stays the same is *everything changes.*

Mother, who was past president of the Auburndale Woman's Club and the Auburndale Garden Club, had become district governor of the Florida Federation of Women's Clubs, representing Polk County and some small rural counties to the south. Most of her closest friends were fellow clubwomen who were older than she, resulting in Mother having, in her later years, the lonely distinction of outliving all her friends.

Daddy was no longer a political force, but the local candidates still dropped by to visit sometimes, thinking he could send a few votes their way. Local politics was about to change, slowly but surely, as lightning struck so hard in Washington that the thunder's rumble could be heard clear across America.

On May 17, 1954, the U.S. Supreme Court ruled unanimously that racial segregation in public schools was unconstitutional. P. E. Braddock said the Southern states would probably never accept race mixing. Cities close to the Mason-Dixon Line—Baltimore, Washington, Louisville, and St. Louis—made plans to integrate right away, but the lower South talked about resisting integration by "interposing" states rights, closing down the public schools, or even seceding from the union again. It was hard for me to imagine whites and blacks attending school together in Florida, *impossible* to imagine it happening in my ancestral home of Georgia.

When I was fourteen, everything I knew about sex was from what other boys had told me. I was embarrassingly naïve and a bit late on the learning curve. I got no help from either of my parents. Three years earlier, about the time I learned there was no Santa Claus, I had asked my mother a little-boy question and she had given me a vague answer. I asked her how babies were made, and she had told me that the man fertilized the woman. When I asked if Daddy had fertilized her, she said "yes," then quickly changed the subject. So, for a long time I had envisioned my father getting a large bag of Gulf Fertilizer, which he used in his citrus groves, and somehow pouring it into my mother. By the time I was in the ninth grade, I was only a few tall tales and dirty jokes wiser on the subject of sex.

We had a new band director, William Miller, who booked a concert in the high school auditorium featuring the marching band from his alma mater, the University of Miami. He made arrangements for the various band members to stay overnight at the homes of members of the Auburndale High School band. Our guest was a band majorette, Sherry Jarvis, who had been the national baton-twirling champion the previous year. She was twenty and beautiful, and the fact that she smoked made her even more intriguing to me.

The morning after the concert, before departing for Miami, Sherry asked me to sit down on the couch (which we Braddocks called the *davenport*) and talk to her for a moment. As we sat down, she touched my hand, and spoke softly, so no one else could hear:

"Bobby, you're so shy. You're fourteen years old. You're a cute guy, but you'll never get a girlfriend being so shy."

"Yeah, I know," I replied, never looking her in the eye. Little did she know that shy Bobby had been in the large closeted hallway the night before, looking through the big old-fashioned keyhole as she emerged from her bath.

So I was inwardly sexual and outwardly "saxual." I had become a halfway decent sax player and joined a small dance band called "The Cool Noters." The trumpet player, Billy Chisholm, was my brother's age, an outgoing guy (and future mayor of Auburndale) who treated me as a peer. The other guys in the band were a year or two older than me, not big men on campus so to speak, and I tended to hang out with them. Paul, a senior when I was a freshman, would see us sitting on the benches between the school cafeteria and the main building, and tell my mother, "Bobby hangs out with a bunch of introverts." He referred to these get-togethers as "vert sessions." I had no best friend in my freshman year, and I was also starting to hang out with some of the school bad boys.

I had a crush on Loraine, a girl with closely cropped blonde hair, but did absolutely nothing to let her know. What good would it have done? I wouldn't be old enough to drive without an adult until I was sixteen. At fourteen, I was only old enough to get a restricted drivers license. Mother took me out on Lake Alfred Road occasionally and let me take the wheel while she sat in the driver's seat. One day, when I was at "the eighty" grove with Daddy, he said, "I'm going to let yoooouu drive home." So I got behind the wheel of his grove car, a 1950 Chevrolet with Power Glide. I drove through the deep metallic-colored sand onto the clay road that led to the paved highway, Polk City Road. I slowly passed a tractor, and my father said, "You're doin' jus-s-s-t fine," as I approached the main road and turned left, toward town. I had dual feelings of empowerment and uneasiness as I carefully negotiated the vehicle past acres and acres of orange and grapefruit and tangerine groves. As we entered the Auburndale city limits, the road, lined with royal palm trees, went into a gradual curve. I wasn't traveling very fast, so someone honked their horn and passed us. I meant to hit the brakes but rammed the accelerator instead. As our car picked up speed, I panicked and lost control. We slammed into a big palm tree.

When one second you're moving along at thirty-five miles an hour, then the next second you're standing still, there is a stunned, surreal feeling of disbelief. I looked over at my father, who was in the floorboard of the passenger side, and said, "I'm sorry, Daddy. I'm really sorry."

"I'll have to agreeeee with you," he angrily retorted, his eyeglasses dangling from the tip of his nose.

My big brother was pretty conventional and generally went with the tastes and mores of his crowd. If it had been decades later, he might have said, "Country music's not cool anymore, so we're all liking black music now." That's not how he specifically put it then, but he and his friends had forsaken the music of Hank Snow and Carl Smith for the rhythm and blues they heard on black radio stations. Rock and roll had already made a cameo appearance with "Shake Rattle and Roll" by Bill Haley and His Comets, but the music hadn't yet exploded across America. Southern white kids going from "hillbilly" to rhythm and blues—that was a sign of things to come.

One night Paul let me go with him and his friends to the amateur boxing matches at the VFW hall between Auburndale and Winter Haven, on Havendale Boulevard. Before leaving Auburndale, we drove into the black part of town, known as "the quarters," and pulled up in front of a juke joint owned by an elderly gentleman named Jeremiah Jones. One of the boys called out "Jeremiah!" and the old man knew exactly what the boys wanted. He brought out a large brown paper bag containing Miller High Life beer and Silver Bar ale. I liked it.

I wanted to do anything to make me appear older. When I went somewhere with my parents, I would scoot my butt way up in the car seat so I'd look taller. Though I wasn't old enough to drive a car alone, I refused to ride my bike anymore because I didn't want to look like a kid. I started smoking Lucky Strike cigarettes and Hav-A-Tampa wooden-tip cigars.

In the summer of 1955, I got my first taste of working in the groves, sawing and pruning dead wood off citrus trees. Paul and Jere Truitt had worked in the groves the previous summer, so they indoctrinated me into the world of what I would come to call the "Green Hell." Daddy paid us every bit of eighty cents an hour. It would have been exhausting enough just to spend ten hours a day, from seven until five, doing nothing but enduring the almost unbearable heat.

Paul and Jere were relentless in the jokes they pulled on me. I didn't have a watch, so one day they turned the car clock back thirty minutes every hour or hour-and-a-half. When quitting time rolled around, the clock read only 1:00 p.m. on what I thought was a day that would never end. They once asked me to get something out of the glove box; I opened the compartment and a big black snake jumped out. Another time, we were in Paul's hot rod, and he wanted me to ride outside on the running board; he drove fast and made sure he went under plenty of protruding orange tree branches that would slap me across the face. When we stopped, I was so angry that I went after him with my handsaw.

I turned fifteen with a vengeance. I was changing, and everything around me seemed to be changing too. Even the crickets and the rain frogs and the whippoorwills seemed to be singing a different song. The orange blossoms still rode the soft midnight breeze, but the wind was coming from a new direction.

September of 1955 probably felt like just another hot summer season to any Northerners passing through Auburndale, but to the locals, there was a slight hint of fall in the air, just enough to turn one's thoughts to football or quail hunting. For a few days, the towering cumulus clouds and the emerging thunderheads were replaced by gently gliding white puff balls that sometimes cast fast-moving shadows over the glistening waters of Lake Ariana.

On a morning in early September, Auburndale men were working hard at Continental Can Company out on Highway 92. Many of their wives were at home but would be making money themselves come winter—during fruit-picking season—when the packing houses hired several hundred women. These people had fewer children than their parents had had, and times were better than during their own childhoods on small peanut and tobacco and cotton farms. Auburndale, once fairly backward itself, was becoming a part of the modern world. With crystal clear reception from two stations in Tampa and one in Orlando, most Auburndale homes now had TV.

On this pleasant morning, Mother was probably tidying up the house and making plans to go to some club meeting or luncheon. Daddy was probably in one of his groves, looking at an orange or a grapefruit through his high-powered magnifying glass, to see if he could find any rust mites. Paul may have been in Lakeland, registering for his freshman year as a day student at Florida Southern College, where he planned to major in agriculture. It may have seemed to anybody else like an ordinary day, but I was walking down the hall, hearing the bell ring in my first year as a real high-schooler.

Determined to erase the last vestiges of anything remotely sissified, I had stopped taking piano lessons and quit the high school band. I started going to the poolroom every afternoon after school. There were three poolrooms in Auburndale; I went to Steve's Billiard Parlor downtown, which catered mostly to teenage boys (girls *never* went to poolrooms). Steve, a small mild-mannered man of forty, didn't allow alcohol or loud profanity in his place. Betting wasn't allowed either (but was sometimes done without his knowledge, for small stakes). The boys respected Steve and usually didn't give him any trouble. My parents didn't like the idea of me hanging out at a pool hall, and I think the only reason they let me was—I can imagine my mother saying—"At least we know where he is."

I made new friends, many of them tough guys or what my father would call "a rough crowd." They had mamas and daddies who came from Alabama or Georgia, most of whom worked in something that was citrus related. The gang I ran around with included Wayne Aman, Edell Carter, and Red Cannon. The only one from this group that I remained close to throughout high school was Red, a good and well-liked boy who spoke with sort of a mumble and wore his hair in a typical Southern 1950s short crew cut, like mine. It was a big night for all of us whenever one of the guys, though underage, got the family car—that meant we would go beyond the environs of Steve's Billiard Parlor.

A typical night out would usually start with a visit to Jeremiah Jones's place to buy beer, a four-mile trip to Winter Haven, then back to Auburndale to a drive-in restaurant, the A&W Root Beer Stand. We would circle it a couple of times to see who was there, sometimes going inside to get a cheeseburger or to play the jukebox. I had an earlier curfew than the other kids, 11:00 p.m., and I could only go out on weekends. My nickname at fifteen: "Sot."

One Friday night, some of my friends and I saw a group of girls congregated around the playground equipment in the Auburndale city park, next to the butterscotch-colored stucco Atlantic Coast Line depot. The girls were from Eloise, a mean-ass little town next to Winter Haven. There were four of us and four of them. We talked them into piling into the car with us and headed out to one of the area's most popular parking places, a small lake in the middle of my father's eighty-acre grove, known as "Braddock's Hole." The girl I paired off with was skinny and probably a year younger than I. My first attempt at being a lover boy was a dismal failure. At the time, I was giving her an F in anatomy, but looking back later from a more experienced perspective, I realize I should have been giving myself an F in geography.

When a traveling carnival came to town, I went there on a Saturday night with Wayne, Edell, and Red. There was a New York–talking guy doing his spiel in front of his shooting gallery:

> "C'mon, c'mon, c'mon
> And shoot da little duck
> For a quarter of a buck
> C'mon and try ya luck
> C'mon, c'mon, c'mon."

Edell started wisecracking, trying to imitate the man's Brooklyn accent.

"I'm lookin' fa shooters, not shitters," the big beefy fellow sneered.

"Well, you *eat* shit," my jackpot mouth shot off.

The large and muscular man snatched me by the collar, whirled me around, then grabbed me by my neck, snarling, "Hey kid, are you sayin' I gotta fuzzy mouth?"

I was so horrified by the raging giant that I was speechless. Then, from out of nowhere, appeared the most feared threesome in Polk County, the Brown boys. They lived on "the lanes," the toughest part of town, with streets named Alabama Lane, Tennessee Lane, and Norman Lane. They had a younger brother, Herman Brown, who was a star athlete at Auburndale High. But there was nothing scholastic about *these* Browns, and the only athletics they engaged in was ass whuppin'. It was not the last time these devil-angels would be watching over me, appearing from out of nowhere.

"You put that boy *down*," Homer Brown demanded in almost a whisper, his eyes burning like coals of fire.

The carnival man seemed to know instinctively that it would be in his best interests to turn me loose, which he did immediately.

"Don't you *ever* put your hands on an Orburndale boy," Homer said quietly as he jabbed his index finger into the man's stomach, before strolling on down the midway with his brothers.

It seemed like someone was *always* looking out for me. One Friday night I was at Steve's poolroom, talking to Jimmy Ray Johnson, a guy my age whose voice was creaky and quavery like an old man's. He told me that his car could be started by someone pissing on the spark plugs, and if I didn't believe it, I could see for myself. I followed him out the back door to a light-colored Chevrolet. Jimmy Ray raised the hood, then positioned himself at the steering wheel, where he could turn on the ignition. "Go ahead," he drawled in his old-man voice. I jumped up on the bumper, unzipped, and pulled out. As I hovered over the engine, Jimmy Ray pointed to the spark plugs, and I took careful aim.

"Stop!" yelled Steve, the poolroom proprietor, as he raced out the door toward the car. "You'll be electrocuted." Just in the nick of time, my manhood, and possibly my life, was saved.

Auburndale had a reputation as a tough, gritty little town. The Auburndale Bloodhounds and the Kissimmee Cowboys were not allowed to compete against each other in high school sports because a big fight would inevitably break out. (Kissimmee, years before becoming Orlando's Disney World suburb, was a cattle town where cowboy hats were as commonplace as in any Texas town.) In fact, my brother had temporarily been banned from Bloodhound games the year before, after allegedly picking a fight with a guy on the visitors' side. In late 1955, the Bloodhounds were, for the second year in a row, undefeated in football and basketball, and the champions of the Ridge Conference, which consisted of Polk and several surrounding counties. They were considered the state's best football and basketball teams from an intermediate size school. Some of the players were big old boys who drank, smoked, and chewed tobacco.

Football was already an important part of the local culture. Practically everybody went to the games, especially the home games. Excitement was always in the air on the chilly fall nights that many people called "football weather." The high school band would be playing "fight songs" and the cheerleaders yelling "Get the BALL you all, get the BALL" (clap clap), "Get the BALL you all, get the BALL" (clap clap). Then when the Bloodhounds became a celebrity team—earning big headlines on the front pages of the sports sections of the *Tampa Tribune* and the *Orlando Sentinel*—there developed a kind of local hysteria. Football coach Tom Terry, a slow-talking country boy from North Florida, was treated reverently. Star running back Terrell Teague, son of an orange picker, became a statewide legend. My mother, a much bigger sports fan than my father, kept a scrapbook on the Bloodhounds, although she had no children on the team. (Paul played football in junior high, but I was the total nonathlete.) On the night of the 1955 Auburndale homecoming game, there were five thousand people in attendance, more than the population of the entire city. Orburndale was a football town.

I was fifteen and Paul had turned nineteen, but our father continued to call us *darling*, as though we were still little kids. When other guys were around, I would usually talk very loud when Daddy started to speak, hoping to drown out his word of endearment. One day Wayne Aman was at our house and said "Hey, Braddock, your daddy just called you *darling*." I turned red.

Paul had a friend named Ronald Calloway who was a bit wilder and more raucous than his other buddies. Daddy decided to give Paul a lecture about Ronald, not realizing that his friend was there with them in the living room, just a few feet away.

"Paul-l-l," he said slowly, "you know, darling, Ron-ald has gotten in a bit of trouble with the police depahhht-ment."

Ronald snickered nervously.

"Annnnd, you know you are JUDGED by the commm-pany you keep. It doesn't be-hoooove you to hang out with a fella like that."

Ronald again snickered nervously as Paul stood there in agony, not knowing what to say or do. I was frantically trying to get Daddy's attention, clearing my throat, looking him square in the eye and nodding my head over toward where Ronald was standing.

"And furrrrthermore, he drives his cah-rr around Lake Stella so fast that . . . " Suddenly, he saw Ronald, looked away, and continued, "I'm afraid he might get hurt, because no matter whaahht people SAY about Ron-ald, I like him a lot, and I think he'll probably turn out just fiiiine. Why, hello there, Ron-ald, good to seeeee you."

Lake Stella was where the city of Auburndale placed a giant

Christmas tree on a raft every December, the twinkling yule lights dancing on the cool, dark waters.

The climate in Central Florida is subtropical; it was very unusual for us to have a bitterly cold midday, but a few mornings a year we'd wake up to freezing temperatures. In the living room, the fuel oil heater would be roaring, but we had no heat in the bedrooms. We just put on flannel pajamas and piled on the quilts and blankets.

I can remember it being so threateningly cold one night that Dad stayed up late, reading the Bible and talking to God Almighty. The rising sun shimmered through the black smoke that filled the Auburndale air—smoke that was drifting in from the countryside where smudge pots and fiery tires were being used in an attempt to thwart Old Man Winter's Arctic assault on Florida citrus. When Daddy arrived back home from the groves, I could see the tension was gone from his face. "It got down to twenty-three-e-e out in the country, but it's already warmed up seven degreeees and I think we're going to be allll-riiight," his deep voice boomed.

I went to school that day, but about half the boys were absent because they had been for hire the night before, firing the area groves. For inexplicable reasons, P. E. Braddock never fired his groves during a freeze nor did he irrigate them during a drought, perhaps letting the fate of his fruit hinge on his relationship with God Almighty.

After I came home from school on that day—or a day very much like it—I sat in front of the family TV set, a large Emerson console, watching a local teenage record hop, broadcast from a station in Orlando. The kids were dancing the jitterbug, as their older siblings and parents had done ten and fifteen years earlier. And in all those years, the music had hardly changed at all. Then the deejay said, "Here's a record that's causing a lot of controversy—some people say this guy's pop, and some say he's hillbilly. Tell us what you think." He then played the Elvis Presley record of "Mystery Train." I would fall in love with this new thing called rock 'n' roll—and the country music and African American music from which it came.

Then, a couple of months into 1956, when Elvis came out with "Heartbreak Hotel," he split the musical atom, causing a wonderfully violent chain reaction. This would be the music of the young for a long, long time to come. The kids of the 1950s weren't overtly rebelling as the kids ten years later would do, but there was something revolutionary in the music they were listening to. And maybe they were getting a little bolder—with each other.

Bob Bobroff, editor of the weekly local newspaper, wrote an editorial about how disgraceful it was that Auburndale's teenagers were kissing and carrying on in the soda fountain booths at Taylor's Rexall Drugstore.

"We're not gonna have this Yankee Jew tellin' *us* what to do," I heard one boy remark.

"And he's a *Russian* Jew at that," one parent said, as though being a Russian Jew, which a majority of American Jewish immigrants were, made him some kind of communist. It was ironic that this liberal Jew from Chicago irritated a small community of conservative Southern Baptists by taking a stand for modesty and old-fashioned values.

Then one night a report went out over the AP wire, datelined Auburndale, Florida, reporting that a cross had been burned in the yard of the editor of the *Auburndale Star*. There was speculation in the Florida press that some old Klan members—and there were plenty of them around in Polk County—had crawled out of the woodwork. The rumor in Auburndale was that it was some young men pulling a prank. A prank it may have been, but had the editor been a gentile named Bob Barton, it's unlikely that a cross would have been burned in his yard.

On an early spring afternoon, a few days after the cross-burning incident, I learned that Mother was going to take Daddy to a doctor in Tampa for some tests. I invited Wayne, Edell, and Red to skip school with me and hang out at our house. By late morning, after a couple of hours of playing poker, we were getting bored, so I had a brainstorm: call Bob Bobroff and tell him to get out of town! Edell placed the call, while Wayne and I stood there listening in. Red Cannon was across the room at the card table, unaware of what we were doing. The housekeeper answered the phone and said that the Bobroffs weren't home. Edell told her to tell Bobroff to "get his ass out of town."

I don't know how word got around so quickly to the high school principal, Mr. Eagleson, but it did. Just a couple of days after the incident, he called out over the intercom for all four of us to come to his office. A well-informed policeman stood at his side. We knew we were trapped, so we owned up to it. We all emphasized that Red was oblivious to what we had been doing that day—however, all four of us were charged with harassment and making a threatening phone call and would have to be tried before the Polk County juvenile judge.

Bartow, the Polk County seat, lies seventeen miles south of Auburndale. Most of Polk County was settled in the latter part of the nineteenth century and still had a bit of a frontier feel even in the 1950s, but Bartow had been settled way back in 1851. A sleepy-looking city of gracious old homes, shaded by tall mossy oak trees, it also had a large African American population and a history of lynching and racial violence. Many Bartow residents worked in the nearby phosphate mines, in an area known as Bone Valley. Polk County not only produced a bigger citrus crop than the entire state of California, but at one time most of the world's phosphate was mined in Bone Valley. There may be something to be said for the karma that comes from living on Indian burial grounds; Polk Countians lived on the graves of *dinosaurs*.

On a warm morning in late May 1956, I rode with my parents to Bartow for my appearance with the three other boys in juvenile court. As we climbed the steps of the courthouse, Daddy was at once urging me to speak the truth and coaching me as to what to say. When I was seated at a large table in the front of the courtroom, my pulse quickened as the big man in black robes assumed the bench. Judge Hart was an unsmiling man with snowy white hair. I had heard that he kept one eye on the defendant while scanning the crowd with the other eye, but to me he just looked cross-eyed.

The procedure was a blur; first, the Bobroffs' black housekeeper on the witness stand, then my father trying to impress the judge with his political resume, and, finally, the sentence of one year's probation, with the stipulation that we boys were not to associate with each other until school reconvened in the fall.

I had been a bad boy and an embarrassment to the family, so my parents wanted to get me out of town immediately. They shipped me off to stay with my Aunt Ruth and Uncle Dick, who had recently moved from Georgia to Sanford, Florida. I stayed there until mid-June, when I was enrolled in summer school to make up the Algebra that I had failed.

The Montverde School was located about forty miles north of Auburndale, in the rolling hills of Lake County. It was an expensive school aimed at kids whose parents wanted them to have to rough it a little, and the students had to perform tasks such as milking cows, washing dishes, cutting grass and weeds, and cleaning up the grounds.

The group that I thought of as the really cool guys didn't want me to hang with them. It's easy to understand why I might not have made a great impression in a new group of people. I had developed a tic: blinking my eyes, not both eyes at once but one at a time, like the turn signals on a car. Though I wouldn't realize it until much later in life, this was Tourette's Syndrome. Tourette's has been so sensationalized that most of us think of it as a condition in which one has the uncontrollable urge to shout out obscenities, but actually only a small percentage of people with Tourette's do the profanity thing. Its most common aspects are habitually clearing your throat or blinking your eyes or twitching your face. My Tourette's includes the blinking and twitching and also a strange stutter, a sort of quick doglike panting sound that I make before speaking. In my book dialogue, I have myself t-t-talking like this s-sometimes because it's just easier to characterize my stutter that way. The condition would be exacerbated in my late teens as a result of amphetamine overdose, but I was already doing it pretty seriously when I was fifteen. So imagine meeting this scrawny kid, eyes blinking like the lights on a Christmas tree, panting like a dog. If you were in a new environment seeking out friends, is this someone you would want to include in your circle?

But there was someone there who really *did* like me. Her name was Joanie, a slightly chubby girl who wore glasses. There were girls at the school who I really lusted after, but Joanie was what the universe gave me. One day she invited me to come up to her room in the girls' dorm that night. If I got caught, it would mean automatic expulsion and repeating my sophomore year in the fall. My parents had already warned me: if I got into any more serious trouble, they would ship me off to school at Georgia Military Academy. But not to worry, I got lost and couldn't find Joanie's room.

The next day she berated me. "I thought you were a real grown-up boy," she said with disgust, "but you're nothing but a *kid!* Just a little *kid!*"

As she turned on her heel and walked away, I could hear the echoes of "Be-Bop-A-Lula," an Elvis-y sounding record by Gene Vincent, coming from the boys' dormitory. The best thing about my six weeks at Montverde School was the music. A guy down the hall had brought his record player and records and I got a really good dose of great rhythm and blues, with songs like "Speedo" by the Cadillacs and "Little Girl of Mine" by the Cleftones.

When summer school was over, my parents came to take me home. I was fidgety on the way back. My father told me he knew I was addicted to cigarettes and to go ahead and light one up. With Mother at the wheel, the smoke-filled Lincoln headed south through the grove-covered hills of Lake County. There were political posters and placards on utility poles, and we approached a billboard displaying the handsome face of Governor LeRoy Collins. Despite Collins's "moderate" racial views, Daddy, an unrelenting segregationist (and 1948 supporter of Dixiecrat Strom Thurmond for president), was nevertheless taken in by the governor's genteel charm. He waved toward the billboard and said, "I think Leeee-roy is a migh-ty fiiine guv-nuh."

LeRoy Collins, a courtly Old South gentleman from North Florida, had been elected two years earlier to finish out the term of his late predecessor and in 1956 was running for a full four-year term as governor. In his short time in office, Collins had already gained national attention as a one-man Florida Chamber of Commerce, traveling around the country and bringing new business and industry to the state, and had won high praise as a governor who truly cared about education. But foremost was the way he dealt with the simmering race issue. Though officially an opponent of race-mixing, as most

Southern politicians were in those days, he decried hatred, and urged people to deal with the Supreme Court's integration ruling calmly, with cool heads. On Democratic primary day, he lost Auburndale, but statewide Collins got more votes than three hard-line segregationists combined. In time, he became a courageous advocate of civil rights, causing him to lose favor with many former supporters. Most historians consider LeRoy Collins Florida's greatest governor.

There's no ocean in Auburndale, but when you live smack dab in the middle of the vacationland of the South, you see a lot of relatives that you might not see otherwise (though we were always glad to have them). One morning in the summer of '56, when my father got up to put on his coffee, he stood in the breezeway at the glass-louvered door, peering through the dim light of early day at a car parked beneath our huge banyan tree. Still wearing his pajamas and bathrobe, he slowly and quietly eased outside and approached cautiously, flashlight in one hand, snub-nosed revolver in the other. The car had Georgia plates, and everyone in it was sound asleep. It was my mother's second cousin Katie, her husband James Humphries, and their two daughters Kat and Janice.

My fourth cousin Kat was one year younger than me. Everything about her defied the rural county in Central Georgia where she was born and raised. She wore closely cropped hair and had an exotic, almost Eurasian look about her. She quoted the masters, discussed politics, and talked about physics—and would grow up to become a multilingual New Yorker whose three marriages were to men from third world countries.

After supper on the day of their arrival, Kat and I were alone in the kitchen as the distant thunder grew louder and lightning lit up the early night outside the window. A thunderstorm raged inside my skinny body as well. As she meticulously washed each dish, I dried every one she handed me, quickly, and stood there waiting for her to hand me another, admiring my cute cousin in the tight short shorts.

As the thunder rattled the dishes we had stacked on the counter, she turned her head and stared straight at me. "Don't look at me with lust in your eyes," she said matter-of-factly. Then the lights went out.

In the pitch dark, I put my hand on her shoulder, moved close, and kissed her on the mouth. She didn't pucker or kiss back, but neither did she pull away. It lasted only a few seconds. Then the lights came back on, and we continued washing and drying the dishes as she talked about literature. For the rest of their visit, we acted as though it had never happened.

I spent the rest of the summer working in the Braddock groves. Though Paul now had a full-time job as a plumber's assistant, his best friend Jere Truitt needed the extra work between college semesters and joined me in the Green Hell. Jere was a chemistry major and taught me some German. He also taught me how to kiss—*girls*, of course.

"I'll be sixteen in a few days," I announced as I clipped off a dead branch with my pruning shears. "I'll be getting my unrestricted drivers license."

Jere, his blond flattop already wet with sweat from the midmorning heat, looked down from his ladder, as he sawed off a large dead limb.

"Well, I guess you're gonna be romancin' all over town in P. E. Braddock's '56 Ford," he said with a grin.

"I dunno. I'm thinkin' about callin' up Jessica Wilkes and asking her for a date," I told him, feeling some embarrassment.

Jessica, who was one year behind me, was one of the most popular girls in school. She was a cheerleader and one of those personality girls who had a smile for everyone. I'd had a crush on this raven-haired beauty the previous year but didn't know her very well and had no idea that she would even go out with me. But I thought she was a doll, and I was determined to try.

"Well . . . whatcha gonna do?" asked Jere, wiping the sawdust off his face.

"What *should* I do?" I countered. "Drive-in movie, then go get something to drink at the Root Beer Stand or the Top Hat?"

"Yeah," said Jere. "Then take her parkin' at Braddock's Hole. And French kiss her."

I had heard of French kissing but didn't know exactly what that was.

"You stick your tongue in her mouth," he said.

"I stick my *tongue* in her mouth? Are you sure?"

"Damn right. Girls *like* that. Just roll your tongue around in her mouth. And lick her ear. That makes 'em *hot*."

So, armed with all this amorous information, the first thing I did when I turned sixteen and got my unrestricted drivers license was go to a payphone and call Jessica. I dialed the number, and a girl answered. Though she had sisters, I could tell that this sweet voice belonged to Jessica.

"Jessica?" I asked.

"Yes-s-s?" she answered in her sweet drawl.

"This is Bobby Braddock," I announced, my heart thumping.

"Oh, hi-i-i-i, Bobby," she said.

Now I don't know *why* in the world I decided to feign a French accent. Maybe I was thinking about the French kiss, I'm not sure. But I suddenly decided to try talking like a Frenchman, or what I perceived a Frenchman to sound like.

"Hey, ba-beee,'" I said. "You, ah, wanna go out some night wiz me, ba-beee'?"

"Wel-l-l," she said, with a pause, "uhh . . . yeah, I could go out Tuesday night."

"Well, how about also Wednesday and Thursday and Friday and Saturday night too, ba-bee?"

'Wel-l-l-l,' she giggled, "I think we should just start with Tuesday night."

The Wilkes house was out in the country on a clay road. There had been a thundershower a half-hour earlier, and the rain was still coming down pretty hard. Instead of pulling up in their driveway, I left the car out on the wet, nasty clay road. I ran up and knocked on the door. I guess her parents had faith in Jessica's choice of dates because she came right to the door, ready to go.

"Why didn't you pull up in the driveway?" she asked.

"Oh, I'm sorry," I said. "You stay here, I'll go get it."

"That's okay," she said with a shrug, and we ran through her yard and through the red mud to the car.

I took her to a drive-in movie—in the rain—where, after a couple of minutes, she rolled her eyes and reached over and turned off my headlights for me. After the movie, we stopped at a curb service restaurant, where I flicked a cigarette ash into her Coke when she wasn't looking, having heard that this would make a girl very hot. I wish I could recall whatever it was I said to induce the girl to "go parking" with me, because undoubtedly it was as dumb as everything else I had been doing. But amazingly, she did let me take her parking, to Braddock's Hole, and she did indeed let me kiss her. I rammed my tongue all around inside her mouth, and then I licked all over her ears, with no subtlety whatever. It was like a dog was licking her.

When I called her a few days later about going out again, she very sweetly informed me that she had decided to start going steady with a guy she used to date, a football player. Paul, who coincidentally was dating her older sister Sandra, said that Jessica told her sister, "Bobby curses too much."

When I was a junior at Auburndale High, the soundtrack for my life blared from the jukebox at the A&W Root Beer Stand on Highway 92 just west of town. It might have been Elvis singing the wild anthem "Hound Dog" or the more melodic rocker "Don't Be Cruel," or maybe it was the black hillbilly sounds of Chuck Berry's "Maybelline" or the mournful country harmonies of Ray Price's "Crazy Arms."

"Crazy Arms"! With its shuffle beat contrasting against the sad melody and words of despair, that song epitomized how much I was falling in love with country music. Rock 'n' roll was in my head and in my feet, but country music had my heart. I also liked "Singing The Blues" by the great Marty Robbins so much more than Guy Mitchell's goofy whistle-tinged pop version. Another favorite was Faron Young's record of "Sweet Dreams," featuring that instrument of love and death—whining and crying without shame—the pedal steel guitar.

And there was nobody I liked better than Johnny Cash—I wasn't sure if it was country or if it was rockabilly like Elvis, but I loved it.

The only one of the old gang who hadn't quit school at sixteen was Red Cannon (whose hair was actually more dark brown than red). My parents were aware that Red was pretty much an innocent bystander in the Bob Bobroff "get out of town" phone call incident, so they didn't mind me hanging out with him. They weren't as sure about Wayne and Edell. What my parents never seemed to realize was that *I* was my own worst influence.

Red was my connection to Don Pace. I had been in the Boy Scouts with Pace, but Red went to Methodist Sunday school with him and had known him longer and better. Because of his friendship with Red, Pace had gone out with our crowd occasionally. Eventually, I got in the habit of dropping in on him at his after-school job of making shipping crates at Hall Lumber Company on Pilaklakawaha Avenue (known locally as P.K. Avenue), next to the Seaboard Airline railroad depot. (*Two* railroads ran through Auburndale.) He was a year ahead of me in school; he would be voted "wittiest" in the Class of '57, and I would be bestowed the same honor—or *dishonor,* since what it really meant was "class clown"—in the Class of '58. He would become my partner in crime, so to speak. In the late 1950s and early 1960s, we would become older versions of Tom Sawyer and Huck Finn. Our adventures would be many, and our Mississippi River would be Polk County and points beyond.

The Pace family had come to Auburndale from McDonough, Georgia, when Don was a small child. Mr. Pace was a big old gentle bear of a man who ran Pace's Pool Room out on Highway 92. Mrs. Pace was a small, cheerful, religious lady who worked at a department store in Lakeland. Don had two older brothers who were more scholarly and studious than he was. The Paces lived in a comfortable screen-porched house with a separate garage on a shady street called Sunset Avenue.

If Don Pace had gone into politics, he would have been a political cartoonist's dream come true. I had sort of a knack for drawing cartoons to depict every major event in our teenage lives, and Pace, big and tall, with a pointy head, pointy little nose, and owlish eyes, was my favorite person to caricature. His odd looks made the funny things he said even funnier. His humor and charisma immediately got everyone's attention when he walked into a room. His double-take, head darting forward and slightly down like a cat about to pounce on a bird, eyes open wide, was comical in itself, often followed by a witty remark. And if that didn't get your attention, his taking a bite out of a drinking glass would.

This big old boy, usually wearing a button-down shirt and chinos instead of the more typical plaid shirt and jeans, was also a big bluffer. If some tough country boys turned up looking for trouble, all Pace had to do was look straight at the leader of the pack—his owlish eyes turning mean and satanic—as he said, "Boy?"

Pace added another dimension to my music appreciation: rhythm and blues, or R&B, as we called it. I had become a huge fan of country music, and I also loved rock 'n' roll. Pace, not at first but eventually, pulled me into R&B as well. With the exception of Johnny Cash, whose records *all* guys liked, Pace didn't care much for white music. He listened to R&B nightly over WLAC in Nashville, the radio in his white Ford always turned up so loud that the music was distorted. WLAC, like Nashville's other broadcasting giant WSM, was a fifty-thousand-watt station that reached half the continent after dark, and it did for the blues what WSM did for country. Their target audience was African American—they beamed out commercials for products like Royal Crown Hair Dressing—but white kids all over the South were tuned in, listening to artists like B. B. King, Muddy Waters, and an up-and-comer named Ray Charles.

Pace had a close friend named Rodney Gelder. One night he and I were waiting for Rodney to get off work at the little store where he bagged groceries after school, up in Polk City, a little town ten miles north of Auburndale. This was the night that Elvis Presley was appearing live at the Polk Theater in Lakeland.

"I wonder where ever'body's *at?*" Pace asked the two old men who were sitting on a bench in front of the grocery store.

"Well," one overall-clad fellow replied as he looked up and down the empty highway, "I reckon they all gone down to Lakeland to see that *Avis Prescott.*"

My junior year love life existed primarily in my own fantasies and dreams. Jere Truitt, Paul's friend who told me all about French-kissing and ear licking, set me up with a girl who quite a few of the older guys had been out with, and he was a little disappointed to learn that all I had done was stick my tongue in her mouth and lick her ears. One night, a classmate and I spent several hours driving around Lakeland because we didn't want anybody in Auburndale to see the girls we were with. And one day Harvey Wooley, a slow-drawling peripheral friend with whom I came to blows a couple of times, announced loud enough for everyone in class to hear, "Hey Braddock, I met this girl from Winter Haven that said she went out with you and *you didn't know how to kiss!*"

There are your closest friends and then there are your friends' friends who may or may not be your buddies too, but the core group that I ran around with in eleventh grade consisted of Don Pace, Red Cannon, and Stanley Cox, a good-natured, laid-back, slow-talking guy I had known for years. Stanley was one friend who was given my mother's unqualified and unconditional stamp of approval. The reason was plain and simple—Stanley's father was a deacon at the Church of Christ. I had known Stanley since second grade, when the Cox family moved to Auburndale from Alabama. Their concrete block house on P.K. Avenue became my home away from home. His parents were young, still in their thirties, and extremely hospitable. When I went there I would chat with Mrs. Cox or Stanley's little sister Gwen, and—if it was in the evening and Mr. Cox was home from his work as an agent for Independent Life Insurance Company—I would have to play "Down Yonder" on their old upright piano. Inevitably, I would end up in a rocking chair in Stanley's bedroom, listening to records.

Stanley turned me on to a lot of the traditional country music, especially Hank Williams, that I had disliked and ignored when it had first come out several years earlier. We also played the current rock'n' roll records and were big fans of the rhythmic Delta-like blues of Jimmy Reed.

Stanley started going out less with his Church of Christ friends and more with Pace, Red, and me. Stanley got a kick out of talking dirty, but he didn't drink quite as much as the rest of us. Even though Don drank as much as I did, he held it better, and I always got drunker. Polk County was the most heavily populated dry county in the state. Beer was legal, but it was the 3.2 percent "military beer," so we had to go twenty miles to Hillsborough County to get the stronger stuff.

Perhaps because he was a year older, and because of his charisma and self-confidence, Pace became the ring leader. Because this position was also somewhat self-appointed, the rest of us jokingly called him "hero" behind his back. Sometimes we would stop the car at his street, get out, and kneel facing his house, bowing down worshipfully and sarcastically.

When I think of this time in my life, I think of girls (that I longed for), friends (that I had a lot of fun with), and music (that I loved). All these factors came into play when I went with my buddies to see Elvis's first movie, *Love Me Tender,* at the Polk Theater in Lakeland. We were gratified vicariously as the girls screamed and moaned over Elvis. When he sang "Let Me," one girl sitting behind us gasped, "*I'll* let you, Elvis, *I'll* let you." This was the Eisenhower era, the age of innocence—it was the time of the Cleavers and the Cunninghams. Yeah, right.

My parents were stricter with me than the other parents were with their kids. Even Stanley Cox's deacon father gave him more slack. I had an earlier curfew, so sometimes I just opted to stay out late and pay the consequences. Daddy would still whip off his belt from time to time, only now I would grab his hands to keep him from hitting me, as my mother shamed me for "fighting your elderly father."

Paul, who had always been my protective big brother, seemingly turned antagonist as I approached puberty, and it continued throughout my high school years. He thought of me as a brat, and I thought of him as a bully. He had been whipping my butt for years now. I often told him that I was going to whip *his* butt on my eighteenth birthday.

And then Paul got married, to a cute sixteen-year-old girl from Winter Haven named Jo Ann Moore. They had met at the skating rink, the social center for Auburndale youth. (I went to the skating rink *only* when it was unavoidable because I had once made a big fool of myself there by skating for just a couple of minutes, then falling down and taking several people with me.) Paul and Jo Ann "ran off to Georgia." That's the way so many marriages began in Auburndale. In Georgia, you could get married quicker and younger, and it was easier to lie about your age. So they went to Kingsland, a little town on the Georgia-Florida line, and were married by a justice of the peace. This youthful union did not initially meet with approval from either family, but acceptance came quickly and a solid marriage would endure for many decades.

The newlyweds would live with us on Lake Stella Drive until they could find a place of their own. At our first meal together (befitting the occasion, it was in the dining room rather than the kitchen) as Jo Ann sat down, I smiled and announced, "Welcome to the family!"

Before she could even say "thanks," Paul mocked me with a snarl. "*Welcome to the family!* How stupid!"

So my brother and his bride, who was four days younger than I, settled down. I was anything but settled, just discovering the world around me and caught up in the frenzy of it all.

In the summer of 1957, there was magic in the air. Teenagers across America were listening to Marty Robbins sing "White Sport Coat" and Ferlin Husky sing "Gone," having no idea that they were hearing country artists. Whether it was this new pop-country or the more traditional kind, I was becoming an aficionado of what was then known as country and western music, and I loved rock 'n' roll almost as much.

My excitement over what was playing on the radio kept me running to the record store or sitting down at the spinet piano in our living room, where I taught myself to play the songs I was hearing. I also worked out the songs that were coming from my *own* head. I sang my ditties with my own piano accompaniment, taping them on a Webcor recorder. Sometimes I played the songs for my friends, who usually didn't seem to think they were very good.

That summer, Daddy let Stanley Cox and Red Cannon work with me in the citrus groves, sawing and pruning dead limbs. Sometimes Daddy's tractor driver, Rosco Wiggins, would work with us, painting hot tar over the saw wounds on the trees. Rosco was a real backwoods Cracker, never having ventured outside a four-county area in his forty-seven years. He had a large muscular body, and his face was almost always filthy from the torrents of dirt that he stirred up when he drove the tractor down the sandy rows as he plowed or sprayed parasites. He wore a railroad cap over his curly graying hair, and he sometimes wore an evil little smile as his eyes grew big behind thick spectacles. The black men who worked in the groves were afraid of him.

"Son," Rosco said to Stanley, who, not liking to be called "son" by anyone but his parents, barely responded. "I seen yore mama down thar at th' Post Office t'other day." He paused, thrusting out his chest as his eyes widened and he smiled wickedly. "That Mizzus Cox shore is a good-lookin' woman."

Stanley remained silent, never looking Rosco in the eye. As the barrel-chested man mounted the John Deere tractor and slowly roared away in a cloud of dust, Stanley, who liked almost everyone, quietly said, "I just don't *like* that old sonofabitch."

Toward the end of the summer, Mother somehow talked Daddy into a trip to see his kin in New Jersey and hers in Maine. Now that Paul was married, it would be just the three of us.

I was the official driver, and my driving kept my father upset for most of the trip. In New Hampshire, I came upon a car rather suddenly and slammed on the brakes. Daddy, who was lying down in the backseat taking a nap, was thrown to the floor, and raised up yelling, "GOD-all-MIGHTY, you're gonna kill us all-l-l before we get to the state of Maine!"

When we got back to Auburndale, Paul told us that our bird dog of twelve years, Brownie, had died while we were gone, but he hadn't wanted to ruin our trip by letting us know before we returned.

I joined Stanley and Red for a couple more weeks of working in the Green Hell, as we anticipated our senior year—my favorite school year of all.

CHAPTER FIVE

Senior Moments

M Y FATHER, WHO LOST his mother at age five, often said that a mother was far more important in the life of a child than a father. Throughout my childhood, I loved my father but I *worshipped* my mother, probably because she was consistently sweet and nurturing, while Daddy went from one extreme— demonstrative affection—to the other— harsh discipline. But as I look back now on my young life, I see that Daddy had the dominant personality and cast the longer shadow. As I approach manhood in this tale, P.E. becomes less germane to the plot. He is by no means disappearing from these pages, because there are still years of good P.E. stories left, but before he steps back from center stage a bit, I feel that a little reflection is in order.

P. E. Braddock was a nineteenth-century man. He was born only ninety-three years after the inauguration of George Washington and a mere seventeen years after the end of the Civil War. My having an old father who was the baby of *his* family gave me a living link to the far-distant past. He sang me songs that he learned first-hand from former slaves. He grew to manhood without seeing one single automobile; he would be twenty-one before the airplane was invented and close to forty before the first radio station went on the air. He was a Florida relic, with roots so deep in the sandy loam that he was an anachronism even in my early life. His pronunciation of Florida's major city was never *Mi-am-ee* but *Mi-am-uh*. (My brother still pronounces it that way.) He used Old Florida definitions that are probably unknown to today's younger natives, such as calling a pine thicket a *bay*. He called a land turtle a *gopher*, a gopher a *salamander*, and a salamander a *scorpion lizard*.

And once Daddy formed an opinion, that was it, forever: cancer was contagious; California oranges were tiny inedible things; George Jenkins, the poor Georgia-born Polk County boy who started the Publix supermarket chain, was actually a Jew because only Jews owned chain stores.

So this courtly old gentleman who washed his snowy-white hair with a bar of black tar soap sold in a tin container, this provincial farmer who truly believed "the citrus industry affects the lives of *every single person* in the state of Flahrr-da," this nineteenth-century man who was nearing middle age when Abraham Lincoln's son died, colored my life and made it richer and brighter. Whatever damage his gloom and his capriciousness and his hard-line discipline might have done to my psyche, he more than made up for it with the gifts he gave me. He taught me to show affection for those I love. He taught me to be kind and courteous to everyone. And despite his old-fashioned prejudiced ways, he taught me to be honest, because the only person I ever caught my father lying to was himself.

As I write these words, I am in the county of my father's birth, though about forty miles southeast of the shores of Lake George (the setting for Marjorie Kinnan Rawlings's great novel, *The Yearling*), where the Braddock oranges grew and the Braddock cattle grazed— and over a hundred miles northeast of Polk County, where Daddy settled as a young man. I am looking out at the Atlantic Ocean from a little cottage. It's a cool, drizzly winter day, and there is no one on the beach. As I hear the timeless roar of the sea, I can imagine myself looking out at the same spot one hundred years earlier, and I can almost see young Paul Braddock stepping out of his carriage onto the hard sand beach, a very young and very handsome man with dark hair and sky-blue eyes that suddenly start to twinkle as I walk down the dunes and give a friendly wave. I can almost hear his deep voice as he comments, in an affable yet almost formal way, about the weather, the seagulls, or anything you want to talk about. It's been thirty-five years since I last saw him, ancient and effete, yet I still feel his strong presence today as I imagine the horse and buggy carrying him on down the hard sand beach, into his future and into my life.

My senior year was my favorite at Auburndale High. We were the

Class of '58. My grades, so perfect in grammar school, had begun a downhill slide in junior high. They hit rock bottom in my sophomore year and had to be made up at summer school. Rarely studying and certainly no honor student, by my senior year I was at least beginning to make good grades in the subjects I loved (history, civics, social sciences) and managing to get by in the rest.

I think I was past doing the "not a sissy," tough-guy routine of my sophomore and junior years. Having *survived* those earlier teenage years was an amazing feat in itself. Back in those days, *nights* actually, I would turn up a bottle of whiskey and chug-a-lug without stopping until falling over and passing out. The time that I drunkenly drove my father's Ford the entire stretch of the Highway 92 overpass *lying down in the seat,* just to show off for Don Pace, who was following in his car, very easily could have resulted in what is known today as vehicular homicide. But by September of 1957, though still full of mischief and rarely missing an opportunity to blurt out something that would make my fellow classmates laugh, I had started to do a little work on my image. I don't think my teachers thought of me as a hoodlum anymore.

So I was getting along better with the teachers. I had always gotten along well with my fellow classmates, except for the bullies. Whenever challenged to a prearranged fight, I was a spineless coward and always got my ass whipped. But I was *fearless* when I lost my temper. There was a guy named Richard Manley who had bullied me the entire previous school term, and he started out senior year the same way. It never happened anywhere except in the boys bathroom, where we all went to smoke. Then one day he gave me a pretty big shove, knocking me against the wash basin. Something went off inside me, and before I really knew what I was doing, I had him down on the floor, banging his head against the commode. From that point on, Richard Manley treated me with respect, and we got along fine.

The 1970s TV sitcom *Happy Days* painted a fairly accurate picture of what it was like to be a teenager in the late 1950s. In my memory, the music was everywhere, as if it were being piped in through the trees and coming up from the cracks in the sidewalks. Rock 'n' roll was the music of the young, and we couldn't imagine ourselves or the music ever growing old. When Elvis's "Jailhouse Rock" arrived at our local radio station, the teenage deejay Ronnie Brown played it continuously for one hour, with no interruptions or commercials. Because I had fallen in love with country music, my favorite rock 'n' roll was by the artists who had country roots, such as the Everly Brothers and Jerry Lee Lewis. I think I loved music so much that one kind of music just wasn't enough for me.

I had one friendship that was based almost entirely on a mutual love of country music. Jim Woodard, a tall gruff-voiced but congenial guy, didn't run around much with my friends and vice versa, but he often came by my house after school. We would enthusiastically listen to the music of Marty Robbins, Jim Reeves, and Ray Price, as well as obscure country records I had ordered from the Ernest Tubb Record Shop in Nashville. Stanley Cox played some guitar, and we would sit around his room and imitate country singers and also listen to the latest rock 'n' roll records. One afternoon we rode around singing a song we had made up about Jack Lopler, a friend of my brother's. Jack's years were said to be numbered because he had an enlarged heart. We sang the song to the tune of Hank Williams's "Your Cheatin' Heart." Our version went:

> Your enlarged heart will tell on you,
> You'll gasp for breath the whole night through.

As of this writing, decades later, Jack Lopler is still alive and well.

To Stanley, playing and singing was sort of a hobby, and I think he viewed my piano playing and songwriting pretty much the same way. He was a slow-talking, soft-spoken, easy-going guy who was a lot of fun. It didn't take much for us to make each other laugh. We knew well enough to not sit anywhere close to each other in Mr. Redig's speech class because one of the classmates had a speech impediment; it's not that we were insensitive, but we knew it would be dangerous for us to look at each other while this unfortunate but brave soul was making a speech. Whereas Don Pace may have seemed a bit worldly to my parents, Stanley had my mother's stamp of approval because she saw this gentle, well-mannered boy at church every Sunday morning, where his father was a deacon. She would have been surprised to find out that one of the things Stanley and I loved to do was drive to the newsstand in Winter Haven and buy a copy of *Sexology* magazine. Then, while one of us drove, the other would read aloud. In that much less pornographic era, the words *penis* or *vagina* printed in a magazine, would set us off into howls of laughter.

For Stanley, Red, and me, self-deprecation was the way to go. Bragging was something one just didn't do—it would take me years in the music business before I learned how to take a compliment. To be rejected by a girl was something for us to share with each other and laugh about. One day Stanley and I were riding around Winter Haven in his father's Dodge when we saw two attractive girls walking around Lake Silver. Stanley pulled up beside them, and I rolled down the window and asked if they wanted a ride. They took a look at us, looked at each other, then rolled their eyes and said, "Shit," as they continued walking. We couldn't wait to tell Red about it.

The *American Graffiti* and *Porky's* type of practical jokes aren't indigenous to my generation. There were high school hijinks in the 1920s, and there were high school hijinks in the 1990s. These pranks are most appreciated by one's peers. My daughter and her teenage friends trying to see how many Nashville restaurants they could get thrown out of in the 1980s didn't strike me nearly as funny as the gags that I had once participated in.

Elmo Woods, who taught shop and mechanical drawing, was the butt of many jokes. It would be a stretch to say that Mr. Woods was Barney Fife, but Don Knotts could have played him. He had a chronic sinus condition, and almost every sentence was prefaced with a *sniff sniff*. The shop classroom was not inside the main hall but was a detached outbuilding next to some woods, and therefore more accessible and vulnerable. Once we left a twenty-gallon jug of pee, a pee bank we had contributed to for many weeks, at the door of Mr. Woods's classroom, with a note saying it was varnish remover. ("Sniff sniff, this stuff smells *awful*.") One night we fed a stray dog a hearty meal spiked with a heavy dose of laxative and sneaked him through a window that we had left cracked; the next morning Mr. Woods was slipping and sliding all over the place.

There was an element of danger in the "truckdriver's wife" joke. It was first pulled on Red Cannon and me by Don Pace. Pace, who had graduated from high school the previous year, was acquainted with some college boys in Lakeland whom the rest of us didn't know. We were told of a truckdriver's wife who loved young guys, and I anticipated a night of wild sex as I drove Red, Pace, and one of Pace's new friends deep into the wilderness. As we climbed out of my father's 1956 Ford and approached what we thought was a house in the pitch-black night, a loud and angry voice pierced the silence, filling my heart with terror.

"You sons-of-bitches been *fuckin' my wife!!!*"

There was a terrible explosion, an echo of gunfire, and a staccato scream as Pace's friend fell to the ground. Then came another blast, and Pace yelled, "*Run! Run! Run!*"

In seconds I was opening the door on the driver's side of Daddy's Ford, and Red was opening the other door. Pace was almost in my face, flailing his arms, "No! No! No! Don't get in the car. Run! Through the woods there, *Run!*"

Without questioning the logic of running through the woods when the car would have had us on the clay road within a few seconds, I did as he told me. I ran into the woods, for about a mile, as fast as I could until I couldn't run anymore. As a tiny moon sliver rose above a pine tree, I could see a dimly lit Red Cannon, squatting and shivering, going "Shhh-h-h." As we saw the glow of the approaching flashlights and heard Pace yelling, "It's a joke," the wheels were already turning in my head. This was a prank we needed to pull around Auburndale.

We found an abandoned house on a lake several miles north of town. One coolish November night, we had a guy waiting inside the house with a rifle. The victims this time were Billy Ray Smith and Wilbur Wolfe. The "truckdriver" yelled, "You sons-of-bitches been *fuckin' my wife!*" and BANG! Stanley Cox yipped and fell to the ground. Our two victims were so horrified that they ran in circles, then smack dab into each other as Wilbur's fingernail cut Billy Ray's face.

"I've been *shot*," Billy Ray hollered. When Wilbur saw the blood in the half moon's light, he gulped and his eyes got *huge*. He jumped into the lake and started swimming away like he was in the Olympics. We yelled Wilbur's name over and over as we searched all the way around the lake, to no avail. We thought he had drowned and felt that we were responsible (and in serious trouble). After two hours of searching and hollering, with heavy hearts we decided to drive on back to Auburndale and call the Polk County Sheriff's Department in Bartow.

Halfway back to town, there alongside the Polk City Road with his thumb out, was a very wide-eyed, wet, and shivering Wilbur Wolfe. As we pulled over, extremely relieved and very happy to see him, he peered into the car and asked, "Who all got *killed?*" After swimming the lake, he had run through about four miles of groves and woods and swamps and finally ended up on the highway.

I was especially anxious to pull a joke on Harvey Wooley, who, the year before, had announced to the entire classroom that he had met a girl who said I wasn't a very good kisser. We told Harvey that one of the best-looking girls in school was "putting out" but didn't want anyone to know her identity so she did it with a blanket pulled over her head. We dropped hints that it was a *particular* beautiful girl. *I* got to be the girl. I was near Braddock's Hole in my father's orange grove, lying down on the backseat of Red Cannon's car, pantsless legs crossed very tightly as they dangled out the open door, the rest of me covered up with a blanket, as Stanley Cox and Harvey Wooley drove up. With only the stars and the lights of distant Auburndale to offer faint illumination, it very well could have been a girl lying there cross-legged. Harvey bent over me and slowly drawled, "Hey, baby, I *know* who you *are.*" He proceeded to pull my legs apart, and within a few seconds was yelling, "You *son-of-a-bitch!*"

The meanest practical joke was played on my goody-goody cousin Tommy Tolliver, who was visiting from Jacksonville. We were riding up the Polk City Road in Don Pace's car. There was an extremely sharp curve that should not have been attempted at more than thirty-five miles an hour. What an unsuspecting passenger couldn't see was that by driving straight ahead instead of negotiating the curve, you would continue to drive right onto a clay road.

"Hey, you're doing ninety miles an hour," Tommy said anxiously.

"Oh, that ain't nothin'," Pace replied. "There's a sharp curve up here that I'm gonna take at a *hunnerd* miles an hour."

"No, that's too fast, Pace, we'll never make it," I feigned excitedly.

"Slow down! *Please, please slow down!*" Tommy yelled.

"Shoot, I'm gonna take this curve at *a hunnerd and ten*," Pace yelled as he moved his hands in a leftward motion over the steering wheel without actually touching it. We came upon the curve, flying like a rocket. Tommy screamed. With a slight jolt, there we were, continuing straight ahead onto the clay road, safe and sound.

When Tommy told his parents what we had done, I thought I saw a tiny hint of a smile cross his father's lips, but his mama was definitely not amused.

My senior year seemed like a kind of way station, a stop between Bobby the kid and Bobby the man. It seemed especially so on one pleasantly cool December day, our last day of school before the holiday vacation. A small group of us decided to break early and left school around noon to go to a café out on Highway 92. It was one of those fine Florida winter days; the temperature was around sixty-five, and there wasn't a single cloud in the Easter-egg-blue sky.

Stanley Cox and I were with Kim Weston and her cousin Margaret. They had moved to Auburndale from Ohio earlier that year. Kim had short hair and wore horn-rimmed glasses; she wasn't so pretty as to be intimidating but had a great figure. I had smooched with her at a couple of parties but we never actually dated. It was okay to talk dirty around Kim and Margaret, and they were fun to hang out with. The four of us were eating cheeseburgers while my favorite Christmas record, Elvis's "Blue Christmas," resounded from the jukebox. We were talking about postgraduation plans. I have no recollection of Kim's and Margaret's future plans, but Stanley and Red were in the navy reserve and planned to be sailing into Hawaii and Japan the next year. I had decided that I would try to be a deejay—I thought of it as a way to get into the music business—and revealed to my companions my long-range dreams of being a musician and eventually a songwriter.

Stanley already knew of my aspirations. I had gotten fairly good on the piano, listening over and over to records of my favorite pianists. Several of my buddies would come by the house after school, always requesting that I play the piano solo from Jerry Lee Lewis's version of "You Win Again," but they didn't seem to think my songwriting was very good. I wondered if it was my songwriting or the way I presented the songs. Or maybe they just weren't totally into country music. I knew that none of them listened regularly to any country radio programs, as I did, so I hatched a scheme. I learned both sides of a brand new Carl Smith record—which went on to become a two-sided hit—then taped the two songs on my Webcor recorder, doing both the singing and playing. I told my friends that I wanted them to hear two new songs I had just written. They listened, and their reaction was the same as when hearing songs I had *really* written: negative. That's when I knew I had the potential to be a professional songwriter.

I had discovered a new magic land, and I went there every night. It was the *Opry Star Spotlight* with Ralph Emery over WSM in Nashville. WSM was a clear channel fifty-thousand-watt station, and on most nights the reception was as good as if the show were being broadcast from right there in Polk County. I turned on the red plastic radio at my bedside every night at 10:30, and listened to the all-night show for at least two hours. Ralph, who went on to be country music's most celebrated TV talk show host, was twenty-six years old and a former rock 'n' roll deejay. He played all the current hits, and his guests included practically every star in the country music constellation. I loved hearing him chitchat with all these famous people whom he knew personally and socialized with. Here was born the dream of someday going to Nashville and becoming a part of all this. I would have been thrilled to know that in ten years I would be Ralph's occasional on-the-air guest, playing his piano and singing live my parodies of the hits of the day.

Every Tuesday when school was out, I drove the family car, a 1953 Lincoln, or Daddy's 1956 Ford "grove" car, to the newsstand in Winter Haven and bought a copy of *Billboard* magazine. I devoured every single word in the music section, all the news, columns, and reviews, and practically memorized the chart positions in the pop field as well as country. I probably knew more about the music business when I was seventeen than I did years later when I was actually part of it.

As Elvis was begging his baby not to say "Don't," as the Silhouettes were urging us to "Get a Job," and as the Champs were playing "Tequila," the cute tight-skirted butts of Auburndale High girls wiggled up and down the hallways, into the classrooms and into my fantasies. I didn't have a lot of dates, but I didn't have a lot of rejection either, because I just wouldn't ask a girl out unless I felt certain she would say yes. Sexy Charlene Crim, known for bending over the teacher's desk in her low-cut blouse to ask a math question and for Alabama-drawling "Hey y'all" to every group of gawking guys who watched her walk by, just seemed off-limits to me. Jeanette Johnston, an Arkansas Freewill Baptist preacher's daughter who had the courage to say she wouldn't mind it if black kids went to school with us and who looked so sexy sitting on her front porch barefooted, just didn't seem interested in me. Gorgeous, ponytailed Fay Dean was only a freshman, so we didn't have any classes together and just spoke to each other in passing. There was a beautiful girl named Carmen Stone, from the little grove town of Dundee, who went out with me a couple of times, but she was seriously involved with a guy she would soon marry. There was a sweet girl from Winter Haven I dated twice, then didn't ask out again when I suddenly realized she was the sister of the most feared guy in Polk County, a boy so mean and vicious that he threw grapefruit at the stomachs of pregnant black women.

But my gigantic crush was on Mary Lou Dunlop, who was one year behind me. Mary Lou was attractive, but she wasn't glamorous and didn't try to be. My obsession with her was one of those things that's hard to explain, but I thought about her constantly. To tell the truth, I didn't really know her very well. Though she was friendly and seemed unpretentious and easy to talk to, we never had that many conversations. She was serious about a guy who attended the University of Florida but occasionally went out with local boys. I finally got up the nerve to ask her out. She said yes, so I picked her up one night at the Auburn Theatre, where she sold refreshments.

"Why did you want to go out with me?" she asked.

"Well, I don't know . . . because I *like* you."

"I mean, you don't date other girls, do you?"

"Yeah, I date other girls," I said, a little defensively. "I went out with Jessica Wilkes." Immediately I wondered if Jessica had told everybody what a damned fool I had been on my very first date.

"I didn't know you went out with Jessica," Mary Lou declared, seeming surprised and impressed.

"I've gone out with girls from Winter Haven and Dundee," I continued.

"Oh, well, I *figured* maybe you dated out-of-town girls," she said politely, trying to save me some face.

We went parking at Braddock's Hole. I loved kissing her but, true to form, didn't know where to go from there. I doubt that she would have let it go any further anyway because it was plain to see that she was hung up on her college guy.

One day I was driving my dad's '56 Ford through Auburndale. As I turned left at the Auburn Theatre, there was Mary Lou standing in the doorway, taking a break from the concession stand. When she saw me, she waved. I threw up my right hand and blew the horn with my left. Instead of making the full turn, the car jumped the curb in front of the theater. Mary Lou hopped backwards through the door. I got the car back on the street for only a second and then back on the sidewalk again, where I hit a garbage can and sent it flying through the air. When I got the car back on the street once more, I grabbed the wheel so tightly that I accidentally blew the horn again. That was the end of any hope for me and Mary Lou Dunlop. For the next few weeks, if I saw her coming down the hall at school, I hid. I was so humiliated, I didn't want to face her.

The crush on Mary Lou didn't disappear overnight, but I knew I needed to put my attention on other things. As I headed down the final stretch at Auburndale High, I started to think seriously about my future.

One spring afternoon, a representative of the Atlanta School of Electronics paid Mother, Daddy, and me a visit. I had read in a magazine about this institute, which offered a course in radio announcing, and had sent off a letter of inquiry. We sat on the front screened porch, our guest in the rocking chair and my parents and I on the glider, poring over brochures and booklets. The man told us the classes were at night and the school guaranteed that they would find me a day job. He also assured us that the school was able to find positions at radio stations for a majority of students who finished the course. There was a boarding house in Atlanta that rented only to A.S.E. students, and at a special low rate. Despite my poor grades in high school, my parents wanted me to go to college, not some school for disc jockeys, but they knew I really wanted to do this. Throughout the years, even when they didn't support me with words, they always came through financially.

Mother, at fifty, was now a grandparent (nothing new for Daddy, a great-grandparent who'd been a grandparent for over thirty years). Paul and Jo Ann had a baby daughter named Carol and were living in an area just west of town called Lena Vista.

One warm late spring night, sixty-seven of us from the Class of '58 received our diplomas at Connie Mack Field, and I'll simply say that I wasn't valedictorian or salutatorian. Several of the girls were teary-eyed, and though I may have felt a bit sentimental, I was ready to move on. Just after graduation exercises, June Bainbridge, a cute, petite girl in the junior class who had a bit of a bad reputation, came up to me and told me she would have gone to the Junior-Senior Prom with me if I had asked her. That was my cue to ask her for a date, and the only reason I didn't was because I had just recently started to date a pretty blonde from Winter Haven.

Beth Kruger was a very Aryan-looking Wisconsin girl who had moved to Florida the year before to live with her grandmother. The kids who came from small towns in Indiana and Ohio assimilated pretty easily with us Southerners, but Beth was from way up in Milwaukee and stood out as very Northern. She kidded me that my "you're a little doll" sounded like "you're a little dull." I was experiencing a pretty major infatuation for this extremely good-looking girl.

Early in our dating experience, she told me she had met an Auburndale guy named Billy Max Jones, who was about my brother's age, and had told him she was dating me. She said when he laughed, she responded, "I think Bobby's very nice," to which he replied, "Yeah, that's what I *mean.*" Then she asked me, "What do you think he meant by that?"

We went out several times, always ending up kissing at Braddock's Hole, with me never carrying it to the next level. No matter what I tried, she never put up any resistance and never said "No" or "Stop." She would let me put my hand on her breast, but that was as far as I would take it. I was afraid of making a fool of myself, not realizing that I was doing exactly that anyway.

After a few weeks, Beth called me up and cancelled a date, saying she wasn't feeling well. I tried two or three times to get her on the phone with no success, so one day Stanley and I drove past her house. There she was, sitting in a sports car that was parked in her driveway, with some deeply tanned blond muscle man, probably one of the water skiers at Cypress Gardens. She had her arm around him. I was heartbroken. I went home and listened to the Ray Price recording of "Invitation to The Blues" over and over.

Stanley was also losing someone he cared about, but he wasn't being dealt rejection as I was. His girlfriend, who was still in school, was moving out of state with her parents. We were both very sad. So what we did was ride around singing sorrowful country songs about some guy being broken-hearted because his baby had run off and left him. We were goofing off and acting like we were *pretending* we were heartbroken. It was our way of laughing at ourselves and each other, and it worked.

Auburndale was a pretty little town, with its small downtown businesses and old Spanish-style City Hall running parallel with the palm-lined city park and the Atlantic Coastline railroad depot. But I was ready to leave it behind. Don Pace had once said he would probably end up living an adventurous life in South America while I stayed in Auburndale all my life. I didn't want that. As a child, I always thought it would be so much more exciting to live in a big city. Auburndale, like my parents, was strict and conservative.

The big growers and packinghouse owners may have controlled Auburndale's purse strings, but the churches had the political clout, especially the Southern Baptists, who were by far the biggest religious group in town. In the 1958 wet-dry election, Polk County remained dry by a fairly small margin; in Auburndale, it wasn't even close. In the last week of campaigning, the anti-liquor forces, operating out of the First Baptist Church, had put together a long convoy of "Keep Polk Dry" cars to go up and down every street in town, honking their horns. As the caravan passed the house of Billy Max Jones—the big guy who laughed when Beth Kruger told him she was dating me—Billy Max stood out in his yard and defiantly raised a bottle of whiskey at the cars.

I liked my town and I loved my parents, but I was ready to leave. On my eighteenth birthday, I drove to Bartow to register for the draft. I had quit wearing my hair in a flattop, and it was getting longer—a Tampa policeman had recently told me that my loud mouth and sideburns would someday get me in trouble. Stanley, Red, and R. L. Pugh, the tall, friendly Auburndale Bloodhounds football hero who hung out with us occasionally, came by the house for a birthday supper and one of Mother's delicious desserts (probably chocolate chip cookies). Afterwards, we headed west into the melted-butter sky, on our way to Lakeland to play miniature golf, or "carpet golf" as we called it. Oddly, I have no memory of anything that transpired in the three-week interim between my birthday and my move to Atlanta. That night, when we finished our game, I'm sure we drove the ten or twelve miles from Lakeland back to the Braddock house where everyone got in their cars and drove home. But in my mind, we all just quietly walked off in different directions: R.L. down to the University of Miami and a track scholarship, Stanley and Red out to San Diego to sail the seven seas, and I up to Atlanta and the world beyond.

CHAPTER SIX

Starvin' in Atlanta

FOR THE FIRST TIME in my eighteen years, I would be living away from my own native soil. I had always thought "Imperial Polk" was more like a state than a county. The population was around 185,000, but it was not densely settled in an urban sense—it just covered a very large area. With 1,861 square miles, it was the size of several other Florida counties combined. Though Lakeland had a population of forty thousand, most of Polk County was rural and small town in character. We led the nation in phosphate and citrus, and ranked fifth in America for the total number of agricultural workers.

Auburndale was exclusively citrus. Winter Haven pulled in a lot of tourists because of the water ski shows at Cypress Gardens; many of the families from up in Polk City and Green Pond were in the cattle business; strawberries were so bountiful around the community of Kathleen that school vacation came in winter instead of summer, so the kids could work in the fields at harvest time. But Auburndale was strictly a citrus town. Most of the people there grew it, bought it, sold it, picked it, packed it, or canned it.

So it was from this cultural garden that I sprang forth. It was a pretty narrow patch. My parents had good vocabularies, and they appeared to be genteel, my father's gentility inherent and my mother's acquired. But they weren't book people. Daddy read newspapers, agricultural journals, *Reader's Digest,* and the Bible. Mother enjoyed magazines and read maybe one book a year. I loved books, but because I had never let a formal education affect me enough to discipline my reading habits, my reading was highly selective. In other words, I read what I *wanted* to read, such as Mickey Spillane's crime fictions, Grace Metalious's revolutionary "nasty" books, or Erskine Caldwell's tales of degenerate Southern white trash girls with big bosoms. I was interested in politics and did keep up with national and world events, but I saw all things through parochial eyes. My perceptions were steeped in misconceptions and myths, and, when I left for radio-announcing school in Atlanta, I was very much the unsophisticated small-town boy going to the sophisticated big city.

One would correctly think of Georgia as being far more Southern and less urbane than Florida. That's certainly true now, and it was in 1958 as well. But Auburndale was a lot *more* Southern than Florida as a whole and Atlanta was a lot *less* Southern than the rest of Georgia.

Redneck was a word that the national media picked up from the Birmingham area in the early 1960s, but it wasn't a word used in Auburndale or in most of the South prior to that time. My friends and I referred to dumb-acting country people as *hicks*. I certainly never thought of *myself* as one. But when I moved to Atlanta, I found out that I was indeed a hick.

Somewhere around Labor Day 1958, Daddy, Mother and I climbed into the family car to head up to Atlanta. I forgot something—I don't remember what it was—and wanted to run back inside the house to get it.

"No-o-o-o," Daddy mooed, "bad luck to go back. We'll *mail* it to you."

Before I could back the car out of the garage, my father had to say the family travel prayer, asking our Heavenly Father to guide, guard, and direct us on our journey. You'd think we were about to embark on a canoe trip down the crocodile-infested waters of the Amazon, which may actually have been less dangerous than riding in a car with me driving.

Road travel was extremely hazardous in 1958. Not only were there no seat belts or air bags, but the Interstate System was still in its babyhood and had not yet reached the Southland. All the major highways were two-lane. On an interstate, if you get careless or sleepy—for sure, it can be lethal—but you'll most likely run through the gravel or maybe bang up the side of somebody's car. On a two-lane highway, a little mistake (just a few inches worth) often resulted in people flying at sixty miles an hour right into a deadly dashboard or through a windshield. There was also the impatient driver, passing everything in sight, whose luck would run out when his judgment erred by a few feet or a few miles an hour. In those days, needless to say, most highway deaths were caused by head-on collisions.

This would be my last turn at the wheel for some time. Daddy had bought me a 1951 Chevrolet a few months before but sold it at summer's end because it had been decided that I wouldn't have any need for a car in Atlanta. Like hell I wouldn't!

We drove up U.S. 27 through the rolling grove-covered hills of Lake County and the horse country around Ocala. We took U.S. 41 through the flat piney woods and tobacco fields of North Florida and South Georgia and into the red-clay country of my mother's childhood in Central Georgia, where we stayed over to visit assorted relatives. In Gordon, I played piano duets with a redheaded female distant cousin whom I had never seen before and haven't seen since. In Macon, I got a twenty-four-hour crush on my third cousin Charlotte Robertson, the jailer's daughter, who had turned into a beautiful fifteen year-old. Back on the road, I looked over at a car speeding past us and recognized the familiar double take, the head darting forward and slightly down like a cat about to pounce on a bird, the eyes comically wide open; it was none other than Don Pace, also Atlanta-bound, going to visit his pharmacist brother for the weekend.

Near Jonesboro, my parents and I sat helplessly in a traffic jam, listening to the distant hideous screams up ahead from a man trapped inside a wrecked tanker that burned too big and hot for anyone to approach. The screaming stopped just before the fire trucks arrived. There was nothing any of us could do to save him. Daddy didn't need to admonish me, "Bobby, for God's sake, pleeease drive *ve-ry* carefully." We continued our journey silently, heading north to Atlanta on U.S. 41, the gloomy ghost of tragedy riding with us.

If New York's the Big Apple, then Atlanta's the Big Peach. By the twenty-first century, it would be an international media center—a big city with Northernlike urban blessings and curses—but in 1958 it was the booster-minded, growth-obsessed capital of Dixie.

We drove up Peachtree Street in the lunchtime traffic as the car radio blared out a jingle, "Vandiver For Governor." Heading east on Ponce de Leon Avenue past the Fox Theatre, we turned onto a shady street lined with big old houses—not run-down mansions, they weren't that bad or that good—but nice old residences that had seen better days. "There it is," my mother announced with a big smile. As I pulled the car in the driveway, I saw several guys about my age, standing around the wide, pillared porch, smoking cigarettes. This was the boarding house that had a special rate for students of the Atlanta School of Electronics.

After getting me settled in, and before driving a hundred miles north to visit my mom's sister, my parents took me to Rich's Department Store to buy me a winter overcoat, an article of clothing not considered a necessity in Central Florida. I picked out a deep green and burnt orange Chinese-looking thing with big square buttons. Then we went by the school and met with the headmaster.

It was late afternoon when Mother and Daddy took me back to the boarding house, or the apartment house, as I called it. Mother had tears in her eyes. To this day, I feel a tad guilty when I recall how thrilled I was to be on my own and not under their jurisdiction. That night I went to a nearby restaurant; the waiter looked at my rather large schnoz and my slicked-back hair (the butch haircut wax that I used made my hair look almost black) and said, "You're *Italian*, like me, right?" I lied and told him I was, and he took my order for pizza and wine. I went to several bars (and got hit on by a couple of guys) until I found a bar that would serve me, then proceeded to drink several glasses of sherry wine. I ended up in the apartment building's backyard making out with a girl who lived in the neighborhood. It was my first night on my own, and I got stinking drunk and stayed up all night. This didn't get me off to a very good start with my landlady/housemother, Mrs. Bunch.

Mrs. Bunch was a short, plumpish lady, probably in her mid-fifties. She seemed very cultured and played classical piano, but she was also a born-again Christian Pentecostal. There was a young man who attended to her needs and drove her to church. She ran an old-fashioned boarding house, serving breakfast every morning and a big

STARVIN' IN ATLANTA • 103

supper every night. (There were several black cooks and housekeepers who lived in a little house in her backyard, like slaves in the antebellum days.) At first, she just didn't like me. She didn't like me staying up all night, and she didn't like me playing rock 'n' roll on her grand piano. I wanted to get along with her, though, so I tried really hard and turned on the charm. I finally won her over, but it took some work.

My roommate was a big, fat, happy, funny guy named Billy Brewer. Billy referred to Mrs. Bunch, behind her back, as "Bessie." He loved rock 'n' roll and looked forward to being a deejay. I had a fairly decent portable hi-fi record player, and he loved to play "Rockin' Robin" on it. "Is this *loud enough*, Bessie, you old heifer?" he would shout with a wild giggle. He was fun and easy to get along with, and on weekends he went home, which was about a hundred miles away in Alabama, so I had the place all to myself.

Billy was in Alabama one weekend, and I was still up, about 3:30 on a very chilly Sunday morning. I was doing this weird thing that I sometimes did—I invented a state and gave names to all its counties, drew an imaginary map, sketched pictures of imaginary political candidates and ran them in an imaginary race for statewide office, never knowing the results myself until adding up the vote in all the counties. I was still up, doing this weird thing that I called a "doodle," when I heard a clap of thunder so loud that it shook the room. How could there be thunder on a clear, cold night, I wondered. I turned on the radio and soon learned what had happened. Someone had set off fifty sticks of dynamite in the Temple, Atlanta's oldest synagogue.

Ironically, it would be disclosed that one of those involved in the crime was a former resident of my hometown and related to one of Auburndale's best-known citizens. After growing up and reading a lot of history, I would become sympathetic to all things Jewish, but at the time I don't think the temple bombing greatly impacted my young life. I knew it was wrong, but I didn't understand its significance. My mind was on breaking into radio and the music business.

My radio-announcing classes, which were held at night, weren't very impressive. The instructor talked occasionally about losing regional accents but spent most of our time talking about funny radio bloopers. One of my classmates was a thin, blond drummer named Louis Wright. Louie, as I called him, was originally from Illinois, but his home was in Gainesville, Florida, where his father was a university professor. Louie had been rehearsing with a couple of musicians who were taking electronic courses at the school. He knew a place that had a piano and invited me to jam with them.

The two guys he had told me about were country boys from the hills of northwestern South Carolina. Willie Williams was an electric guitar player who was a walking, talking hillbilly stereotype, somewhere between Jethro on *The Beverly Hillbillies* and Gomer Pyle. He was a tall boy, but his partner—singer-guitarist Dwight Hicks—was even taller and very skinny. Willie was talkative and giggly while Dwight was humorless and slack-jawed. Dwight pronounced "rock 'n' roll" as "rotten roll." "We're a rotten roll band," he told me.

I don't remember how it was arranged, but we got a nonpaying gig, a party at a black elementary school. Long, lanky Dwight swayed backwards and forwards as he sang "Hard-Headed Woman" to the children who looked on in wide-eyed amazement. Afterwards, when Louie asked me excitedly (Louie was very excitable), "Did they like us?" I told him I honestly didn't know.

My day job was actually a half-day job, at Decca Distributors, the Southeastern distributor for the MCA family of Decca, Brunswick, and Coral Records. The building was located on Forsythe Street, downtown, about a half-hour walk or a five-minute bus ride from where I lived. My job was to go to the large bins and pull the records that had been ordered by record stores and department stores throughout the region.

My supervisor was Horace Brown, an African American. A black boss was something new for me, but I learned my first of many needed life lessons on race when I saw that he was the smartest person in the building and a bona fide expert on record distribution. I had been brought up in a society where blacks didn't achieve because they weren't *allowed* to achieve. For an African American to be given such a position of responsibility was unusual at that time in the South, even in a big city like Atlanta. The Decca southeastern distributorship was run by a New York–born Jewish man.

One morning I saw a stranger walking up and down the aisles, looking through the record bins. He was short and plumpish, pale-skinned, pug-nosed, and wore his dark hair in an almost-ducktailed pompadour. I figured he was a few years older than me—actually he was ten years older, twenty-eight.

"Hey, I'm Dub Dalton of Dub and Debbie. I wanna copy of the Kalin Twins record; wanna make sure those mothas (as in "mothers") aren't stealin' our sound."

I was familiar with the Dub and Debbie record "Lolly Poppa." It wasn't a hit, but Dub and Debbie were sort of a poppish rockabilly act on Decca, and I had seen a few copies of their record around.

"Yeah, here it is, 'When' by the Kalin Twins," I said. Since Dub and Debbie were on Decca, I figured it would be all right to give him a copy. I introduced myself and told him I played piano with a little rock 'n' roll band.

"Hey, man, we about to go on tour with the Everly Brothers. I need a band right away. When can I hear you cats?" Dub was a Southern hipster, speaking kind of a white/black jive talk, in both vocabulary and dialect.

"Uh—uh—we can play for you over at my apartment building, most any afternoon," I stammered. This opportunity seemed almost too good to be true. I was wondering if we were good enough to play with an act that had a major recording deal. "How about tomorrow afternoon?"

He protruded his lips as though he was saying "pooooh" while he moved his head around in a circular motion, then thrust his torso forward and snapped his fingers and said, "Thas *it!*"

"I know I can have everybody there at four o'clock tomorrow," I told him as I wrote out the address.

"I'll see ya tomorra, Bobbeh," he said as he sort of waddled away with just a hint of a choreographed dance step.

That night after school, I told the guys about Dub. Louie, the thin, blond excitable drummer was jumping up and down. Willie Williams grinned big, babbling and saying, "Goll-leeeee." Somber Dwight Hicks just said, "Damn."

The audition was a blur. We ran through two or three songs, not very well, I thought, but Dub told us we were hired! It's almost as though he had made up his mind before he even heard us. He said the tour would be starting right away, a few hundred dollars a night in twenty-first-century dollars.

Rehearsals were to begin right away. We all immediately quit the Atlanta School of Electronics. I liked Dub's 1958 black Ford Fairlane so much that I went to a Ford dealership and told one of the salesmen that I would be coming back soon to purchase a black 1959 Fairlane. My hometown weekly paper ran the headline "Auburndale Boy Touring With Everly Brothers"—for the past year and a half, everything the Everly Brothers had put out had been a major pop hit. I was giddy over the prospect of heading for the big time.

Because I was no longer attending Atlanta School of Electronics, I couldn't stay at Mrs. Bunch's place for the same rent, so I moved into a basement apartment where the other guys in the band were living.

Dub said there had been a delay in the tour. We stayed busy, but not busy making music. Dub had lived around Atlanta all his life and was constantly taking us somewhere. One night he took us down to East Point to stand guard outside his house all night because he said there had been rash of burglaries in the neighborhood. While we were standing guard, he waddled out with some rakes and said, "They's leaves all over the yard. Get out there and rake those boys up." He took us to a drugstore where he had once been a soda jerk, got behind the counter, and started making a soda. He said, "Hey, Bobbeh, you know they don' let just *anybody* come in here and do this," as though it had something to do with having star status. We kept asking him when the tour would start. He finally said, "Well, mothas, I'll just call up ol' Owen Bradley and find out when our next record's comin' out."

Dub pulled over to a telephone booth to place a call to the legendary Owen Bradley, head of Decca Records' Nashville office and producer (a position then called "A&R man") of Brenda Lee, Patsy Cline, Webb Pierce, Bobby Helms, and Ernest Tubb, all of whom were close personal friends of Dub's, he assured us. ("Oh yeah, I know Elvis *real* well, he's just a regular down-to-earth boy.") He fed a bunch of coins to the pay phone after he gave the operator the number for Decca Records in Nashville.

"Hello, this is Dub Dalton, lemme speak to Owen, and make it snappy." He gave us a big wink. "Hey, Owen, you ol' sonofabitch, it's about time we went out and played a few holes of *geef*." He winked at us again, then burst into convulsive laughter, exclaiming "Owen, you just too much! Hey, when we gonna cut another record?" He protruded his lips as though he was saying "pooooh" while he moved his head around in a circular motion, then thrust his torso forward and snapped his fingers and said, "Motha, thas *it!* See ya in a couple weeks."

Later on, Louie told me he was a little worried. I asked him what was the matter. "When Dub got through talking, he kinda nonchalantly reached into the coin return and pulled out a bunch of coins." Louie shook his head. "He didn't call Owen Bradley. He was just *faking*."

Dub and Debbie *were* on Decca Records, but this guy was a major bullshitter, that was clearly evident. We knew we couldn't wait around forever for this tour to take place. Our parents, at first elated about our newfound success, were growing impatient, and were griping about the school tuition that had gone down the drain. Dwight called a man who was in the Jaycees back in their little South Carolina hometown, and they worked out plans for a show in the local school auditorium, featuring themselves and Decca recording star Dub Dalton.

We left Atlanta on a cold Wednesday night in November for the boys' hometown. Dub was to meet us there late Friday afternoon before the show. We didn't sleep *at all* that night.

The next day Louie and I walked around the courthouse square with the two hometown heroes, Willie and Dwight. There were signs up on telephone poles and in store windows advertising the show. Dwight ran into a guy he went to school with.

"Whatcha up to these days, Dwight?"

"We got a rotten roll band."

Louie went with Dwight to spend the night at his folks' house, and I went with Willie, up a winding road through the hills. Willie's parents and grandmother lived in a farmhouse that had a barn out back. Willie was the baby of the family; his older siblings had all left home. As the twilight shadows darkened the hills, we all sat down to a big meal.

"Dad gum it, Willie," his father said at the kitchen table. "We done gone and bought you a nice set of suitcases fer that tour. I hope it ain't money throwed away like the money we spent on that school in Atlanta."

"Aw, Daddy, Dub said we're about to start up most any time now," Willie said with a hangdog look on his face.

His father took a bite out of a pork chop. "Son, how come ol' Dub don't get on TV like Arthur 'Guitar Boogie' Smith in Charlotte?"

"But, Daddy," Willie said incredulously. "Arthur Smith is *heeel-beeely!*"

That's about the last thing I remember because, having had no sleep at all the night before, I fell asleep with my face in the plate. I finally got up and went to bed where I had terrible screaming nightmares. Early the next morning, I overheard Willie's grandmother saying, "There's somethin' bad wrong with that boy."

Dub got to town just in time for the show. He was carrying his wife's pink overnight case. We all walked into the high school auditorium for the big Jaycees shindig featuring two local boys and a major label recording act. We went in through the back door and walked out on stage to set up and get tuned. Then we found the school library, which served as our dressing room. The guy from the Jaycees asked us to wait awhile because there weren't many people there, and he thought if we started about a half hour late there might be a few last-minute stragglers coming in. At about 8:40 he came into the library and told us, "Well, y'all might as well get started." Besides Willie and Dwight's families, there were a total of five people in the audience. After the show, the Jaycees paid us fifty cents each. I told Louie that was our rotten roll money.

"I'm gonna be frank for *tellin'* you boys, that was jus' plain *embar-*

rassin' last night," Dub told Willie and Dwight the next day. They were going to stay in their hometown for a few days before going back to Atlanta. That was the last time we ever saw them. Louie and I rode back with Dub.

I woke up in the middle of the night while we were riding through some little town. "Where are we, Dub?" I asked from the backseat where I was stretched out.

I could see his torso thrust forward and hear his fingers snap as he said, "Man, *we* in *Pootysville!*"

We couldn't have a band with just piano and drums. Louie knew of a bass player in his hometown of Gainesville, Florida, named Sam Lawson. Louie called him up, put Dub on the phone, and Sam agreed to come to Atlanta. Dub said we shouldn't worry about a guitar because there were plenty of good guitar players in Atlanta. So within just a few days, we were at the airport picking up Sam Lawson and his bass.

Sam was our age and about my height, which is medium—a nice-looking guy with sort of a butch haircut in the process of growing out. He was loaded with personality, very funny, and had a passion for music. He was also moody and sometimes just plain weird. One day when someone at a store told Dub that the Everly Brothers had been in the week before, Sam squealed.

Dub wanted Sam to meet his singing partner Debbie. I had only been around her a couple of times. An attractive brunette about Dub's age, Debbie was from a locally well-known musical family. She was married to Jim Komas, a handsome young furniture store owner whose family was prominent in the Atlanta Greek community. After introducing Sam to everyone, Dub and Debbie started writing a song. Debbie's husband kept jumping up and shouting, "It's a goddam hit! It's a goddam hit!"

Dub had originally suggested that we move in with him and his wife Florence (which he pronounced "Flawnce"). They lived in East Point, a suburb that actually is not east but south of Atlanta. I'm sure that three guys moving in didn't sound like a good idea to Florence, so we ended up renting a whole section of a house from an older couple, Mr. and Mrs. Tom Bell, who lived just down the street from Dub and Florence on West Washington Road.

Florence was a tall, attractive blonde and very pregnant. She was one of the most miserable people I've ever met, and I assumed the source of her misery was Dub. She was a country girl from South Georgia, a long way from her mama and daddy. She was sweet to me, and I think she was pretty smart, but she usually gave a blank stare and sat around with her mouth open. It was the look of total despair.

"Flawnce?" No response." Flawnce!" Still no response. "*Hey, Flawnce!*"

"What *is* it, Chester?" she barked. Dub Dalton's real name was Chester Hawkins.

"Me and Bobby and Louie and Sam gonna go up to Nashville to see Owen," he said.

"I don't care, *go on*," she said, as though she were shooing away a fly.

Dub told us that we needed to go to Nashville so he could get their recording session set up. The trip was unforgettable. There was sleet falling on Monteagle Mountain northwest of Chattanooga. I was scared to death that we would be taking a thousand-foot tumble. In Manchester, Tennessee, we hung out for a while with a carload of girls about my age or a little younger. One of them told me, "You'd look just like Elvis Presley if it wasn't for your nigger nose." So much for small-town Southern enlightenment in the late 1950s.

Around 9:00 p.m. we pulled up behind an old two-story house on 16th Avenue South in Nashville. Owen Bradley had converted two rooms into a small recording studio, then eventually added an annex, known as the Quonset Hut. The Quonset Hut housed a much larger recording studio. Mr. Bradley, then in his early forties, was and would over time increasingly become one of the most respected music business figures in the world. He said fewer than a half-dozen words to Dub, who treated him with total deference, and it was obvious that there would be no "Hey, Owen, you old sonofabitch."

We walked through the back door of the Quonset Hut, right into the recording studio. Mr. Bradley's younger brother, Harold, a guitar player, sprang up out of his chair and greeted Dub with a handshake and pumped our hands as we were introduced to him. He grabbed up four chairs for us and told us to enjoy the session. Country music legend Red Foley was recording an album of old pop standard "sing along" songs, an attempt to cash in on the popularity of the *Sing Along with Mitch* TV show. I watched in reverence as just a few feet away my musician heroes Floyd Cramer, Buddy Harmon, and Hank Garland were in the process of making a record. Nashville's two leading background vocal groups, the Jordanaires and the Anita Kerr Singers, were both on the recording date. Today, a lot of this would be scheduled on separate sessions and recorded on at least thirty or forty tracks. In the late 1950s, everyone played and sang at the same time, on just a couple of tracks.

What we experienced would never happen today. Strangers would not be allowed at a recording session without the explicit invitation or approval from the artist or the producer, and then they would sit in the control room, not out in the studio with the musicians. One cough, sneeze, or giggle would have ruined an entire take.

I don't know if it was self-delusion, wishful thinking, or out-and-out lying, but in a letter dated December 5, I wrote my parents, "Dub's managers don't want the cross-country tour to begin until the record is out so we can all work for BIG MONEY!" Dub had some kind of big plan pending, as usual, so it looked like I wouldn't make it home for the holidays. Though I sometimes craved my mother's good cooking, especially her cowpeas (a Florida-grown legume similar to crowder peas), I never actually got homesick until Christmas approached. Having no income except what I could squeeze out of my parents, I bought presents for them and for my brother's family at the Dollar Store.

Then, a couple of days after Christmas, Dub told us that Florence wanted to visit her mama and daddy in South Georgia, and if we wanted to come along, he would drive us on down to Florida. So off we went, four guys, a pregnant girl, and a car full of luggage.

"I gotta piss like a flyin' racehorse," Dub announced about two hours out of Atlanta.

"I just saw a place back there for flyin' racehorses to piss," I piped in from the backseat.

Dub laughed loudly, then said, "Hey, Flawnce." Silence.

"Hey, Flawnce." Florence sat there with a blank stare on her face, with her mouth open.

"Hey, *Flawnce!*"

"What *is* it Chester?" she barked.

"Did you hear what Bobbeh said?" he asked.

"Whutt?" she replied, barely loud enough to be heard.

"I said I had to piss like a flyin' racehorse and Bobbeh said he saw a place back there fo' flyin' racehorses to piss."

Florence smiled.

After leaving Florence with her parents in South Georgia and dropping Louie and Sam off in Gainesville, Dub and I headed south for Auburndale. On Highway 33, a lightly traveled twenty-seven-mile stretch between Groveland and Polk City, Dub had his Fairlane going wide open, about 115 miles per hour. The orange groves, piney woods, grazing land and swamps flew by in a frightening rush. When I told him he didn't have to drive that fast, he said, "But we wanna make it to your mama and daddy's by suppertime."

"Welcome to Auburndale, Flahrrr-da," my father told Dub as we climbed out of his car around dusk.

As we feasted on heaping servings of fried chicken, cowpeas, creamed corn, buttered spinach, and piping hot buttermilk biscuits served with orange marmalade, Dub amazed my parents with stories about the music business and the trials and tribulations of being a "star."

"Mrs. Braddock, one night I was performin' and a bunch of girls ran up to the stage screamin'," Dub said softly and philosophically, like a war hero modestly recounting a major battle. "One of 'em reached up for my leg and pulled off a handful of hair."

"Well, I'll swannee (Southern for "I'll swear")," Mother declared as Daddy smiled and shook his head.

After two hours of hearing Dub's motor mouth, of being regaled with show biz stories and assured over and over how he was going to look out for "Bobbeh," Mother beamed her biggest smile and said, "Well, Dub, I sure feel *a lot better* about Bobby now."

Dub spent the night and left in the morning. A couple of days later, someone drove Louie and Sam down from Gainesville. The three of us saw 1959 come in as we passed around a bottle of blended whiskey on a train bound for Atlanta.

It was good to get back. I liked the hustle-bustle of Five Points in downtown and the feeling that something was always going on. I found it hard to believe that this city was even *in* Georgia, the severely Southern land of my ancestors. One thing I especially loved in Atlanta were Krystal burgers, the tasty, small, low-priced, square-shaped hamburgers with the tiny chopped onions.

The three of us had nice living quarters in the home of Mr. and Mrs. Tom Bell in East Point. The rent was low, and Louie and I were paying all of it from our occasional checks from home. The Bells were friendly country folks well into their sixties, originally from the mountains of North Georgia. Mr. Bell would sometimes pour us a glass of ice cold, clear-as-water mountain moonshine.

We spent a lot of time doing nothing but waiting for Dub and Debbie's record to come out. We listened to the radio a lot. Sam would squeal over a certain bass lick on "Sixteen Candles," and I would act like I was in orgasmic paradise every time I heard Connie Frances singing "My Happiness."

One morning Mrs. Bell was knocking on our door and shouting, "Hey boys, it's a-*snowin'* outside." Louie had seen plenty of snow as a child in Evanston, Illinois, but Sam and I were native Floridians and had never seen it on the ground. We had snowball fights the rest of the morning.

Another day we were riding around downtown with Dub. While we were stopped at a light, two pretty young girls walked by, their elegant figures discernable even beneath their heavy overcoats. Sam and I jumped out of the car and started walking with them. This might be considered some kind of harassment today, but in that simpler, gentler time, it wasn't considered inappropriate; maybe a little on the bold side but not inappropriate. I directed my conversation to a very attractive honey blonde and Sam to a short, cute brunette. They were both our age, came from small towns in Central Georgia, and lived at a dormitory-like apartment building that rented exclusively to young female students and office workers. We made dates with them for the next night, a Friday.

My "date" with Ann Chafin, a nursing student, consisted of sitting and talking in the lobby of her apartment building. It was fairly easy to take an imaginary leap into the future and picture what Ann would be like as an old lady because she didn't care for rock 'n' roll and had very old-fashioned values. After we saw each other a couple of times, she told me she wouldn't date anyone else but me as long as I was living in Atlanta. There would be no kissing, which she thought was improper for an unbetrothed couple; only hand-holding was allowed. I remember her as being a very nice and sincere person.

Sam's experience with Judy Winder was quite different from mine with Ann. He told her he was in love with her, somehow forgetting to tell her that he was still madly in love with his high school sweetheart Wendy. He also led her to believe that he was a big shot in the music business. Shades of Dub.

Our patience with Dub was wearing thin, and we were trying to figure out some way to make money in this profession we had so prematurely gotten into. When we talked to Dub about it, he decided that we should go to Nashville once again. While we were driving through Chattanooga, Dub exclaimed, "Man, I gotta find a fillin' station before I crap in my pants."

"There's a station up there, Dub," I said.

"Godamighty, boys," he bellowed, "I might be too late. If I've crapped my pants, you gonna have to find a department store and get me some boxer underpants."

Tires screeching, he wheeled into the station, slammed to a stop, then jumped out of the car and ran to the bathroom on the side. In a few seconds, the bathroom door opened. Dub poked his head out and yelled, "Size forty-two and make it snappy!"

I don't recall Dub seeing Owen Bradley at all on this particular trip. We went by the Quonset Hut that night, but it was a Columbia session, not Decca, so Mr. Bradley wasn't there. Lefty Frizzell, who nine years earlier had been a twenty-two-year-old overnight super-star, was in the studio rerecording his earlier hits with a more modern sound for an upcoming album. Lefty looked over at us, naturally; here were all these strangers sitting in the studio at his session. "Ol' Lefty knows who I am," Dub whispered. "Did you see him nod his head at me?"

On our way back to Atlanta, we heard on the radio that rock 'n' roll stars Buddy Holly, Ritchie Valens, and the Big Bopper had died in a plane crash. The news cast sort of a pall over us. And that's about the time that everything in Dub's life started going really, really bad.

Dub had to pass his own house on West Washington Road in East Point on the way to Mr. and Mrs. Bell's house. Parked facing out of his driveway were two men in a brown Chevrolet. When they saw Dub, the driver blew his horn and pulled out into the street behind us. "It's the mob, they *after* me!" Dub hollered as he hit the gas.

I thought, "Oh my God, we're going to be killed. Those guys are going to shoot us." Dub started passing every car he could get around, weaving in and out of traffic. He was speeding down alleys, making U-turns at busy intersections, and cutting through people's yards. I was thinking, well, if the police stop us then we'll probably be safe from those criminals who are chasing us. It appeared, though, that Dub had successfully outrun them.

"Who *were* they," Louie asked excitedly, "and why are they after *you*, Dub?"

"Gangsters, Louie. They wanted to invest in my career and I wouldn't let 'em. I said, 'No way, mothas' and now they tryin' to *kill* me."

He took us home, and the three of us talked all night about how we didn't want to get killed because of Dub. We were all about ready to move back to Florida. Late the next morning, after only about three hours sleep, we heard a pounding on the door. Sam got up and opened it. It was Dub.

"Those mothas stole my car," Dub said dismally. I don't think it took us very long to figure out that the men in hot pursuit weren't Mafia guys, but repo men. Dub's Fairlane had been repossessed. Two days later his furniture was repossessed. And then Florence's parents drove up from South Georgia to repossess *her*. When the landlord kicked him out later that week, Dub moved in with his mother, about half a mile away.

A day or two later, Dub was knocking on our door again. He was going into Atlanta to see his managers, and he wanted us to go with him.

"How are we gonna get there?" I asked.

"Well, motha, we'll stick out the ol' thumb," he said, as his lips protruded and his head swiveled. He was wearing a white t-shirt, leather jacket, tuxedo pants, and old tennis shoes.

Still tagging along, still hoping, our trio stood with Dub at an intersection on West Washington Road with our thumbs out, looking for a ride to Highway 41, then north into downtown Atlanta. After about a half hour, a big beefy middle-aged guy in a Pontiac pulled over and motioned us to get in.

"We don't usually do this," Dub told the man as he slid into the front passenger seat. "My car's in the shop."

After we got downtown, the man went three blocks out of his way to drop us off at a large office building on Peachtree Street. We took the elevator up to the offices of Dub and Debbie's managers. Dub introduced us to the two men, then asked us to wait in the reception area. I think his purpose in bringing us along was to prove to the managers that there really was a band.

It was too cold to hitchhike back, and we couldn't afford a cab— "Damn, boys, I left my wallet at home!" Dub said—so we took a city bus to East Point. On the long ride, Dub went on and on about how he and Debbie were going to record in two weeks and that their managers were starting to line up a long tour with the Everly Brothers. When the bus finally got to our street, Dub got off with us, instead of continuing down the street to his mother's house.

"Aren't you going to your mother's house?" I asked him.

"Bobbeh, I need to borr' your record player for a day or two, need it to learn some songs for the tour."

So I let him have my portable hi-fi. He said he was going to walk on to his mother's house and would talk to us the next day. He waddled off down the road with just a hint of a choreographed dance step, my record player tucked under his arm. I didn't see him or hear from him for several days. Whenever I called his mother, she would curtly tell me that Dub was "out." Then one afternoon, I ran into him at a neighborhood grocery store.

"D-D-Dub, I want my record player back right away."

"Man, I'm sorry I've took so long. Had a lot more songs to learn than I realized."

"Well, I want it back tomorrow," I told him impatiently. "If you don't bring it to me tomorrow, I'm gonna go tell your mother that you *steal* things."

"Bobbeh, don't do that. I ain't stole nothin' from you. I'll have it back to you by tomorra, I promise."

The next day, I just happened to be looking out the window at the bus stop which was half-a-block away. There was Dub getting off the bus with my record player tucked under his arm. The bus was one that had originated downtown and was heading *toward* and not *away from* his mother's house. When he returned my hi-fi, the case handle still had the pawn shop string tied around it.

Louie, Sam, and I were getting behind on our rent, which was very low in the first place. Mr. and Mrs. Bell were more than understanding. "I know you're gettin' a dirty deal from ol' Dub," Mrs. Bell told me.

We ate whenever Louie or I got a little check from home. I had too much pride to let my parents know that they were my only source of income. We stayed hungry much of the time. There were two single ladies about sixty years-old who lived nearby and felt sorry for us. They had us over to eat occasionally. One of them was a professional woman who had a nice figure for a woman her age; Sam was constantly telling us he would like to have sex with her.

Sam could be pretty scary sometimes. He showed me a photograph of his old girlfriend in Florida, a very attractive girl named Wendy. Sam seemed obsessed with her, and I assumed it was Wendy who had ended the relationship. When I commented on how good-looking she was, he got a crazed look in his eyes and said, "You're talking about her tits. You want to *screw* her because you like her *tits.*" He grew angrier and angrier. Louie and I agreed that Sam was potentially dangerous.

There was a neighborhood grocery store on West Washington Road that was run by a man and his wife and their teenage son and daughter. Every one of them had red hair. Occasionally, these good folks would let us have a little food on credit. We had become the neighborhood charity case. One day I was talking to the lady.

"We ought to be getting some Florida watermelons here in March," she said.

I was going to tell her that I thought Florida watermelons were harvested in February. What I intended to say was, "I thought Florida . . . ," but what came out was, "I fart . . . " I stopped right there with the word dangling in the silence. We both just stood there by the produce case, embarrassed, as I felt a hot crimson wave wash across my face. I turned on my heel, walked away from her, and walked on out the door. I knew I would not go back there.

The next time I got a check from home, we decided to use it to cut a record. Sam and I had written a folk ballad called "Red Rose," and I had a rockin' piano instrumental, "Dogleg," that I had written back when I had access to a piano. We went to a recording studio owned by a middle-aged man named Candler, of the Coca-Cola Candlers. He was independently wealthy and recording was his hobby. Mr. Candler was the first person I had ever heard say, "Flattery will get you everywhere." We thought that was hilarious, and laughed and laughed. So Sam sang "Red Rose," and I played "Dogleg." Mr. Candler handed us an acetate copy of what we had recorded, and I handed him our food money.

We stayed so hungry and malnourished that all we wanted to do was sleep; three eighteen-year-old boys sleeping around the clock, sometimes eating nothing more in one day than a candy bar with a carton of milk.

One day I was riding on a downtown bus carrying several kids—I heard one of them say they were in the second grade. I often think that my life is filled with synchronicity, and redheaded people seemed to be a recurring part of my Atlanta experience. Of this group of kids, I especially noticed a cute freckle-faced boy with bushy scarlet hair.

He got off the bus with three or four other children, and before we could start moving again I heard the loud screeching of brakes. I looked out the window and saw the little boy face down, zooming past me on the street, as though he were attached to a rocket. When he came to a stop, his body quivered for a couple of seconds, then became very still. A policeman was there immediately, and everyone was ordered to stay on the bus until an ambulance arrived. I searched the newspapers the next day but found no account of the accident, so I don't know if he lived or died. But it haunted me for several days, and I had nightmares about it.

I also dreamed of food, my mother's food. I dreamed of her cowpeas and her fried chicken and her key lime pie. The combination of being hungry all the time, not having enough money to take Ann to a restaurant or a movie, then seeing the little boy hit by a car was just too much for me. The next time the two old ladies had us over for a meal, I thought, "By God, while I've got some strength, I'm going to hitchhike to Auburndale." The only reason I hadn't moved back much sooner was pride; I kept remembering that headline in the *Auburndale Star*: "Auburndale Boy Tours With Everly Brothers." Now it didn't matter.

I got up early the next morning, ate a drumstick the ladies had given me the night before, and started packing. I had too many belongings to take with me, but I managed to cram a lot of it into my two big suitcases. I told Sam and Louie that I would probably be back in a few days. I hitched a ride with a salesman who happened to be headed for Highway 41 South. He also picked up two sailors who were stationed in Pensacola. They said "Pensacola sucks," and that was the first time I had ever heard *suck* used that way. The salesman was going as far as Ft. Valley, Georgia. I didn't care much for the sailors, so when we got out, I walked down the road to a truck stop and got a ride with a truck driver to the end of his run, which was a few miles north of Ocala, Florida.

I was standing alongside the road when a late-night thunderstorm erupted. Before I got very wet, a yellow Buick pulled over. A middle-aged African American man beckoned me to hop in, so I did. He said he was a school teacher. It didn't take me long to realize that he was a very drunk school teacher. In a couple of minutes, he pulled off the road and reached into his glove compartment and pulled out a revolver. He didn't aim it at me, he just held it in his hand as he continued to drive. He wasn't speaking coherently. While his demeanor didn't seem friendly, he wasn't threatening me either. I think he was just drunk out of his mind. I wasn't worried about him intentionally shooting me as much as I was afraid the gun would go off by accident. Before long, he stopped at a service station that was still open.

I said, "This would be a good place for me to have my parents pick me up." He said nothing, just stared at me as I got my suitcases out of his car.

I walked inside the station, grabbed the key to the men's restroom, then walked slowly around to the side of the little building. When I got to the men's room, I kept on walking, slowly, in the drenching rain. I walked into a wooded area then turned left and started walking fast, heading south towards Auburndale. I stayed in the woods and fields about one hundred feet off the highway. In about forty-five minutes, I was in the middle of Ocala, wetter than wet—cold, exhausted, and hungry. The suitcases felt like they weighed a hundred pounds each. I just stood there in a waterlogged daze, shivering, when a police car pulled up.

"You hang around downtown here, I'm gonna have to run you in for vagrancy."

I pointed to a phone booth and told the officer I was going to call my parents who lived ninety miles away. He said, "All right then." Mother and Daddy didn't seem too thrilled about making a four-hour round trip at 11:30 on a stormy night. I huddled close to the door of a Rexall drugstore, trying to stay as dry as I could, staring at the empty rainy streets of Ocala and looking for the headlights of a 1953 Lincoln.

As I wolfed down grits and eggs and link sausages late the next morning, Mother told me, "Well, I'm just going to have to keep feeding you 'til you gain back about twenty-five pounds, Bobby." My parents were appalled that I was so emaciated. I had literally been starving in Atlanta.

We all drove back up to Atlanta the next day to get the rest of my belongings. Daddy paid Mr. and Mrs. Bell on my back rent, but I don't think he paid them enough. Louie had decided to stay in the Atlanta area for a few more weeks and play with some musicians he had become acquainted with. Sam had split, and took along a coat and a sweater of mine that he had admired. "Sam's as bad as ol' Dub," said Mrs. Bell.

On the way back home, Daddy was saying very little. He had been a bit sullen ever since they picked me up in Ocala. He definitely wasn't pleased with me. Though he didn't say so, I knew what he was thinking: I had been a *failure*.

Mother was giving me lectures, punctuated with nervous laughs. Though she didn't say so, I knew what she was thinking: I had been a *fool*.

"Bobby, you're going to have to remember, you can't believe everything people tell you," she said with a coral-snake smile.

"Mother," I reminded her, "who was it who said, 'Well, Dub, I sure feel *a lot better* about Bobby now'?"

Her smile disappeared. I turned up the car radio; Johnny Cash was singing "Don't Take Your Guns to Town."

CHAPTER SEVEN

Speedin' in Miami

SPRINGTIME IN CENTRAL FLORIDa could be the time for a late winter chill or an early summer swim. Except for the occasional violent weather, it was quiet; the winter residents and visitors, the "snowbirds," had gone north. There weren't as many trucks on the back roads because most of the citrus fruit had been picked, and the migrant workers had moved on to other places until the next harvest. Spring is a good season to come home to, even when you don't intend to stay, because it's a time of freshness and new beginnings.

Daddy said he would hire me to hoe orange and grapefruit trees until I found work that I liked better. I think Mother was really happy to have me back home to enjoy her cooking. Where else could I get guava jelly or watermelon rind preserves? When I was a child, I told anyone who would listen that she was the best cook in the world, and I still felt that way.

I can't say enough good things about my parents. The worst thing I can say about my father is that he had a bad temper. The worst thing I can say about my mother is that she was an inveterate snoop. The absolute worst—and funniest—of Mother's snoopings happened right after I came back home from Atlanta. Before I moved up there, Don Pace had begun dating a girl named Alladene Gordy. He was having a sexual relationship with Alladene, but he definitely didn't want to marry her. He sent me a letter in Atlanta in which he had posted this afterthought: "Remember, a dick can screw a man as well as a woman." As crude as that sounds and as 1959 sexist as it was, it was an adage that meant a man's organ could screw up his life by getting some girl pregnant and causing him to have to get married. He thought Alladene was pregnant. But when Mother ran across this little morsel, she saw it as Don Pace propositioning me, trying to talk me into letting him have sex with me. I explained to her exactly what it meant, but I don't think I thoroughly convinced her. Whenever Pace came around, she was polite to him but a little distant, undoubtedly having visions of him grabbing my butt. I believe Mother thought for the rest of her life that this big, tall, rugged, turkey-hunting, motorcycle-riding, girl-loving guy was gay.

On a Wednesday night, soon after Mother had found the letter, Pace and I went out to Club 92. The colossal nightclub was located on Highway 92, out towards Lakeland, and featured a live country band on Friday and Saturday nights. The owner was trying something revolutionary for Club 92; he was hiring a rhythm and blues band, all black, to play on Wednesday nights. The band was great, and it was going over huge. In the Florida of 1959, however, blacks were not allowed to patronize the club, so the audience was entirely white.

That night I ran into a country deejay from Winter Haven, Bunny Brown, who was also a drummer. He said the club was hiring a new band for weekends; they wanted one that could play country *and* rock 'n' roll, and would I be interested in rehearsing and auditioning with them? I said yes. After one rehearsal, we auditioned and got the gig. It was essentially a hillbilly band whose rendering of rock 'n' roll was pretty countrified.

So I was hoeing Daddy's trees during the week and playing piano at Club 92 on weekends. Of course, I loved country music, but the rock 'n' roll gave me a chance to show off. The grand piano at the club had a simple organ attachment with just a couple of octaves and no settings, but it was perfect for me to play a new rock 'n' roll hit called "The Happy Organ." On the piano, I played "After Hours," a blues song from 1940 that was the theme song for one of the R&B shows on WLAC in Nashville. I didn't play it right, not then, but nobody seemed to notice or care. A lot of people were telling me I was good, and I was loving it.

The featured singer with the band was Jumpin' Jack Jubal, a twenty-four-year-old Georgia boy with wild eyes and a devilish grin. He wore his curly hair long for the time and looked like a younger and handsomer version of Larry of the Three Stooges, the one with all the curly hair on the sides—except Jubal wasn't balding. He sang things like the Jimmy Reed rockin' blues "Ain't That Lovin' You Baby," with a touch of Hank Williams and George Jones, but he also jumped around all over the stage. Sometimes Jubal would get down on the floor and roll around, doing sort of a holy-roller male hoochie-coochie thing. It was pretty suggestive. Some of the women thought it was sexy; a lot of people thought it was funny. When he did that, his hair got *really* wild. Jumpin' Jubal definitely had something different and was quite entertaining.

Jubal was a likable character, and Pace and I had fun hanging out with him. He had a wife named Jenniebill, and several little boys, and he loved them all, but he was a wild, hard-drinkin,' pill-poppin' musician who ran around with a lot of women. Imagine this young, unbald Larry Stooge with wild dark eyes, and crazy grin, and mischievous chuckle.

Jubal was my introduction to amphetamines, later known as speed. We referred to them as *bennies*, a nickname for Benzedrine, or simply as pills. Taken as prescribed, they were diet pills, though using them is not a really healthy way to diet because they sharply elevate the pulse as well as the blood pressure. Ingested in the quantities that we took, they cause a feeling of great energy and euphoria. They made me feel as though I could stay up—and talk—forever. Pace once took the pills before teaching his Sunday School class at the First Methodist Church, and got so wound up talking to his young students that the minister had to send someone to tell him to dismiss his class, that church services had begun.

The down side to the bennies was coming down *off* the stuff. There was a feeling of major anxiety and depression and forlornness. I soon learned that drinking buttermilk helped a little. I didn't stop with the pills, though. Following Jubal's example, Pace and I started purchasing a now long-defunct product called Rexall Inhaler. It looked like any other inhaler but contained a cotton strip soaked in Dexedrine, which was similar to Benzedrine. The trick was to cut off a little piece of the cotton with a razor blade and down it with a beer, a ritual that was called "chewing the cotton" and had an effect that was like getting high on several bennies. We also started buying codeine in a cough syrup known as Codinate A-H. One night I drank a whole bottle of it and sat there on stage as though I was in a trance, somehow playing the piano but oblivious to everyone around me. I even started drinking bottles of vanilla extract so I could have my own little fix that nobody else took.

Club 92 became my regular hangout, even on weeknights when our band wasn't playing. Pace was a rhythm and blues enthusiast, so he and I always made it a point to hear the all-black band from Tampa that played there every Wednesday: Gene Franklin and the House Rockers, featuring Texas Ray. As the band played, Pace and I would keep time with the snare drum's backbeat by banging the bottoms of our beer bottles on the table top. This was a first-rate R&B band, and Ray was a super-talented singer and harmonica player, as well as a knockout entertainer. The sets were about an hour-and-a-half long, and Ray was featured on the last half of each set. In the segregated South, black musicians sitting at the tables during their break was taboo, so they had to go hang out in the kitchen. Pace and I started going to the kitchen to talk with Texas Ray on his long breaks.

Texas Ray was very dark-skinned and a few years older than we were. He had a small curly goatee and wore the coolest clothes we had ever seen. His laugh was instantaneous and infectious. Pace and I didn't agonize over the fact that he couldn't sit at the tables with us, nor did we spend much time wondering if *he* was bothered by it. But those Wednesday nights we spent in the kitchen at Club 92, drinking beer and carrying on with Texas Ray, were an important and defining part of my life. They heightened my interest in African American music and peeled away a couple of layers of old racial attitudes. I had never been taught to dislike blacks, but I had been taught that tradition forbade whites and blacks to be social partners. The fact that I would fraternize and drink with this man but couldn't sit down to eat with him was totally irrational. Surely, even in the unenlightened days of 1959, there must have been some little voice inside me, trying to get my attention, asking, *"Why?"*

One Wednesday night, Pace and I took Jumpin' Jack Jubal to the kitchen with us. After a few minutes of free and easy conversation,

Texas Ray made a remark about Jubal's clothes, clothes that were almost as wild and colorful as his own.

"Why, you black sonofabitch," Jubal said, not hatefully but definitely crossing the line.

"Well, you tallow-ass motherfucker," Ray shot back.

Everyone exploded in laughter, none laughing louder than Jubal. Pace and I later decided that blacks had their names for us just as we had our names for them.

One Saturday night, after playing to a packed house at Club 92 with our no-name band, Jubal and I hooked up with a couple of attractive girls, the White sisters. They spoke the language of the North Alabama hills and said *arn* for iron and *tard* for tired. Jubal was with Rosie, who said she was twenty-five, and I was with Margaret, who said she was eighteen. We soon learned that Rosie was thirty-three, and Margaret, who was Rosie's *daughter*, was fifteen. Mama was a peroxide blonde, well-endowed and flashy. Margaret was thin and shy, with curly brown hair and big brown eyes. Jubal had a brief fling with Rosie that got him into some trouble with her husband. Margaret and I had a few dates, and I developed a crush.

One night, after a Club 92 gig in late spring, I took Margaret parking at Braddock's Hole. She had the faint scent of too much fast dancing on a hot night. There was just enough moonlight to see the sparkle in her big eyes.

"Bobby, sometimes ah jes' wanna throw mah arms around yuh an' tell yuh ah love yuh," she said softly. But this was the end of our time together, because of something my mother had done . . . and would come to deeply regret. She had run across a classified ad in my *Billboard* magazine about an opening at a Miami nightclub for a piano player and a singer, and called it to my attention.

"Hello, I'm calling Danny Star."

"This is Danny."

"M-m-my name is Bobby Braddock, and I saw your ad in Billboard about needin' a piano player and a singer."

"Yeah, Bobby. Ya called the right man. I gotta band I'm bringin' into Club 17 down here." He had a clipped Northeastern accent.

"Well, I play the piano and I work with a guy who's a really good singer."

"Gotta do both country and rock 'n' roll."

"That's . . . exactly what we do. We're playin' with that kinda band right now."

"Where ya live, Bobby?"

"Do you know where Polk County is? Lakeland, Winter Haven?"

"Nah, I'm from Connecticut, just came to Miami a few years ago."

"W-w-well, I live between Tampa and Orlando."

"Yeah, yeah, I know where that is. Well, jeez, ya wanna come on down here and audition next Sunday? There's gonna be an afternoon jam session. You and your buddy can sit in, gimme a chance to hear ya."

"His name's Jumpin' Jack Jubal. He not only sings good but gets down on the floor and rolls around."

"Jumpin' Jack Jubal, huh? Jesus, this I gotta see."

So Danny Star (stage name for Daniel Dante Salvatore) gave me his address in Miami and told me to meet him there for lunch the next Sunday.

Miami didn't even exist until the 1890s, making it one of the youngest of America's big cities. By the time I was born, it had surpassed Jacksonville as Florida's largest city and was already more Northern than Southern. My father had often said that if he'd had a hundred dollars to invest in some lots in "Mi-am-uh" when he went there to visit his Uncle Henry in 1900, he would have been "a millionaire many times over."

When I went to Miami in the summer of 1959, Fidel Castro had been in power for only a few months and the huge exodus from Cuba, which would eventually make Miami a Cuban-American town, had just begun. The Miami I was being introduced to was an American melting pot but not yet a Latin American melting pot. There were a lot of Southerners in the white working-class areas of town, the kind of people who would come to the clubs I worked. The northern part of town, in and around an area known as Liberty City, was heavily black. The biggest group in Miami was comprised of those who had moved there from outside the South, particularly from the Northeast. This was truly the *New* world: New York, New Jersey, New England. In 1959, the surnames listed in the phone book of this future New Havana were Jewish, Italian, English, and Irish.

Jubal and I drove down to our Miami audition and took along Don Pace and his friend, Alton Holloway. We drank gin and grapefruit juice as we followed Highway 27 down through the cattle country, then around Lake Okeechobee and into the Everglades. What I found so ironic about the Gold Coast, that glistening megalopolis of North-in-the-South that stretches from the Palm Beaches down through Ft. Lauderdale and Hollywood to Miami, was that it was surrounded, not too many miles out to the west and to the south, by the most fertile farmland in America, dug up out of the swamps, black muck so rich that almost anything would grow on it. Driving from this Deep South country into the Gold Coast was like crossing directly from the Mississippi Delta into Manhattan—except Manhattan doesn't have palm trees.

Highway 27 approached Miami running parallel with the Miami Canal. As we entered the outskirts of town, the road was adorned with Australian pines and little houses that looked almost like huts. And then, there it was, the tropical metropolis of Miami. Houses were in assorted colors and in the various South Florida styles—old wooden frame with big screened porches, 1920s Mediterranean stucco, and 1940s art deco. Danny Star lived in a newer, yellowish concrete block house with coconut palm trees in the front yard.

Danny was a big, engaging man in his early to mid-thirties. His hair was jet black, and his pearly white teeth were always clamped together and exposed, either in a grin or a grimace.

"Well, jeez, you brought the whole gang with ya, huh? Hey, the more the merrier. This is my wife, Polly." He explained that Polly, a friendly lady with a sweet smile, was a Polish girl from Michigan who knew how to cook him great Italian meals.

I told Danny about our trip down, how Pace had put his hand out the window and loudly banged the exterior of the passenger door while Alton Holloway was napping, and how we had convinced Alton that I had accidentally hit one of the people fishing by the canal.

Danny laughed and remarked that they'd just been having a lazy Sunday. He said that was typical, that they never went to church.

"Don't you believe in God?" asked Pace, looking out of the corner of his eye, head down like a cat about to pounce on a bird.

"I'm Catholic," Danny replied, his grin turning into a grimace. "Does that sound like I don't believe in God?"

"Oh, no," said Pace, digging into Polly's lasagna.

Later we drove north up 17th Avenue to the Sunday afternoon jam session at Club 17, where I sat in and played piano. Jubal got up and sang "Whole Lotta Shakin' " à la Jerry Lee Lewis. When he hit the chorus, he started rolling around on the dance floor, hunching and thrusting as he contorted his face and held the hand mic close to his chest and chin. After the set, Danny had a conference with Mr. Berger, the short New York–born Jewish man who owned the club. When they emerged from Mr. Berger's office five minutes later, Danny was wearing a big grin.

"Okay," he said, looking at me. "You got the job, but ya gotta join the union. And your stage name is Bobby King."

I didn't like the idea of changing my last name but went along with it. The idea of being a full-time musician was pretty exciting. Six nights a week, six hours a night.

Still looking at me but motioning his head toward Jubal, Danny continued, "Now, *he* can come in and clean up the club in the afternoons, if he wants the job." The pay wasn't much. "He can do his routine two or three times a night, to see how it goes over. Mr. Berger isn't sure people are gonna like it."

"I'm forty-four years old," Mr. Berger said stoically, his deep voice resonating rabbinical wisdom. "I've been there."

"Well, hell, let's do it," Jubal said with a crazy grin, wild eyes flashing. Danny knew of a nearby apartment house where I could get a room fairly cheap, so I told Jubal he could stay with me for free.

That next week I made the official move to Miami. The distance was 220 miles; it might as well have been a million.

Danny Star wasn't polished—as Danny Salvatore, he had grown up poor, the son of immigrants in New Haven, Connecticut—but he was smart. I got the impression that he operated on the periphery of organized crime, but I had no evidence of it. He would prove to be very generous to me, giving me clothes and often inviting me over to eat. He was a terrible bass player, but he always made sure that the other musicians he hired were really good. Danny Star was, above all, a hustler.

The band had a good singer and rhythm guitar player, a superfriendly aw-shucks country boy from South Alabama, Billy Swafford. Billy was a gentle red-headed soul who gladly took what the universe had to offer him: good-looking women. He was a little guy, early twenties, sweet-natured, with a Southern accent so thick that even *I* noticed it. He confided that he was really excited about a girl he had met the night before.

"Bobby, I think I love huh," huh rhyming with "uh" and meaning "her."

"W-well, what about your wife up in Alabama?"

"Bobby, I think I love huh too," he replied with a sweet earnestness.

The rest of the band consisted of a tall, squinty-eyed Georgia boy named Slim Byrd on the electric guitar, and drummer Tony D'Amato, an agile little New Yorker who always wore a Stetson hat and who had just recently started dating a pregnant girl.

We had two or three rehearsals, and I fell into the songs pretty easily. I liked pounding out the triplets on Elvis's "One Night" and the guys seemed to like the way I played Floyd Cramer's rockin' boogie song "Flip Flop and Bop." After our final rehearsal, Danny took me down to join the musicians' union, and I felt like I was the real deal.

My first gig with the Danny Star Band was fun, but the crowded club on a South Florida summer night felt like an oven. Danny's bass playing wasn't good, but the loud drums, electric guitar, and amplified piano sort of drowned him out. Jubal's rollin' on the floor was a big attention-getter, but as we later walked the short distance to my room, both my tux and his rock 'n' roll clothes soaking wet, he said he might not stay in Miami; he wanted to be a singer, not a clown.

After a few nights, Jubal went back to Auburndale, but I was enjoying Miami and starting to get quite a bit of self-confidence.

From my rudimentary perspective, I saw the band as pretty solid. Billy Swafford gyrated as he sang like Elvis, while Danny Star spun his big acoustic bass around and around. Toward the end of the set, Danny sang a dirty version of "Happy Birthday," then announced the upcoming slow song as "body contact music." This sure wasn't Polk County! When break time came, a middle-aged man approached me as I hopped off stage.

"Hey, really, *really* nice piano," he said.

"Aw, I'm not so good," I said modestly, "but thanks for saying so."

"Oh," he said quickly, and then paused, "uh . . . well, sure, your playing is okay, but what I meant is that piano up there . . . it's a really nice one."

I climbed down, feeling like a fool and wanting to hit the man on the top of his head. Danny walked up to me and started straightening my bow tie.

"Jesus, ya look like Farmer Brown. How ya gonna get laid if ya go around lookin' like Farmer Brown?"

During the break I hung out at the bar, talking to the bartender, Danny's cousin Eddie, who had just gotten out of prison. While I listened to Eddie talk about how much he hated "cowboy music," I watched Billy Swafford work the room, spreading around his Deep South down-home sweetness and earnestness that won him a lot of friends and got him a lot of girls. The jukebox played a favorite of mine, Chuck Berry's "Memphis, Tennessee," the B-side of his latest hit. The main reason I was hanging out at the bar was a beautiful waitress. Nan was a tall brunette, in her early twenties. She had seemed very friendly, so I was getting up the courage to find out just how friendly she could be. I asked her if she'd like to get breakfast after closing time. She said she would.

Around 4:00 a.m. in Miami, in the Royal Castle hamburger joints, at the truck stops and the all-night restaurants and cafes, you could always spot the musicians and their dates eating breakfast. I took Nan to a place that she had suggested. We took a corner booth where she ordered waffles and I ordered grits and eggs. Nan was a native of Miami and recently divorced. She suddenly started to open up to me, telling me her problems and then started crying. I felt great sympathy for her, held her hand, and told her I would be her friend, that everything was going to be all right.

When I took her to the house where she lived, she said, "I can't ask you up to my room, because this is only the first time we've been out. But I can do *this.*" She then took my head in her hands and gave me a big long kiss. I stood at the door of my blue Chevy and watched her shapely body gracefully swing and sway toward the rear entrance of the old white frame house. She turned around and blew me a kiss. I was thunderstruck.

I had to get up fairly early the next day (which meant late morning) because Danny had asked me to go over a couple of songs with a guy from out of town, Joey Miller, who was going to sit in with the band that night. I knew who Joey was because he was a regular on a country music TV show in Jacksonville. He was a good-looking guy, early twenties, Mister Personality. We hit it off instantly, and after going over the songs, we went to get a drink at a nearby bar and he shared some pills with me. He told me about growing up poor in Jacksonville, and I told him about Nan, the beautiful waitress at the club. As the afternoon wore on, he said he needed to go check into a hotel somewhere. I told him he was welcome to crash on my couch that night, and he said he'd take me up on it.

I was speeding that night, not in my car but in my brain, from Joey Miller's pills, as I walked from table to table at Club 17, almost uncontrollably loquacious as I talked to anyone who would listen, about anything I could think of, amazed at how much wisdom I possessed, daring my brain to be damaged and tempting my heart to stop beating. When I abused my body, I liked to boast that I wouldn't live to be forty, not realizing how soon forty would come, thinking it was light years away.

There was a tap on my shoulder. It was Joey Miller, pulling me aside.

"Hey Bobby, would you mind if I took Nan home tonight? I know you went out with her, but I didn't know if you were serious. I won't do it if you don't want me to, man."

"Oh, no, I don't mind," I lied, "but she's a nice girl and won't *put out.* She wouldn't even let me come up to her room with her."

"Oh, I don't care if she puts out or not, I just thought I'd give her a ride. She doesn't have a car, y'know. Maybe take her to breakfast."

"Sure, I don't mind. Here, I've got an extra key, in case you get to my place before I do."

After our last set, Billy Swafford invited me to go get a bite to eat with him and a girl he had been seeing, so I followed them to an all-night diner down around 8th Street (later known as Calle Ocho). I pulled my '57 Chevrolet up behind Billy's '56 Ford and followed him and his pretty strawberry blonde girlfriend inside the diner.

"Bobby," Billy said, with all the earnestness and concern of a Baptist preacher talking to me about my soul, "do you mind Joey goin' out with huh?"

"Naw, I don't mind. She's a nice girl, and he seems to be a pretty good guy."

"I sweah to God, Bobby," he said, looking me in the eye and pulling my arm as if he were asking me to accept the Lord, "I don't think I'd trust him."

I chatted with Billy and his girlfriend for a while, paid my ticket, then got in my car, and headed for my place. I was coming down off the speed pills and not feeling too well. I was ready to crash.

Little splashes of sunrise were appearing over the housetops and through the palm fronds as I opened the door to my room. It was still fairly dark inside, but it appeared that Joey was in my bed instead of on the couch. As I switched on the lights, my disbelieving eyes saw Joey *and Nan* in my bed together, sleeping in the nude. As Joey began to rub his eyes, I clicked the lights back off again, then quickly and quietly withdrew from my room.

I drove over by Biscayne Bay and thought about taking the causeway to Miami Beach and looking out at the ocean. Instead, I just parked my car and walked around. I was worn out and depressed from the bennies I had taken several hours before. My heart felt like it was on the bottom of the bay, but I think my wisdom had floated up to the surface. The hell with it. I needed to go somewhere and find some buttermilk.

When I saw Nan at the club the next night, she acted as though the thing with Joey had never happened. She probably didn't know that I knew; she may not have even known they were in my room. We exchanged pleasantries and never discussed it. It was soon thereafter that I met Jean.

Danny pulled me aside when we took a break one night and said, "Hey, there's a girl that really likes ya. You're gonna get some head." Head? I hadn't had basic sex yet.

Jean was a tall pale girl with short dark hair, not beautiful but attractive. She was from Alabama and had a husband in prison. There would be an irony—a contradiction—throughout my life, in that I would never be unfaithful to anyone I was committed to, but I would have no qualms about other people breaking *their* commitments to be with *me*. My bad judgment in going out with married women would have its beginnings on this night.

I had the usual trepidation that I wouldn't *do it* right, but Jean was putting me at ease. She was twenty-three years old and was very sweet and nurturing.

"I just *love* country music," she said, as we turned off 17th Avenue onto the street that went to my place. "'Specially Johnny Cash. Lord, I just *love* Johnny Cash." A girl who loved country music! I was enjoying being with her, no matter how the night turned out.

The night turned out very well. I wish I could say I was guilt ridden that my first sexual experience was with a married woman, but the truth is I felt *wonderful*. I had actually *done it*. Done it *twice*, by God, and I was thinking that she couldn't even tell it was my first time. I was eighteen—damned near nineteen—and at last, I had lost my virginity.

The next night, Jean came to the club. While we were sitting around a table on break, most of the guys in the band nearby and in earshot, she took my hand and announced, "He might be just eighteen, but he's *all man!*" She couldn't have made me feel better if she had handed me a thousand dollars.

One night, during a break, Jean was sitting between me and an accomplished guitar player with whom I had become friends, Fred Sutton. She was holding my hand and had just told me how crazy she was about me. Fred leaned over and whispered in my ear, "Look where her *other* hand is." I pulled up the table cloth and saw that it was between his legs.

Fred Sutton was a character. He was a balding thirty-two-year-old North Carolinian who resembled a young Bob Newhart. A bachelor, he totally eschewed smoking and drinking and absolutely had to have his eight hours sleep every night. He told jokes and stories in various dialects. There was one thing he could not stand, and that was rock 'n' roll. He pronounced it like he was trying to vomit it up. "*Rrrrrock 'n' roll!*" Fred would gag with revulsion. "At least some of the country songs have five or six chord changes. *Rrrrrock 'n' roll* has three chord changes and *that's it!* A five-year-old could play it." When the Beatles came along a few years later, I remember thinking their music was rock 'n' roll that Fred Sutton might like.

The greatest rock 'n' roll moment in my life—after Elvis and before the Beatles—happened on my day off, a Monday, when I was making the long trip from Miami to Auburndale for reasons I can no longer remember, probably just to visit my parents. As I drove through the little farming town of Bean City, I heard a song on the radio by Ray Charles, the Genius, the King of Soul. "What a funny sounding guitar," I thought at the beginning of the long instrumental intro. When I heard the higher keys, I realized that it wasn't a guitar at all, it was some kind of piano. It was, in fact, a Wurlitzer electric piano, and the song was "What'd I Say, Part I and Part II." Pace had already turned me on to Brother Ray, and I had loved "I Got a Woman" and "Hallelujah I Love Her So." I was a fan of his singing but also his piano playing, which I tried to mimic. But *this* record was like none I had ever heard—the wildest, the most energetic, and the most sexual. In Part II, it sounded like Ray and his female backup group, the Raylettes, were having group sex in the recording studio. I had to have this record . . . immediately.

I breezed right on through Auburndale and headed for Martin's Record Mart on North Florida Avenue in Lakeland. Before moving to Miami, I had become a regular there. It was owned and operated by Martin Ribbe, a New Jersey transplant in his fifties. He had always taken up a lot of time with me, talking about the record business, patiently answering every question I asked. He carried all kinds of records, but his specialty was R&B. His store was in the middle of Lakeland's black section, and people came from as far away as Orlando and Tampa to find their favorite songs.

I was talking the second I walked through the front door. "What'd I Say, Ray Charles," I said.

Martin looked toward me through thick spectacles and gave a frustrated smile.

"This customer just bought my last copy," he told me, gesturing toward a large African American man who said he had come all the way from Tampa to buy it.

I looked up at the big man. "I'll give you five dollars for it," I proclaimed. Forty-five rpm singles were then selling for eighty-nine cents.

"Mm-m, I . . . I don't know," the man muttered as he rubbed his chin.

"Six dollars," I said with finality, as though this was as high as I could go.

"You can have it." He handed me the record with the Atlantic label. I gave him the six dollars, then went to my parents' house where I played it over and over.

The next day, I drove back down to Miami. Billy Swafford had to go home to Alabama for two weeks of National Guard duty. Danny had been telling me about this supertalented singer/musician kid who was going to substitute for Billy.

Supertalented was not an exaggeration. Charlie McCoy was the most talented musician I had ever met at that time. He was a multi-instrumentalist who would go on to become the most recorded harmonica player in the world. He would play on records by Simon and Garfunkel, Bob Dylan, and Elvis, as well as for most of the big country singers of the next three decades. He would one day say that his favorite harmonica part he ever recorded was the one on George Jones's recording of a song I co-wrote, "He Stopped Loving Her Today," in 1980. But in 1959, he was a young man known mostly for playing school dances in the Miami area. He was the first white person I ever heard who could play blues harp like Jimmy Reed and Little Walter.

Though Charlie and I were the same age, he was very short and looked about twelve. I had long sideburns and hair slicked down with Butch hair wax, and probably looked twenty-five, so I bought Charlie's beer for him.

When Billy Swafford got back in town, Danny decided there would be a nineteenth-birthday party for me and that we would all go to the beach. Billy brought along a beautiful eighteen-year-old blonde named Jan, and she brought along her friend Lynne, a reasonably cute girl who had two years of high school left. My pelvic partner, Jean, had suddenly moved back to Alabama for some reason, so I was looking for a new girlfriend. Lynne seemed to really like me, but I wanted Billy's girlfriend in a bad way.

As it turned out, Lynne lived with her family about one block from where my room was. She would come over and bring me something she had cooked, and we'd sit on my couch and kiss, but she knew that I liked Jan. She told me, "Jan says she knows that you like her, and she thinks she could get you to do just about anything for her."

The next afternoon, Billy Swafford and I sat around the swimming pool at the motel where he lived. He mentioned Jan, and I told him how beautiful I thought she was.

"Bobby, you wouldn't fuck huh, would you?" Billy Swafford asked me like a Baptist preacher discussing the unforgivable sin. When I told him I wouldn't, knowing that Jan probably wouldn't let me anyway, he picked up his guitar and sang me an autobiographical song he had just written. "I got tooooo many women," he wailed, "an' I cain't turn none of 'em downnnnn."

Billy had a weakness for women all right but, unlike many singers and musicians, he wouldn't have anything to do with drugs. Some of the Miami musicians were using marijuana, which was a whole new world to me. It would be many years before I actually smoked pot myself because I was afraid it would cause instant addiction. Tony, the drummer, told me it was "like getting drunk, only you don't get sloppy and stagger around."

The next day, we had a rehearsal at Club 17, working up a couple of new songs including Elvis's "Big Hunk o' Love." A club that hasn't been cleaned up from the night before is one of the most disgusting places in the world, with cigarette butts floating around in half-finished drinks, hundreds of glasses, many wadded-up napkins, and stinky overflowing ashtrays. After we had finished rehearsing, Danny wanted us to congregate outside on the sidewalk, in front of the club, where Mr. Berger couldn't hear the conversation.

"Hey guys, I got us a gig that pays a little more money, up at Polumbo's Ace of Clubs." I had heard a lot about the Polumbo family and how they made their money. Old Santo Polumbo had moved down to Miami from Jersey many years before, and, besides owning the nightclub, was engaged in other business ventures. His son, Sammy, who was thirty-one but looked much older (and who resembled Tony Soprano), would sometimes sit in with us at Club 17 and sing a torch song, such as "You're Breaking My Heart."

I wasn't really nervous about working for people who were reputedly in the Mafia because one night, during a break at Club 17, I saw a carful of thugs drive by and snatch up one of Mr. Berger's bouncers. They drove away, then returned ten minutes later and poured him out of the car, beaten to a bloody pulp. My rationale was that such a thing would probably never happen to one of *Polumbo's* bouncers, so I'd be safer at the Ace of Clubs than at Club 17. Besides, I'd heard some people say that Danny was connected to the mob, and *he* was always nice to me, whenever he wasn't calling me Farmer Brown.

On our first night at Polumbo's Ace of Clubs, there was a gorgeous girl there. She had dark eyes, raven hair, and a beautiful olive complexion. It was obvious that she and Billy Swafford were attracted to each other. The only problem was that the girl was old man Polumbo's niece, visiting from New Jersey. When we broke after the second or third set, Santo Polumbo walked up to Billy and put his arm around him. The man looked the part, with his still-handsome Sicilian face and curly white hair. I thought he was going to tell Billy that his niece was a nice girl and to please be a gentleman with her.

"If you *ever* touch that girl," he said in a stage whisper loud enough for me to hear, "I mean if you even *touch* her, your body will be at the bottom of the Miami River."

"Yes, *suh*, Mistuh P'lumbo, I mean *no suh*. I won't *evuh* touch huh. I swear to *God*."

He patted Billy on the back. "Good boy. Just don't forget what I said."

"No, *suh*," a dazed Billy kept saying, even after Polumbo had walked away. He never *looked* at the girl again.

The younger Polumbo, Sammy, seemed to have taken a liking to me. One night the club closed before midnight because some repairmen were coming in, so he invited me to go out on the town with him and three of his "bouncers," who looked and acted more like bodyguards. We went to a swanky club in Miami Beach. I was enjoying the floor show and the drinks that Sammy wouldn't let me pay for when he suddenly swiveled around toward me and demanded. "You *are* twenty-one, aren't you?" I was scared to tell him I was nineteen, so I told him I *was* twenty-one. For the rest of the night, I was scared because I had lied to Sammy Polumbo.

The stage at the Ace of Clubs was in the center of the room and slowly revolved, so it was possible to see everyone in the room. We were usually packed, especially after 2:00 a.m. when some of the other clubs had closed. Our late-night clientele often included a man and wife who were jazz pianists and came by after their gig (or gigs). Why these jazz musicians wanted to hear a country rock band, I don't know. He was a big guy with curly black hair and horn-rimmed glasses, just the way one would expect a jazz pianist to look. She was thin and had a constant look of anguish on her face. They were snobbish and would barely speak to me. Whenever I saw them come in, I would try really hard to impress them with my playing, but they seemed to look right through me as though I weren't there. When I did my fast key tickling on the high notes in "After Hours," all I got from Mr. Jazz was a blank stare.

One night, there was a girl sitting at the bar who kept staring at me, wearing the sweetest smile. She was a little overweight but still attractive, with pretty eyes and long, curly brown hair. I bought her a drink and we chatted a while. She said she would go out with me after work. She was in her early twenties, and her name was Christmas. And, coincidence of coincidences, here was another Alabama girl who had a husband in prison. We didn't even make it to breakfast and did the dirty deed in my car, in the parking lot.

What I didn't know was that Christmas's husband was getting out of prison the next week. A couple of weeks later, Danny said a mutual female friend told him that Christmas had made an assortment of confessions to her husband, and one of her disclosures was about this piano player down at the Ace of Clubs, screwing her in the parking lot. The word Danny got was that Christmas's husband didn't like musicians anyway, and he was going to kill him one goddamned piano player.

I was a nervous wreck. Sometimes between numbers, Tony D'Amato would hit a loud rim shot on his snare drum, and I would pop up off the stool, thinking I was being shot at. Sammy Polumbo pulled me aside—it would be much later that I realized he was just pulling my leg—and he said, "Hey, Bobby, if you're gonna get shot, please try to make sure it happens outside. My dad and I don't want any bloodshed inside the club, okay?"

I made up my mind to give Danny my two weeks notice the next night. The Polumbo family saved me the trouble (and maybe my life). When I walked into the Ace of Clubs, there was another band playing on the stage. Tony D'Amato said they couldn't do that to us, he was going to the union. Danny Salvatore, knowing better than to cross the Polumbos, urged him not to, promising that he would find us another gig. I took it as my cue to get out of town.

I told all the guys good-bye. Danny told me he would keep in touch. Slim Byrd, the tall, squinty-eyed guitar player, gave me an affable nod and a handshake. Billy pumped my arm, looked me in the eye as if he were proclaiming that we would meet someday in Heaven, and told me he knew we'd be playing together again soon. Tony the drummer said I was a good guy and "the only one in the band who gets along with all the others."

The next day, Lynne, the girl from down the street who sometimes brought me something she'd cooked, dropped by my place on her way home from school, just as I was packing up my car. She asked if I would be coming back to Miami, and I told her I was sure I would someday. As I drove away, I waved good-bye to Lynne. I turned onto 17th Avenue and said good-bye to the dry cleaner's and the drugstore and the filling station. I headed north on Highway 27 and said good-bye to Miami Springs and Hialeah and the little hut houses and the Australian pines along the Miami Canal and all of this strange, tropical world that was about a million miles south-southeast of Auburndale.

Miami had been a city of firsts for me: my first full-time job as a musician, my first real sexual experience, and my first time being around Italians, Jews, and Northeasterners, people from outside my familiar cultural habitat.

For the second time in seven months, I was moving back in with my parents, this time with a bit more self-confidence and this time not half-starved.

Unless there's some hurricane churning in from out in the Atlantic or down in the Caribbean, October in Central Florida is usually pretty nice. The stifling heat is gone; the days are comfortable, and there's a nip in the air at night.

Upon my return home from Miami, Daddy once again created a grove job for me, something for me to do until I found something better to do.

Stanley and Red were in the navy, so for the next few weeks it would be The Adventures of Braddock and Pace. We drank obnoxious concoctions like beer mixed with milk, engaged a girl in a game of strip poker with a stacked deck, followed the Texas Ray show around to black nightclubs and juke joints, got in a car wreck that earned me a night in jail, and once we outran a crazy man in Lakeland who was chasing us with a gun.

In late November, Pace's good friend Rodney Gelder was home on leave from the army. We went to pick him up at his folks' place up toward Polk City. They lived in a small white frame house on a clay road surrounded by the family's small orange grove. I caught a glimpse of Rodney's little sister, and she caught a glimpse of me.

She had a mass of light reddish-brown frizzy hair, but was attractive nonetheless, had a warm smile, freckled nose, and nice figure. I told Rodney his sister was cute. He suggested that I call her up and ask her out. I did, and she said yes.

There were several Gelder kids, and Gloria, at fifteen, was the youngest. Her father Henry was in his late sixties. His grandparents had been German immigrants who settled in southeast Georgia. He talked Southern but, with his hawkish nose, high forehead, and hairless dome, he looked like an old German baron. His wife, Vivian, was forty-seven, but her extra poundage, wild white hair, and warty face made her seem older. A backwoods Florida Cracker, Vivian Gelder called a wish a *woosh* and a sheriff a *high shurf*; her favorite answer was "*I* reckon" and her favorite comment was "You *reckon*?"

On our first date, Gloria came bounding out the front door with a big smile and a "Hi, Bobby!" She seemed to never be at a loss for words. Pace had told me she seemed really nice and that he understood she was very popular at school.

We had a typical date: drive-in movie, drive-in restaurant, and then went "parking," not at Braddock's Hole, but by a lake down the road from Gloria's house. The same lake, in fact, where my friends and I had pulled the joke about the truck driver's wife about a year before. We talked and kissed and enjoyed each others' company so much that time got away from us. I turned on the interior light; the clock on the dashboard read 3:45.

"I'd better get you *home*, Gloria," I said as I started up the car, only to find that I had parked too far off the clay road and was *stuck*. The more I tried to back up, the farther down toward the lake the car slid. Finally, I gave up, put on the emergency brake, and walked Gloria to her house. Her mother met us at the door. To my surprise, she didn't seem at all upset that I was bringing her fifteen-year-old daughter home at 4:00 a.m. on a first date.

"I'll git Rodney up and have him run you home," Mrs. Gelder said. "I'll betcha David kin pull you out tomorrow with the tractor." David was Gloria and Rodney's twenty-five-year-old brother.

"I had a really nice time," Gloria bubbled as I followed Rodney out to the Gelder family car. "I guess I'll see you tomorrow."

The next day was the big Gelder *car pullout.* You would think I had told them there was buried treasure down by the lake, and they seemed only too glad to go get it. The old man had a gruff voice but was cordial. Mrs. Gelder was rough edged, almost manly, but very friendly to me. Rodney, who had his father's hawk nose, was cynical in an amusing way. David, the brother who was going to pull me out with the tractor, was handsome, sweet-natured, soft-spoken, and down to earth.

Gloria and I started seeing each other fairly often. She was talkative and sometimes stuck her foot in her mouth. If she seemed a bit unsophisticated—after all she was only fifteen—she was warm and pleasant and easy to be around. And there was a definite attraction between us.

It was during this period, when Gloria and I first started going out, that Pace and I hooked up with Jumpin' Jack Jubal on a Sunday afternoon and decided to share a Rexall Inhaler and "chew the cotton." The objective was to take a razor blade and cut off only a tiny slice of the Dexedrine-soaked cotton strip, but just to be obnoxious, I cut off a very big piece and washed it right down with a beer. Within the hour I was wired so hot that I called up everyone I knew and talked and talked for hours.

That night, I was unable to sleep. When the sun came up, I was still wide awake and my pulse was so fast that I couldn't count it. My mouth was full of white, dry, chalk dust. There were other physical effects that I won't recount here. I was scared to death, certain that I was about to die. I went to the local doctor, Dr. Tanner, who gave me a good scolding and told me if it hadn't killed me by now that it probably wouldn't, then admonished me to never do it again. He gave me something to help me sleep that night.

For the next few days, I was a nervous wreck, pains all over my body, especially in my head. One night I had a pain radiating from my left elbow to my shoulder and was convinced that I was going to have a heart attack at nineteen. Sometimes I got palpitations, even when I wasn't exerting myself.

The night after Christmas, Pace and I were at Club 92 where we ran into the White "sisters," Rosie and her daughter Margaret, the now sixteen-year-old with big brown eyes who had said "sometimes ah jes' wanna throw mah arms around yuh an' tell yuh ah love yuh" right before I moved to Miami. I made a date with her, but the more I thought about it, the more guilt I felt. I had been seeing Gloria a lot and didn't really want to go out with anyone but her, so I called Margaret and told her I couldn't make it.

On New Year's Eve, I took Gloria to the Polk Theater in Lakeland, then to my parent's house to watch TV.

"*Hi,* Mr. Braddock. *Hi,* Mrs. Braddock." Gloria was a walking bubble machine.

"Hi, Gloria," my mother said, her smile maybe just a little stiff.

"Come in, come in," Daddy said, "and make yoursellllf at hooome."

"We went to a movie and started to ride around but Bobby said well why don't we just go over to the house and watch some TV and then go outside and listen to the firecrackers going off around Auburndale when the New Year comes in," she said, in a slow-paced babble. "Gosh, can you believe it's gonna be nineteen-sixty already and it seems like nineteen-fifty-nine just got here," and on and on and on.

Gloria and I sat alone on the front screened porch, holding hands, looking out at the street lights dancing on the waters of little Lake Stella. I told her about me making, then breaking, the date with Margaret.

"Oh, Bobby, I don't want to go out with anyone but *you either.*"

As we kissed, there were fireworks, firecrackers pop-pop-popping in the distance and the occasional *whoosh* of a Roman candle somewhere in the neighborhood, as 1960 came in from the east and clicked into place in our time zone. There were pains in my arms, my chest, and my head. I entered the 1960s thinking I was falling in love but also believing I was going to die.

CHAPTER EIGHT

Crazy in Orburndale

W ELL, 1960 WASN'T REALLY the sixties. There were a few American military advisors in Vietnam but not yet several hundred thousand American soldiers. There were a few thousand beatniks in the coffee houses but not yet millions of hippies in the streets. Rock 'n' roll was for dancing but not yet for editorializing. The sun was out and the skies were still blue, but the conditions were right for a storm, and keen observers saw the towering thunderheads forming on the distant horizon.

As the new decade dawned, there was a kind of fear across the land. It was not the jumpy, reactive kind of fear that anticipates a recurrence of something that has already happened, such as the fear of suicide bombers and highjackers that would traumatize America in the 2000s. It was a deep apprehensive fear of the *unthinkable:* unfettered nuclear war and a fiery worldwide Armageddon.

In January of 1960, America knew nothing about fanatical Muslim terrorists. Our grave concern was about a people who didn't believe in *any* kind of God: the Communists. After the downfall of the old Soviet Union (Russia and its surrounding territories), the declassification of formerly secret documents indicates that they were never our nuclear equal, but in 1960 we didn't know that. All we knew was that there were more of them than there were of us and, after all, didn't Soviet premier Khrushchev say, "We will *bury* you?" So went the Cold War. One little miscalculation could have triggered the end of civilization.

Our president was Dwight D. Eisenhower, who called himself a "modern Republican." His World War II–hero status had catapulted him to two terms in the White House, and he remained popular throughout his tenure. Both houses of Congress were controlled by the Democrats, but the Southern Democrats were at least as conservative as the Northern Republicans, so together they constituted a coalition that made most liberal legislation unpassable.

In 1960, many Christians still distrusted Jews. Many Protestants were openly anti-Catholic, often speaking out against them from the pulpit. African Americans were not allowed to vote in the Deep South and weren't allowed to use public accommodations in about one-third of America.

Most Americans (especially men) smoked, myself included, knowing that it might cause cancer but clueless about arterial damage or emphysema or the fact that second-hand smoke was dangerous. All TV was black and white; cable was unheard of. Cell phones were twenty-five years in the future, but there was a phone booth on every corner. Nobody had a personal computer. Nobody had AIDS. Jogging was for serious athletes, and low-cholesterol diets were strictly for heart patients. Cars were death traps. More people lived in cities and on farms back then; not nearly as many people lived in the suburbs as today. Each city and county had its own distinct accent or dialect, and this was especially true of my parents' generation; they had learned to form words without any audio influences from outside their region, such as sound movies or radio.

Change was in the air, no doubt. Black people were losing their patience, and young people were losing their virginity. The coming gap between the generations was showing up on cultural seismographs all over the country. There was overt sexuality in the music. The movies were beginning to lose their innocence; no *s* words or *f* words yet, but a lot more *damns* and *hells,* and even though there were no sex scenes, they sure talked about it a lot.

And so it was, all around me. The status quo was still in place, but you could feel the first breezes of the winds of change. Hope springs eternal, and this was true in January of 1960, but there was also that nagging fear of the unknown and the unthinkable. It was going on in the world around me, but it was also going on in my own little world, deep within my psyche. Just as the world was pondering the possibility of annihilation, I was afraid something catastrophic was about to engulf *me*. Everyone has to make the passage from youth to adulthood. Mine was like a trip across an ocean: sometimes dark and ominous, sometimes sunny and pleasant; some nights cruising along in a boat, other nights slipping back into the gloomy depths; on a good day living the good life on a tropical island, on a bad day being swept back out to sea in a storm.

Becoming an adult isn't easy; getting there emotionally disturbed is *really* hard. It could have been worse. I wasn't dying, I only *thought* I was. There were genuinely bad times for me, but many people had it much worse. After all, I was living in a free country, my family wasn't poor, and my friends stood by me. For a long time, I looked back on this period of my life as an embarrassment. Now I view these misadventures and tragedies and comedies as good story fodder, though I must admit that I approach the telling of them with much trepidation because I know I'll be walking back through haunted houses and stirring up old forgotten ghosts. But tell it I must. Everyone who survives their youth has their story, and this is mine.

The Dexedrine overdose, the month before, had turned me into a disaster waiting to happen. I was already a bit skittish as the Braddock family embarked on a wedding excursion one unusually cold day in mid-January. My brother Paul and his wife Jo Ann left their little daughter Carol with her other grandmother and joined me and my parents on a trip to South Georgia.

Both of my half-sisters, who were approximately my mother's age, married men who were foremen with road crews that paved a highway through the swamps between Lakeland and Auburndale back in the late 1920s. Louise's husband Carmon Coker worked his way up through the ranks in the Florida State Road Department. Lucille's husband Earl Olson did the same thing with the Georgia State Road Department. The children of the two couples were my half-nieces and half-nephews. To avoid confusion over me being an uncle to people who were much older than me, I simply said they were my cousins.

Lucille and Earl's children, Diane and Eric, were raised in Tifton, Georgia. They spoke the Deep Southern but choppy dialect of their region, like Jimmy Carter and my singing friend Billy Swafford. ("Bobby, I think I love huh.") Eric, who was four years older than I, was marrying a pretty Southern belle named Betsy. The wedding was to take place in Albany, Georgia, so we stayed with my Uncle Junior, who was stationed there at a military base. On the Friday night that we arrived, there was a big pre-wedding party. My parents' feelings were hurt because while Paul and Jo Ann and I were invited to the party, they were not, apparently because it was assumed that Daddy would disapprove of all the drinking.

I was the hit of the party with my piano playing, and every request was accompanied by a glass of champagne. I staggered into Uncle Junior's house so drunk that I fell down twice. My mother had to drag me out of bed for the wedding the next day. At the reception, Eric told me I needed to get me some sugar water—he pronounced it "sugah wotta"—so I grabbed a big, tall Tom Collins and, escaping the reproachful eyes of my parents as best I could, proceeded to get drunk once again.

On our way home the next day, we were about an hour north of Auburndale, and I was at the wheel. Suddenly, I became so weak that I could barely hold on. I pulled over to the side of the road and let somebody else drive. I fell down in the seat, unable to sit up. I wasn't paralyzed, but it was as though all the strength had been sucked from my body. There is no doubt that a megachunk of cotton from the Rexall Inhaler had screwed with my nervous system, but in addition, I was probably having a blood sugar attack from a weekend of getting drunk. This was the beginning of two-and-a-half years of panic attacks, hypochondria, and depression.

"I'm having a heart attack. I . . . can't . . . breathe," I gasped. Actually, it was the opposite: I was doing *too much* breathing. When they took me to the Winter Haven Hospital, I was huffing and puffing and jerking and trembling. When the nurse took my pulse, it was close to two hundred beats a minute. The doctor gave me a shot of morphine.

Let me tell you about every little fear and every little pain disappearing within a few seconds. Let me tell you about floating on clouds and smiling down at the rest of the world. Generations before heroin was widely manufactured from morphine, so the story goes, there were thousands of crippled addicts hobbling down to their basements, amputees headed for their smokehouses and barns, on canes and crutches, their old Yankee blue or Rebel gray jackets draped around their shoulders as they went to get their fix. I'm glad this was the only day the drug was ever made available to me, because it sure felt better than being crazy, and I'm sure it would have been easy for me to get hooked. Thank God I didn't know where to get heroin.

One warm spring night, I pulled my car off the clay road onto the sandy trail that wound through my father's citrus grove to the tiny lake known as Braddock's Hole. I looked over at Gloria, whose face was illuminated by the dashboard lights. She had a high forehead and light reddish-brown frizzy hair, but she had an attractive face, an expressive face that put on display all of her varying emotions.

"G-G-Gloria, I really think I have a brain tumor," I said gravely.

"Oh, Bobby, maybe we should get married soon . . . before, you know, something *happens* to you," she responded, her look of noble concern fading to black as I turned off the ignition and the lights.

We pledged undying love beneath the hot stars and cold planets. A soft breeze gently stroked the grapefruit trees as the snakes slid silently across the sand, and the crickets and rain frogs sang their crazy Southern song. If the night has a thousand eyes, those eyes would have seen the vague form of a car among shadowy trees in the almost total darkness, then, in a few minutes, the orange glow of a cigarette through the windshield.

We became almost inseparable. Gloria would walk to my house after school, wait for me to get home from working in my dad's groves, and then eat supper with us. After supper, we would go to a movie or ride around, then go parking. Our last stop was usually the drink machine in front of Nail's Grocery Store in Polk City, where we would each get a strawberry soda. Finally, I'd take her home, which was about eight miles north of where I lived.

For her sixteenth birthday, I went to Kay Jewelers in Lakeland ("*It's okay to owe Kay 'til pay day*," went the TV/radio jingle) and bought Gloria a beautiful six-hundred-dollar ring. For the twenty-first century, multiply that amount very many times. My small income came from working in the orange groves (whenever I wasn't too sick or crazy to leave the house) and playing with a band on weekends. I signed a contract, agreeing to pay the jewelry store ten dollars a week.

Gloria squealed with delight when I gave her the engagement ring with the little diamonds. She hugged and kissed me and danced all around the little Gelder living room.

"Well, I'll be," sighed Mrs. Gelder with a twisted smile as she ran a hand through her wild white hair. "That shore is purty."

In Florida, with parental consent, males could marry at eighteen, females at sixteen. Without parental consent, both parties had to be twenty-one. There is no doubt that Mr. and Mrs. Gelder would have both signed off on the marriage. Not so the Braddocks.

"Now, Bobby," my mother said, smiling with her mouth but not with her eyes, "when you save up a thousand dollars, then we'll sign for you."

"But, Mom," I whined. I had started calling my parents Mom and Dad, instead of Mother and Daddy. "That's gonna take awhile."

"Well, I don't think you have any business getting married until you have a thousand dollars saved up."

Appalled at the thought of us getting married, Mom later admitted, she came up with that figure thinking that I would *never* save that much money. My parents' lack of confidence in me and my own lack of self-esteem seemed to feed off each other.

The emotional free-fall that I was in just made me feel increasingly worse about myself. I am now, in effect, walking back into those old days and shining a flashlight on that jumbled mess, trying to make some sense of it. I was a bit fragile to begin with. Though never afraid of *people* in the physical sense—certainly I got into more than my share of fights—I was afraid of *things,* like embarrassment and humiliation and spiders and snakes and heights and closed-in places and nuclear war and, of course, airplanes. No doubt, chewing too much cotton played havoc with my nervous system, causing twitches and tremors and pains. The effect that these symptoms had on a born worrier—with a wild imagination—was often crippling and incapacitating. Almost every day became filled with anxiety, the small annoying kind that keeps you on edge (even in your dreams) and the big menacing kind that makes you think you're in the middle of a major disaster when you're not.

I then became a prisoner of depression. Like so many depressed people, I didn't even know I was depressed. I thought my surroundings really *had* turned horribly bleak. I thought the giant hand pushing me down to the ground was the whole universe ganging up on me. Depression made me think I was dying, and thinking I was dying made me depressed. I wasn't merely a hypochondriac; I was seriously out of touch with reality. A headache became a brain tumor, a gas bubble became a heart attack, and a lingering pain became a cancer. The books I was reading made my bedroom look like a medical student lived there. Auburndale's Dr. Tanner had a new young partner, the Barney Fife–like Dr. Koons, who took Dr. Tanner's night calls. He started receiving frequent calls from me in the wee hours; I recall him angrily responding, "Oh, good grief, what's the matter with you *now*?"

At first, my parents and Gloria thought as I did, that it was my *body* that was sick. But the words of the medical men, that it was all in my head, soon began to resonate with everyone but me. Doctors gave me old-fashioned tranquilizers that simply changed me from *crazy* to *crazy and sluggish*. Alcohol was fire water that temporarily turned a coward into a crazy fearless fool who always woke up the next morning in a lonely room with his anxious, frightened self. Sometimes, I was the old fun-loving me, but more often I was an emotional cripple, certain that death was lurking just around the corner.

Generally, I was a little better when I was making music. I had hooked back up with Jumpin' Jack Jubal. We were playing at a club that was secretly owned by a former Auburndale mayor. The place was called Club 17 (coincidentally, the same name as the club I had played in Miami the year before). It was located on Highway 17 between Winter Haven and Lake Alfred. We had a pretty decent band, which included a couple of country boys, Bobby Joe Barlow on guitar, and a big old guy with thick glasses, Richard Ruskins, on electric bass. The drummer was Arnie Levin, a kid from New Jersey who was a student at Florida Southern College in Lakeland.

There were a few adventures at Club 17. One night, from out of nowhere, appeared the Brown Boys, whose very names struck terror in the hearts of Polk Countians, those devil angels who had saved me from being choked by a carnival barker when I was in high school and who rescued me once again at Club 17 from some drunk guys who were about to whip my ass.

Another night, after singing "Keep A-Knockin'" and while chuggin' a bottle of beer that I kept on the piano, I was arrested by a deputy sheriff for drinking underage and had to be followed by Gloria in my 1960 Ford (which my dad had bought me in a surprising display of generosity) to the county jail in Bartow where my brother came to bail me out.

A lot of my Club 17 recollections are just of me getting in trouble and being obnoxious. The most obnoxious Three Stooges–like thing that I did was to hit a guy for absolutely no good reason. The band was through playing, and I was fairly hammered. And hungry. I went to the food counter in the front of the club where you could order burgers and sandwiches. Sometimes Gloria didn't go with me when I played out, and I don't think she was along on this particular night. I sat down at the counter and ordered a burger, then got up to go to the bathroom. When I came back, Richard Ruskins, the tall, obese bass player with thick glasses, was sitting at the counter with his large girlfriend, who was occupying my stool.

Now, Richard was a very sweet guy—country, slow-talking. Sometimes he would look right at me, eyes crossed behind his thick glasses, and say, "Bobby, I really like you."

What I did that night was unconscionable.

"I'm sorry, Irene, but I was sitting here. I just ordered a cheeseburger," I told Richard's girlfriend.

"Well, by God, *hell no,* you ain't sittin' here *now,* buddy," she said. "Get your ass away from here."

"Richard," I announced, "I can't hit a lady, so I'm gonna have to hit *you.*" I then punched him in the nose. My only excuse is that I was drunk. I probably apologized to him every single time that I saw him after that night.

"That's alright, Bobby," he would say. "She di'n't have no bidness talkin' to you that-a-way."

Jumpin' Jack Jubal, who was still rolling all over the floor while he sang, had a friend who started showing up and sitting in with us regularly. He was a first-rate country singer named Ray Jackson, an East Texas boy who was married to an Auburndale girl. Ray had co-written "Who Shot Sam," which had been a hit for George Jones the year before. He took a big interest in a song I had written the previous year (when my mind was clearer and more creative) called "Forbidden Fruit," a Texas shuffle-type song that I envisioned Ray Price singing. Ray Jackson liked it so much that we went into a radio station in Winter Haven so he could do a demo (demonstration recording) of my song, which he wanted to use to try to get himself a record deal. Ray was an even more serious abuser of alcohol and pills than Jubal was. Though he was only twenty-seven, he looked much older. Already showing wrinkles around his smiling glossy blue eyes, Ray would live only another five years. Knowing that he was from George Jones's hometown and had written songs with Jones made him a celebrity in my eyes. Ray Jackson's confidence in me as a songwriter was a better shot in the arm than the morphine.

Sometimes Gloria showed a little jealousy if she thought some girl at the club was flirting with me from the dance floor, but generally we got along pretty well. She was sweet and understanding about my heart attacks and brain tumors. I was her first real boyfriend, and I think she thought she was in love with me. She held on to her mental snapshot of when she first knew me and thought I was so carefree and cool. She kept hoping I would be like that again someday. We said goofy and mushy things to each other that are so embarrassing that I won't recount them here.

I was so crazy and vulnerable; I think I had a kind of needy love for her. It's obvious what bad stuff *I* brought to the relationship—I was emotionally screwed up, a self-absorbed hypochondriac. And there was something in her that reared its ugly head occasionally, a man-hating thing that could be attributed to a lifetime of her mother's laments about men in general and Mr. Gelder in particular; Gloria's tirades came and went like summer storms, always followed by sweet apologies.

With his perfect posture, beakish nose held high and his large bald dome, Mr. Gelder looked like an old German baron, but when he opened his mouth, out came this quavery, high-pitched voice, like a stereotypical impersonation of an old country-talking man. He was always pleasant and cordial to me, but Gloria told me he didn't like the way we were always hugging and kissing on each other around their house. With *Mrs.* Gelder, however, Bobby could do no wrong.

I think my parents thought Gloria's mother was on a mission to get her married off to me because of the Gelders' assumption that the Braddocks had money. I never heard this from Dad; now that I was grown, he wasn't as likely to confront me. He would tell Mom the things about me that upset or bothered him, and then *she* would confront me. However, my parents were nice to Gloria and didn't typically do anything to make her feel unwelcome.

Mrs. Gelder was large and rough-edged, a bit masculine and shared my dad's passion for agriculture. She worked at a canning plant during the fruit season, but the Gelders owned a twenty-acre grove that surrounded their house, and she had about as much to do with its upkeep as Mr. Gelder did. She definitely didn't connect with my mother as well as she did with my father. Whenever she came to our house, she would walk right past Mother, muttering, "Hey, Miz Braddick," without even looking at her, and head on into the living room and start talking up a storm to P.E.

"Are your 'June blooms' comin' in purty good, Mr. Braddick?"

"Ohhhh, yes, we have some good looking ahran-ges out there, Missus Gelder. I wish you could see-e-e-e them."

"I'll run by there an' look' at 'em on the way home. What kinder fertilizer you use on this yur's crop?"

He'd sing the praises of Gulf Fertilizer, and then they would talk on and on about the different types of oranges: Valencias, pineapples, and Parson Browns.

"You know, a good navel ahrrrange, afta it's been in the refrigerator for awhile, is awwwwfully hard to beat," Dad would say, practically licking his lips.

As Mrs. Gelder carried on in her country accent about the citrus business, Mom would be in the next room with a cute smile, almost but not quite rolling her eyes. Had it been decades later, she probably would have been saying, "What-*ever!*"

Dad's love for agriculture wasn't passed on to me. As a grove worker, I was absolutely worthless. When I wasn't napping on the job, I might have been chasing an armadillo down a sandy row or feeding a large garden spider to a city of ants—or just staring at the sky and hoping for an afternoon rain so I could knock off and go home.

There was a lot of dead wood to be cut and sawed from my father's trees, so Dad hired a large crew, all black men. The foreman, a man known as Wilson, was very light-skinned but deferential, always calling me "Mister Bobby." It didn't appear to be forced, though, he seemed to be genuinely sweet-natured. Wilson and I had worked out a deal in which we would cover for each other whenever my father showed up. Once a day, Wilson, cross-eyed but an otherwise nice-looking middle-aged man, would drive in to Auburndale in the early afternoon and pay a visit to a female friend. He would be gone about forty-five minutes. If my dad asked where Wilson was, I told him he was working over on the other side of the grove or that he broke his saw and had to go into town to get another one. And for an hour or two every morning, worn out from the previous night's insomnia or death nightmares, I would take a nap in my car, which I always parked on the shady side of the biggest tree I could find. Wilson would yell, "Fire in the hole! Fire in the hole!" When I heard these code words for "boss man's coming," I would jump up from a sweaty slumber and dive into the nearest tree, saw in hand, as I heard Dad's Ford-o-matic Drive working hard to pull through the deep sand. As he pulled up even with me, I would be sawing away.

One day when I got home from the groves, Mom told me I had gotten a call from Miami. It was from Ash Bodden, a drummer. He had heard about me through Charlie McCoy. Ash said that he and a sax player named Corky Ventura were looking for a good pianist. He said they did mostly Louis Prima–style jazz and show tunes, and if I were a good shuffle player, I would get the job. Although I liked that kind of music, I certainly wasn't an aficionado, but I *did* know how to play a shuffle. They had some club dates booked in upstate New York. We agreed that he and Corky would come up to Auburndale to audition me.

I had really mixed feelings. With all my fears and phobias, I dreaded leaving home, and I didn't want to be away from Gloria. But there was also that old longing to be free, that same kind of yearning to be on my own that I had felt when I finished high school.

The boys got to Auburndale around suppertime one early summer afternoon. Ash Bodden was a tall, skinny, dark-haired Miamian whose parents had been British subjects from the Bahamas. Corky Ventura was a short blond-haired guy from Pittsburgh who wanted to make sure everyone understood that his people were from *northern* Italy. Both of them were fairly quiet as they sat around the dinner table with Mom, Dad, Gloria, and me. For some reason, Gloria felt very shy and intimidated in their presence, and in the middle of the meal she jumped up and ran from the table, closing herself up in my bedroom.

We ran through some songs; they liked my playing and told me I had the job. We had a gig at a lounge in Kingston and would drive up to Schenectady in about a week and rehearse for a few days with an electric bass player who lived up there. The next morning, I woke up with a severe headache, sore throat, and high fever. Dr. Tanner told me I would probably be in bed for at least two weeks. I told him I absolutely *had* to be well enough to go to New York the next week. I don't know if he gave me antibiotics or an antiviral drug, but he doubled the dosage to see if that would help. It helped knock out whatever I had, but it gave me really bad side effects: upset stomach, sores on the tongue, and zero appetite; I couldn't even force myself to eat ice cream. I wasn't well enough to ride up with Ash and Corky, so we decided they could get started with the rehearsals in Schenectady for two or three days and I would take a train up.

The old Atlantic Coast Line railroad depot, a little butterscotch-colored stucco building built around 1920, was in the middle of the Auburndale city park. I stood there among the palms and the gravel with Gloria and my parents as the big iron beast approached. Riding a train was usually pretty exciting to me, but having lost ten pounds in a week, I was almost too weak to carry my suitcase. My tongue was bloody, and I still couldn't eat. I had forced down a little soup before we left the house. As the train pulled up, I looked at all the railroad cars and thought of this as a cortege, the funeral being mine. I was terribly depressed. Gloria held me tightly and told me she wished I wasn't going. Suddenly, my mother burst into tears.

"I just don't like you going away in the condition you're in. You don't really know anybody up there," she sobbed.

As I took my seat, I was tempted to get up, grab my suitcase, and get off the train, but I didn't. I just sat there looking out the window at Gloria as she mouthed "I love you." I was feeling pretty low, watching my loved ones waving good-bye as the train slowly pulled me away from them.

Luckily, I had the best possible travel companion, a seventy-eight-year-old man named Gus, who happened to be going as far up into New York state as I was. Gus had a very young attitude and was wearing a good-looking three-piece suit. He said he had been visiting his girlfriend in St. Petersburg. We immediately hit it off; we even smoked the same brand of cigarettes, Pall Mall. The old gentleman knew I was sick and insisted that I try to eat some soup. Not only did I have no appetite, but my tongue was now swollen and anything I placed in my mouth caused me great pain.

By the time Ash and Corky picked me up at the station in Albany, New York, I felt as though I had been traveling for twenty-four *days* instead of twenty-four hours. I was so weak and sick that they had to help me into Ash's car.

"We need to get this guy to a hospital," Ash told Corky.

"I've got a better idea," Corky replied. "Saratoga Springs."

"Ohhh-h-h-h," Ash howled softly.

"You remember?" Corky asked,

"Ohh-h-h yeah, I *do* remember."

We drove north for about thirty or forty minutes. In this old resort town, there was a beautiful park area with lush greenery and cascading water. There seemed to be a drinking fountain every few feet. It was late in the afternoon, and there must have been two hundred people on the grounds, most of them elderly, lined up to get a drink from the various underground springs. These mineral waters were reputed to have medicinal and healing powers.

"You need something to help your appetite," Corky proclaimed. He walked around and conferred with a number of old folks and finally told me he had found just the one for me. We stood in line for a couple of minutes, then I leaned over and got a drink from an ordinary-looking drinking fountain. But the water sure didn't *taste* ordinary. It tasted like Alka-Seltzer.

The guys figured by the time we got back to the Albany-Schenectady area that I might be a little hungry, but within fifteen minutes I was begging them to stop. We pulled into a diner. My tongue was no longer swollen, and I had a voracious appetite. I ate two cheeseburgers, sausage patties, and an order of pancakes with syrup. After we left the diner, we checked into a hotel in Schenectady. I slept like a baby. When I woke up, the sores on my tongue had completely disappeared and my stomach was fine. I ate a huge breakfast and felt like a million dollars.

The gig in Kingston was short-lived. I got to do some singing, which was fun; I sang the Eddie Boyd blues song, "Five Long Years." But for some reason, our bass player quit, and I don't think we sounded very good as a trio. So when our little stint came to an end, I didn't care; I was ready to go home and see Gloria. My time had not been wasted. Ash Bodden was a great drummer, and we would become band mates and close friends in the future. And it had been worth the entire trip to experience the miracle waters of Saratoga Springs.

I was sitting on the sunset side of the streamlined train when nighttime descended on the swamps, piney woods, citrus groves, and small towns that whizzed by my window. The electric lights started coming on across Central Florida. When the train started slowing down, I looked out at Auburndale. My parents and Gloria were there to meet me, almost in the same spot where they had sent me on my way.

"Awwww-fully good to have you ho-ome, Bobby boy," Dad said as he hugged me, and in the ancient Southern tradition, kissed me on the mouth. He didn't know what to make of this sickly son who couldn't hold a regular day job, this troubadour who traveled around the country, playing music. There had been nothing in his life to prepare him for the likes of me.

"Well, Bobb-*eeee*," Mom said, her voice jumping an octave, almost like Minnie Pearl saying *how-deeee*, "I've fixed you some cowpeas, and made a key lime pie and baked you some chocolate chip cookies." My sweet mother loved me so much, and I was such a disappointment to her. There were so many things that she wanted me to be that I *wasn't*: a baptized Christian, mentally healthy, more formally educated, and gainfully employed.

Gloria and I were holding hands, glad to see each other. This was not a mad, passionate love affair. I would know many of those, and this wasn't one of them, not for either of us. It was a normal boy-girl relationship, to be sure, we definitely liked each other in that way (even with her name changed, I'm trying to give Gloria as much privacy here as possible), but it wasn't an I-can't-wait-to-get-my-hands-on-you sort of thing. How deep did it go? She was in love with my attention and my need for her, and I was in love with her nurturing. I thought I loved her more than anything in the world, and it was the same way that I had loved my mother when I was a little boy. As long as I was in a mental rut, I wouldn't realize that this wasn't the way romantic love was supposed to be.

And so, back to Florida for me. I tried sales ("H-h-how are you today, ma'am? Y-y-you don't want to buy any aluminum siding, do you?"), then ended up once more working for my father. One day I was riding with Dad through his groves. He was at the wheel and my friend Don Pace was sitting in the backseat. The car seemed to have a little bounce to it.

"Mr. Bradduk," Pace said, "I think you might have a flat tire."

"No, Don," Dad replied in his W. C. Fields–Foghorn Leghorn voice, "if you talk about a flat tiiiire, you'll *get* a flat tiiiire."

P.E. continued down the metallic-colored sand rows. The '56 Ford seemed to be having a harder time of it.

"Mr. Bradduk, I sure think you got a flat tire."

"No-o-o-o, Don, you *talk* about a flat tiiire, you GET a flat tiiiire."

When the car started bucking, Don blurted out, "Mr. Bradduk, I swear . . . "

"TALK about a flat tiiiire, you GET a flat tiiire," he retorted as he slammed on the brakes.

We all hopped out of the car and looked at a very, very flat tire. Dad looked at Don and sternly barked, "SEE?"

So I was doing piece work for Dad during the week and playing weekends with a thrown-together band at Club 92. One Friday night, Gloria had decided to go with me to the club. Her brother Rodney was home on leave from the army and decided to go with us. Rodney had dark blond hair, worn in a flattop. Muscular and of medium height, he was a nice enough looking fellow, despite the beaklike nose that he had inherited from his father. Rodney had a dry sense of humor and accented his words or phrases by rocking his head back and forth from left to right to left to right. "And *that's* (left) the *way* (right) it *is* (left) to*night* (right)." The only thing I disliked about Rodney was the big-brother-to-little-sister condescension he sometimes showed toward Gloria.

The guitar player I was using at Club 92 was a Pennsylvania transplant named Joe Glimp. He was a wiry guy with a bit of an attitude, probably a couple of years older than me. His wife Liz was a local country girl with long dark hair, gorgeous but tall and big-boned.

During one of our sets, the drummer kept hitting his entrance licks at the wrong place in an instrumental I was playing. I yelled at him when it was time for him to hit the extra licks on his snare. It was the only way I could think of to communicate to him at the moment, but it probably did seem as though I was yelling at him angrily. The drummer had no problem with it, but Joe Glimp did. He later told me he was a wreck because his father had recently died, but I didn't know that when he turned to me on our break and hissed, "You'd better not ever yell at *me* the way you yelled at that drummer. *I'll* kick your *ass.*"

That's all it took. I punched him as hard as I could, and we were into it, rolling around on the floor hitting each other. Gloria was hysterical and tried to separate us. Joe Glimp's Amazon wife thought Gloria was hitting her husband, so she attacked *her*. Poor Gloria, who was susceptible to occasional asthma attacks, had a major one on the dance floor of Club 92. The club owner and a bouncer picked her up and carried her to the lobby and laid her on a table. The owner's wife unbuttoned Gloria's blouse to loosen it. As Gloria lay there gasping for air, I took her hand and told her she was going to be all right. Rodney, in an exhibition of chivalry that his sister would never forget, covered her body with a blanket he had found, then asked the gawking crowd to move on and leave her alone.

That summer with Gloria was sometimes good, sometimes not. We had started to have skirmishes, sometimes because I was an emotional wreck and sometimes because she was moody and withdrawn. It was hell when those two negative forces coincided. But for the good and the bad of it, we were almost always together, seeing B-movies at drive-in theaters with names like Filmland and Silver Moon, or watching TV at the Braddock house.

When we rode around, the radio was usually on. Pop stations were playing "Alley Oop" and "Itsy Bitsy Teenie Weenie Yellow Polka Dot Bikini." Country stations played cheatin' songs like "Please Help Me I'm Falling." And of course we went parking, in what was probably not the ideal setting for romance: a cramped car in the middle of a mosquito-infested grove on a hot and humid Florida night. But that was the only place we knew to go to be romantic. It was nicer when there was some moonlight or a soft breeze. Sometimes we would open the doors and just sit and talk for a long time, while a baritone bullfrog sang, "Knee deep, knee deep," backed by a giant choir of rain frogs and crickets who offered up Stravinsky-like harmonies. Sometimes there would be the howl of a distant dog or the hum of an airplane overhead. A pair of large raccoons may have been emerging from the woods at the other end of the grove to see if there was any summer fruit left for them to steal.

It was September of 1960. Every day, Gloria, a junior at Auburndale High, rode a school bus down from Polk City. I, who *should* have been a junior in *college*, was riding a bus to Nowheresville. Summer's hot kiss was beginning to cool. It was football season, deer hunting season, the fall TV season and, where we were, hurricane season. One of the biggest storms of the century—Hurricane Donna—slammed into the Florida Keys with gusts up to 175 miles an hour, killing several people. Donna continued up the Gulf coast and went inland near Ft. Myers, staying on a northerly course and heading directly for us.

I wanted Gloria to be there with me during the storm, so we got everyone's permission for her to spend the night, though Mom told me later that Dad didn't really approve and thought it didn't look good. Gloria would sleep in my bed, and I would sleep two rooms away on the living room couch, the davenport, as we called it.

Donna continued to be a major hurricane as she moved up the peninsula. She hit Auburndale head-on after suppertime, with steady winds of 120 miles per hour. The moaning and howling and creaking brought back childhood memories. Gloria and I stepped out on the front porch and immediately felt the water spraying and stinging through the screen. The palm trees, a few feet in front of us, were almost horizontal.

"This is exciting," she said.

"*Bobby Braddock*," I heard my mother call as her voice fought the wind's voice, "you'd better *not* be out there on that *porch!*" When you live at home, they still treat you like a child.

Suddenly, the wind stopped, almost like someone had hit a switch, and the stars came out. I could see the school gymnasium, which was located across the street from the entrance to our long dirt driveway. A lot of people who lived in really small houses or in trailers were spending the night there. Many of them apparently thought the storm was over because they were getting in their cars and leaving. They must have moved down to hurricane country after the last big one and didn't know about the eye of the storm. But I knew we were sitting in the eye and that the other side of the giant watery wall of wind and rain would reach us any minute. Cowardly about things I should have been brave about, I was, conversely, fearless about things I should have been afraid of. I ran out the door and started up the driveway to warn them. Mom, Dad, and Gloria yelled at me to come back. Before I made it to North Bartow Avenue, the wind suddenly started blowing hard. I immediately turned around and ran back to the house. Within a couple of minutes, it was a full-fledged hurricane again.

Gloria and I stayed up long after Dad had his last talk with God Almighty about the weather. Mom kept getting up until she was satisfied that I was on the couch and Gloria was in the back bedroom. As the screaming winds quieted down to a low moan, I drifted off to sleep.

The next morning, when there was nothing left of Donna but light rain, I drove Gloria home. Roofs were blown away, poles were down, trees were uprooted, and the ripening little oranges and grapefruit, just two or three months away from picking time, blanketed the ground. On one mile-long stretch, with Lake Juliana on one side and a swamp on the other, both shoulders of the Polk City Road were paved with dead snakes, many of them water moccasins. There must have been tens of thousands. I had no idea there were that many snakes in the entire *county*. These guys from the lake and the swamp had found the higher ground but that, too, had been flooded during the storm. Even water snakes have to come up for air.

That night Gloria and I went to Lakeland. There was not one spark of electricity in the entire city of forty thousand people. We drove past a Royal Castle restaurant on South Florida Avenue, filled with customers, candles burning on the counters, burgers cooking on gas grills.

A few days after the storm, I drove down to Bone Valley, that treeless, whitewashed, strip-mined, Saudi Arabia–looking part of southwestern Polk County and applied for and got a job in the phosphate mines, at the F. S. Royster Guano Company. Basically, guano is fossilized bird shit, and Bone Valley was full of it. They made fertilizer out of it.

I was a stockroom clerk, and my job was to issue tools to the electricians at Royster. I never really understood *what* it was that those guys were doing, and, for that matter, I didn't really know what *I* was doing. I don't even *want* to remember all the mistakes I made at that place. I also had to do a lot of filing, so I turned it into a game; I was keeping my own file on who was using which tools the most. Also I was obsessed with one electrician who had committed suicide at his home during the hurricane. I kept going over any work sheets he had filled out during his last few weeks, seeing if I could find any clues about his mood. Needless to say, since I was doing so many things that I wasn't hired to do, I was doing a very unsatisfactory job at what I *was* hired to do. And, believing that I was practically at death's door, I was chronically absent. When I told my boss that a doctor in Lakeland had advised me to develop a don't-give-a-damn attitude, he told me I needed to find a new doctor or a new job.

There was a presidential election going on. The electricians at Royster were union men and all John F. Kennedy supporters, with the exception of one man who was a Bible-totin' Pentecostal who vowed to never vote for a Catholic. There were a lot of Baptist and Pentecostal preachers in Polk County speaking out about JFK's Catholicism, and because of it many lifelong Democrats would be voting for Richard M. Nixon, their first vote ever for a Republican.

Gloria's mother griped about some neighbors voting for Nixon just because their preacher told them they should. "I'm ashamed of 'em," she snorted, "votin' fer a *Republican!*" If someone had asked Mrs. Gelder why she was a Democrat, she might have said it was because her daddy always voted Democratic and so did his daddy before him, or she might have said it was because the Democrats were for the poor folks. Voting Democratic in the South was a tradition that went back to the Civil War when the Republicans were the antislavery party.

My parents had voted Republican before, for Eisenhower, so it was no big deal when they decided to vote for Nixon because of Kennedy's Catholicism. They didn't feel passionate about either candidate, and neither did I. I was yet to develop a real political philosophy, and, besides, I still wasn't old enough to vote (the voting age would not be lowered to eighteen for another twelve years). However, I favored JFK because, in my emotional state, I had a terrible fear of nuclear war and, remembering Nixon's much publicized "kitchen debate" with Soviet premier Khrushchev at an American exhibit in Moscow, I thought Kennedy might be less apt to get us into a war.

Needless to say, the F. S. Royster Guano Company chose not to

continue paying me for suicide analysis or keeping my own files, so
before the year was out, I was once again in the market for a job. In
the meantime, I kept working in various bands. I landed a gig playing at a New Years Eve party for the Lakeland Junior Woman's Club.
I was hired by a guy named Robert Holmes, a trumpet-playing detective with the Lakeland Police Department. I asked Gloria to go with
me, so we could see 1961 come in together.

We drove around Lake Mirror into downtown Lakeland. Green,
red, and blue holiday lights shimmered and danced on the water.
Two old white stucco hotels and the Marble Arcade office building
dominated the city's little skyline. Gloria sat close to me, wearing
the white furry jacket I had given her for Christmas the week before,
along with a tight red dress that showed off her nice figure, especially
her shapely derriere. As we pulled up next to the building where the
party was, she was holding my hand and I thought everything was
fine.

Around 9:45 p.m., just before it was time for the band to start
playing, Gloria told me she wanted to walk down the street and see
the late movie at the Lake Theater. I didn't want her to go; I wanted
her to be with me when the New Year came in, and I thought it was
dangerous, her walking the streets by herself at night. I just didn't
want her to go. She insisted, said she was going and that was that.
We were standing in front of the building, and she started to walk
away. I jumped in front of her, and she told me to get out of her way.
For the first time since I was a little boy, I struck a female; I slapped
her face, causing her chapped lip to bleed. Tears came to my eyes
as I begged her forgiveness. She started softly crying and said she
would stay. There were times ahead when our relationship would
get so bad that we would yell and scream at each other. There would
even come a time when she would calmly tell me that she had seriously thought about murdering me, right down to planning out the
details. But this was the first and last time that I would ever lay an
angry finger on her.

We kissed that night after the playing of "Auld Lang Sine." After
the band knocked off, we drove on toward her house, holding hands,
calling each other silly pet names that I will never divulge. In my

craziness, I was glad that Gloria and I were in each others lives. But I also remember hoping there would never be another year as bad as 1960. I started the first few days of 1961 in a deep, dark depression.

My self-esteem was at an all-time low. The only employment I had was a menial grove job that Dad had created for me, doing work that an illiterate person could do. There wasn't even a weekend band gig. I felt that I didn't have the respect of those who loved me, and, I wondered, why should I? I thought of myself as an embarrassment to myself and to my family.

After two or three days of feeling totally despondent and sensing utter hopelessness ahead, I decided to issue an invitation to the grim reaper whom I had so often feared. I went into the closet of the bathroom next to my bedroom, where I kept hidden pictures of beautiful movie stars. Dad kept two of his shotguns in his office in the breezeway and, for some reason, he kept one—a twenty-gauge Browning automatic—in my bathroom closet. I loaded it, took the safety off, and sat on the commode with my finger at the trigger and the barrel at my head. I sat there for about fifteen minutes, trying to get up the nerve.

"Hey, Miz Bradduk," I heard a muffled voice speak loudly across the house. Don Pace said *Bradduk*, almost like a hiccup.

"Is Bobby here?"

I jumped up from the toilet, put the shotgun in the closet, and quickly closed the sliding wooden door. I told myself that I would shoot myself after Pace left.

Pace wasn't sensitive, and he wasn't compassionate. He didn't have to be. He was all he needed to be: he was fun, and he was funny. When he left a half hour later, I no longer had the slightest intention of killing myself.

Soon I got two jobs, one on weekdays and the other on weekends. The full-time position was membership representative for the American Automobile Association; in other words, selling triple-A memberships door to door. The part-time job was sort of a dream come true.

Radio station WBAR in Bartow needed someone for weekends, from sign-on Saturday morning until sign-off Sunday night. I told the station owner/manager about my radio announcer course in Atlanta and about my musical knowledge. He thought I was a good reader with a strong voice, so I got the job.

From day one, there was absolutely no one at the station but me. The place was out in the country, a small concrete block building that sat underneath a giant radio tower. That first day, I somehow managed to push all the right buttons and get the station on the air. There were dual music formats; one was general non–rock 'n' roll pop music with some country thrown in, and the other was white Southern gospel quartet music, plus a lot of civic announcements and live remote church services on Sunday.

When a highway patrolman came by the house one day to pick up my driver's license for too many speeding tickets, there went my short-lived triple-A job. (Mom went by the AAA office and told my boss, "I just wanted to take a look at somebody who would kick a boy when he's down.") So the radio job was now my only job, and I was determined to do it so well that I would be hired full time.

Since I had lost my driving privilege for a couple of months, Mom or Dad would take me to the station in the morning, and Don Pace or Stanley Cox (Stanley was out of the navy) would pick me up in the evening.

"You're listening to double-yoooo-beee-ay-arrrr, one-four-six-OH on your ray-dee-ohhhh," I said, lowering my voice to the bottom of my register, speaking as resonantly and distinctly as I could. When I spoke, I knew not to trail off at the end of a sentence.

A hot spot in the news was a Congolese province in Africa called Katanga. Some of the personalities involved had names like *Tshombe* and *Lumumba*, and there were cities with names like *Lubumbashi*. I don't know if I was pronouncing the names correctly, but if I wasn't, nobody in Polk County seemed to know the difference.

Sitting there in my lonely lair, I had access, of course, to hundreds of albums. Particularly striking were the album covers of the Julie London records. In middle age, Julie London would be known for her role as a nurse in the TV series *E.R.*, but in the 1950s and early 1960s, she was a beautiful young jazz singer, most famous for her sensual rendition of "Cry Me a River."

So one Sunday morning, as soon as I switched over to the Sunday morning services, broadcast live from the First Methodist Church in Bartow, I lit up a cigar and lined up several of Julie London's album covers in a nice panorama across the control panel in front of the turntable. A few amorous moments passed as the Methodist choir sang "Abide With Me." Suddenly, the phone rang. "Oh, damn, should I get it?" I thought. I decided I should, since it was unusual for WBAR to get a phone call.

"What in the *hell* is goin' on down there?" the loud male voice demanded. I knew it was the owner/manager.

"Uh . . . uh . . . nothin', sir, the uh . . . church service is going on."

"The church service may be going on in *the control room,* but there's been nothing but *silence on the air* for *several minutes.* You didn't turn on the *remote* switch."

So there went my second job.

For the few weeks that I didn't have a driver's license, Gloria would come by after school and drive us around, then we would get one of my friends to go with me when it was time to take Gloria home. Several of my friends were out of the service now, so I started hanging out with the guys a little more. About the time I got my driver's license back, I received a call from my singing buddy from the Miami days, Billy Swafford, who wanted me to play in a band with him around South Alabama. I told Gloria I felt that I should give it a shot.

Billy was living with his parents, younger siblings, and grandmother in a prefabricated house out in the woods near Shorterville in Southeast Alabama, near the Georgia line. The women in the Swafford family were wonderful cooks, and all of Billy's folks were very nice to me. He and I played bars and VFW halls in places like Ozark, Troy, and Dothan. Billy was very talented, but the other musicians weren't all that great, and it didn't take me long to see that this wasn't going anywhere.

There was a filling station attendant in Shorterville, a chubby guy in late middle age, called E-bob. One night E-bob heard Billy and me talking about oral sex. "Oh, go on, y'all *makin' that up!*" he said in disbelief. He had never heard of men and women doing such things to each other.

Billy had a girlfriend he was serious about who lived in a little town across the Georgia line. He wanted me to go on a double date.

"She's a beautiful girl, Bobby, I think you really gonna like huh."

"But Billy, I have a steady girlfriend back home," I protested.

"We don't have to call it a date, then," he said. "Just come on along and we'll have fun, Bobby."

I'm sure the girl had a terrible time, as I reiterated to her over and over that I was engaged to a girl who I was in love with, a girl down in Florida named Gloria. Nobody had a very good time, in fact, and it was a mistake for me to go along in the first place. On the succeeding nights that Billy went out with his girlfriend, I stayed at the Swafford house and read. I was enjoying a biography of Franklin Roosevelt, *Affectionately FDR,* and a book that would influence my political thinking in the early 1960s, *Conscience of a Conservative,* by Barry Goldwater. Within a few nights, I called Gloria and told her I was coming home.

As I headed back into Polk County, I once again descended into depression. It was like I was wearing funny glasses that distorted everything I saw, only it wasn't very funny. My dad's citrus groves seemed like a prison camp. My parents house was like a sanitarium, and the irony wasn't lost on me as I looked from the front porch across Lake Stella and saw Kersey Funeral Home staring right back at me. Dad would joke, "When I diii-ee, you all can put me in Lake Stella and give me a big shove, and I'll just float on acrosssss to the funeral ho-ome," but I didn't see anything funny about the mortuary across the little lake and often imagined my cold embalmed body lying over there.

Only music seemed to make me feel good. I sat in my car one warm day in P. E. Braddock's "Green Hell," taking one of my ultralong water breaks, twisting the radio dial. When I landed on a pop station, I was drawn in by a ballad that started off with a dramatic Spanish march rhythm that kept building and intensifying throughout the song. It was Roy Orbison's electrifying record of "Running Scared." I became excited that music could be that original and that powerful. I remember how it totally changed my mood and how I went back to work feeling happy.

I spent hours in the family living room learning to mimic Nashville piano guru Floyd Cramer's "slip note" style—steel guitar licks played on the piano—listening to the record of his monster instrumental hit, "Last Date," over and over. My mind was too foggy to be very prolific or proficient at songwriting, but I was working hard at learning piano licks. I had first-rate teachers: Floyd Cramer, Jerry Lee Lewis, and Ray Charles, all living in my record player.

I think I had an amorphous dream of going to Nashville and getting a job playing piano for some country music star and eventually making a living as a songwriter. I'm not sure if I was waiting for a sign or waiting for someone from Nashville to come knocking on my door or what. So I kept on living in my world of menial work, bad love, disappointed parents, emotional illness, distorted images, big dreams, and no plan.

Every night I would lie awake in the same room, in the same bed, by the same window where I had lain awake as a small child, listening to the same sounds: the crickets and the rain frogs singing their haunting song, along with an alligator occasionally grunting its approval; cars hitting the bump on Bay Street, on the other side of the lot behind our house; the lonesome toot of a train, first in the distance, then getting closer and closer until the train rolled through town, its rumble echoing across Lake Stella. But I did not lie awake in awe anymore, feeling the magic and the mystery of young childhood. The only magic was the black magic that held me in its cold and clammy grip. The primary activity in my life was the marching of time. The biggest dynamics were the amplification of fear and the toning down of joy. The man who used to give me piggy-back rides and the lady who used to listen to my prayers were a few dozen feet and many years removed. I felt certain that I loved Gloria, but why did I feel so far removed from *her* at times like that? I was in my own little world, and I was in it all alone.

CHAPTER NINE

I Saw the Light

M Y FATHER, LIKE A STRONG plurality of Southerners, was raised a Baptist. The Baptists firmly held that unrepentant sinners went to a literal, burning Hell, and the Baptist list of things sinful was a long one. Dad had his own personal relationship with God Almighty, however, and wasn't really a churchgoing man. When I was a child, required to visit the Lord's house every Sunday, I envied my father's stay-at-home religion.

My antecedents on my mother's side, the Valentines, were Baptists, too. But at the dawning of the twentieth century, a few years before my mom was born, an evangelist came through Wilkinson County, Georgia, and converted scores of Baptists, including the entire Valentine clan, to the even more fundamentalist Church of Christ. Mom's father and two of her brothers became elders and auxiliary ministers in that faith.

Being raised up in two faiths, I attended Sunday School at both churches, but because my mother was a regular churchgoer, I gravitated toward her church. As I became more psychiatrically challenged and fearful of all things, I also became more concerned about the condition of my soul.

One sunny Sunday morning in April, Gloria and I went to the Church of Christ on Orange Street in Auburndale, the one my Uncle Lloyd had built with his own hands in the 1930s. The Churches of Christ, an autonomous confederation of the most literal and fundamentalist interpreters of the Bible in all of Christendom, generally carry on a quiet, conservative service. But Thurston Lee, the big olive-skinned, thinly mustached, hair-parted-in-the-middle minister there—he did indeed look like a Mafioso or a movie villain—must have listened to a few old-fashioned Pentecostal or hard-shell Baptist stump preachers when he was growing up, because he definitely spoke with that cadence.

"If there is one here AH who is not a Christian AH, one who has *not yet obeyed* AH the Gospel of our Lord and savior Jesus *Christ* AH . . ."

Oh no, here it comes, I said to myself, the invitation hymn was about to begin. Long convinced that the Church of Christ, more than any other religion, followed the teachings of the Bible, I had come close so many times to relenting to Christianity's clarion call.

"Christ said AH he who believeth and is AH *baptized* will be saved, but he who believeth *not* AH shall be *damned!*"

I was afraid to submit but I was afraid *not* to. Maybe *next* week, I thought. The next Sunday, I promised myself, I would go forward and confess my sins and be baptized. *Next* Sunday.

"As we rise AH and sing the invitation hymn AH . . . "

The *invitation hymn*. A song written to frighten you, designed to give you that final nudge up to the alter. Songs like "Are You Ready for the Judgment Day" or "Almost Persuaded" with that scary last line:

Almost . . . but lost.

"Open your AH hymn books to page forty-nine and AH . . . "

Oh no, I thought, even though it was broad daylight, the invitational hymn was going to be the scariest one of all, "O Why Not Tonight."

As the congregation rose and started singing—all Church of Christ singing is a capella because the Bible says nothing about playing, it says to *sing*—I was torn. I wanted to wait. I didn't want to walk up there in front of two hundred people. I wasn't ready for that big commitment, but I was also afraid of dying and going to Hell.

> *Wilt thou be saved*
> *Then why not tonight?*

I stepped forward and started to walk out into the aisle, but lost my nerve.

O sinner, harden not your heart.

My hardened heart started pounding . . . and racing. I was having trouble breathing.

"Honey, are you *all right?*" Gloria inquired.

As I looked at her, I felt my chest tighten. There were pains in my arms. I was . . . I was having a heart attack. And then came that scary line.

Tomorrow's sun may never rise.

I threw down my hymn book and hit the aisle like there was a snake in the pews. I walked double time toward Brother Lee. Maybe there would be time for him to baptize me before I died. Thurston Lee, not a really warm and fuzzy man, beamed as he saw me approach the altar. Mom later told me that Stanley Cox's father had tears in his eyes.

As I stood before the congregation, Brother Lee asked me if I was confessing my sins. I said I was. He spoke a few more words, then it was baptism time. The Church of Christ people were so adamant about baptism being essential to salvation that I needed to get into the water as soon as possible, and that was fine with me because if you died of a heart attack one second before you were ducked under, tough luck, you went to Hell. One of the church elders led me to a back room where I pulled a rubber suit up over my Sunday clothes.

I returned to the altar where a curtain had been opened, revealing the baptistery. Brother Lee had on *his* rubber suit. As we stepped down into the water together, the congregation sang one verse of "Won't It Be Wonderful There." After the big frowning man grabbed my nose and pinched it shut, thrust me into the water then just as quickly jerked me back up, the congregation sang another verse of "Won't It Be Wonderful There." It was a good day. There was reason to rejoice. Bobby Braddock was going to Heaven after all.

From the moment I was baptized, I was out to save the world. I felt that only by following the holy scriptures to the strictest letter of the law would people be allowed to enter into the Kingdom of

Heaven. And if I had any doubts, well, I just wasn't going to question it anymore. It would now be my obligation to show all my friends and relatives the true way. Poor friends. Poor relatives. Especially, poor Gloria.

I felt that this new path I was traveling was a doctrinal one, and it was a practical matter of how to get to Heaven. I saw no scriptural directive to change my lifestyle. For example, most of the elders and deacons smoked—Brother Lee himself was a *chain* smoker—so there was no need to give up cigarettes. Where in the Bible did it say that smoking was wrong? And though Lee would strongly disagree with me, I held that since the Bible said Jesus turned water into wine, then there was biblical license to drink; hell, it was practically a *commandment!* I *would* quit playing in nightclubs for a while because I was afraid people would misunderstand and that I might set a bad example. But I could find scriptural justification for continuing just about everything else in my life. To me, religion wasn't about being a goody-goody; it was as though the world was going to be destroyed, and I knew where the rocket ships were that would get us out of there. And I felt it was my *duty* to show everyone that the Church of Christ way was the *only* way to salvation. So, basically, besides giving up the nightclubs, the only big change in my life was that I became a proselytizer. Trying to save the soul of Gloria, who felt that her Baptist soul was already saved, certainly did not help save our relationship.

Three weeks later, after I was the featured speaker on Young People's Night, Thurston Lee congratulated me. "You did better than most people who've been Christians for *years and years,* and you're only *a babe in Christ.*"

A couple of weeks after that, the babe in Christ guzzled a beer as he took his girlfriend to her Junior-Senior Prom. After the prom, we headed west, away from home. We drove through Lakeland and continued past the strawberry fields around Plant City and Dover, across the cobblestone streets of Tampa, and over the big bay into the sleeping city of St. Petersburg and didn't stop until we reached a small beach town on the Gulf of Mexico. With the little waves lapping at our feet, we held hands and looked out at the water. We stayed on the beach for a long time and were still there when the sun sneaked up slowly behind us and started washing all the stars away.

I dropped her off late the next afternoon. It didn't seem to bother Mrs. Gelder that we had disappeared, but my mother was very chilly the next time she saw Gloria and didn't warm back up to her for a long time. Who should have borne more responsibility for running off like that, the seventeen-year-old school girl or the twenty-year-old babe in Christ?

I spent a lot of time trying to convert people to my new religion. I wrote long letters to my Catholic half-sister in Jacksonville and my Spiritualist Uncle Bright in Montana. I debated Don Pace's Methodist minister at his parsonage, and I gave poor Gloria an unrelenting daily dose of the gospel message. One Sunday when she refused to watch the syndicated Church of Christ TV show, *The Herald of Truth*, I lost it and ran screaming down to little Lake Stella, threatening to throw myself to the gators. This method proved ineffective and is not recommended for winning souls to Jesus.

I also tried to buy Gloria the title of Polk City Watermelon Queen, an honor determined by the amount of money in the contender's jar. Mrs. Gelder and I dropped enough money in Gloria's jar to make her the runner-up.

That summer, I had some major competition myself: Gloria had gotten eyes for someone else. After a year and a half in a relationship with a crazy person, I think what happened was understandable as well as inevitable, though I certainly didn't see it that way at the time. It was in the dog days of August, and I had just turned twenty-one.

Gloria had met a civil engineer who was involved in the building of Interstate 4, which would run about two miles south of the Gelder house. His name was Jeff Richards, and he had invited Gloria to go out on a Saturday night. She told me it would be an early date and that she would meet me at the Auburndale Teen Center, where I was playing with a band, around 10:30.

I was devastated. Gloria *loved* me, I *knew* she did. How could she go out with someone else? My legs would carry me, and my piano-playing hands would function that night, but I would be in a mental holding pattern until I saw Gloria face to face after her . . . date? How could she *do* this to me?

The band got through playing about 11:00 p.m. Gloria wasn't there. I waited until 11:30 and walked down to a pay phone and called her house. Perhaps there had been a misunderstanding and I was supposed to meet her *there*. Mrs. Gelder said no, she wasn't home yet. I could tell that her mama wasn't happy that Gloria had gone out with this guy. I waited another half hour, sitting in my car across the street from the Teen Center. A nearly full moon shimmered through a live oak tree next to the little building. I stared at the mossy midnight moon with a pang of fear in my belly. I started the car, pulled out into the empty street, and headed north to Lake Stella Drive, then took North Bartow Avenue to Ariana Boulevard and drove around the big lake until I got to the Polk City Road. I hadn't the slightest idea how this night would end.

There was something foreboding about any trip to Polk City because there seemed to be a kind of darkness there. Polk City was a little town, but when you said "Polk City," you were also referring to the huge rural expanse of northern Polk County, a land of poor Crackers, and also of cattlemen who looked and talked like poor Crackers but were, in fact, quite wealthy. Drownings, car wrecks, and homicides, particularly crimes of passion involving lovers or family members, were all too common around Polk City.

As I raced over the clay roads that led to the Gelder house, my heart was pounding in my chest and in my head. I wasn't scared of dying, but frightened about what the night held in store. I pulled up in the Gelder driveway, got out of the car, and ran to the door. Mrs. Gelder said Gloria hadn't come back yet and that she didn't like it one bit. She asked me to come in but I told her I'd just wait outside. I sat in my car awhile until the sorrow and fear and anxiety made me get out and walk up and down the clay road. A giant cricket choir laughed dissonantly as a night bird called out "fool" from across the little lake. The moody moon looked down into the water to see its own face. I went back to my car and sat there wondering what Gloria was doing. Was she holding him? Was she kissing him? Was she . . . ?

Every now and then, in the shadows of the moonlight, I could see Mrs. Gelder standing inside the screen door, arms akimbo, chin moving up and down in nervous agitation.

Finally, about 2:00 a.m., I heard an engine start and saw headlights go on, way down the clay road by the little lake, in the same spot where my car got stuck on my first date with Gloria. The car headed my way, toward the Gelder house, and sure enough pulled into the wide dirt driveway and stopped to the right of my car. Jeff Richards, a tall, thin, dark-haired guy who appeared to be maybe two or three years older than me, got out of the green Chevrolet. Gloria popped up from the other side, and said, bubbly, as though she were arriving at my house from school, "Hi Bobby!"

At that moment I heard the Gelder screen door slam hard as this large figure with wild white hair came running toward Jeff's car swinging a baseball bat.

"Gloria," the young man exclaimed, "get in the car, quick!" Both of them jumped back into the car then slammed the doors shut and locked them. Mrs. Gelder stood in front of the car, wildly swinging the bat, and I thought she was going to bust the windshield before Jeff was able to back out of there.

"You sorry thaing, you cain't stay here tonight! Git on outta here!" Gloria's mother screamed at her.

As the large woman stomped back into the house, yelling something about locking the door, Jeff pulled his car back into the driveway and rolled down the window and said, in a kind but rather whiny voice, "Bobby, I'm sorry. I had no idea until tonight how close you and Gloria were."

"I'm so *embarrassed*," Gloria sobbed, as she ran from Jeff's car to mine.

"Take good care of her, Bobby," he said, as he pulled away.

I told Gloria we would think of something to tell my folks and she could spend the night there, and that her mom would be all right the next day. She told me she wasn't going to date Jeff anymore, and I believed her. I had forgotten that Gloria was born on April Fool's Day.

Gloria and I seemed to be okay for the time being, but the incident had taken its toll on my already fragile psyche. I was an emotional cripple who was just getting crazier and crazier. My parents were flabbergasted. Gloria was confused about me and about her feelings. My sense of self-worth was nil. My only accomplishment was a record that I had recently produced on a local singer named Dot Anderson, whose husband owned the little record label. It was played a couple of times on the local radio station.

Then came the horrible Polk City Road panic attacks—hideous, gripping, debilitating events. The first time I had one, I was absolutely certain that death had come to claim me at last. After I'd had several attacks, I realized that they all took place at the exact same location, right before I got on the clay road that led to Gloria's house. I understood that they were psychosomatic and directly related to seeing Gloria, but that didn't keep me from having them *or* from seeing Gloria.

My solution was to have my mother or Don Pace or Stanley Cox go with me to pick up Gloria because I was afraid to drive alone. Eventually, Gloria started keeping my car at her house, coming by to pick *me* up. My parents felt that I had given my car away.

The following exchange took place between Gloria and me, not just once, but as a ritual that happened every night, sometimes several times a night:

"I love you," I said, along with a pet name.

"I love *you*," Gloria replied automatically.

"As much as ever?" I plied insecurely.

"More than ever," she answered robotically.

A picture of me from this era shows me with my hair cut off, shaved very close, military style, wearing a bathrobe and with a look of fear in my eyes. It could easily be someone locked up in a mental ward.

There were times when I felt just fine and happy. And there were times when I felt like I had my finger stuck in an electric socket. My *normal* feeling was angst. That's not good, when your ongoing day-to-day feeling is angst. In September 1961, Mom, finally realizing that salvation doesn't automatically induce sanity, got me an appointment with a psychiatrist, Dr. Izard, in Tampa. The nurse came to the waiting room and called my name, and Mom became very huffy when she was told that she couldn't sit in on my therapy session. Dr. Izard tried to be a regular guy with me, told me to feel free to smoke as he lit one up himself, talked about sex, and tried his best to put me at ease. When I told him about my fear of dying, he told me something that made me feel a lot better: "Oh, you'll probably die at eighty-five from pneumonia."

I remember thinking, "Yeah, pneumonia, okay, like George Washington."

On the ride home from Tampa, I felt more humiliated than helped—and there was something that was never far from my mind. Back in 1942, my mother's father, Ira Sylvester Valentine, had died in the Florida State Mental Hospital in Chattahoochee.

I still had fun when I was around my friends Don Pace and Stanley Cox. Gloria and I arranged a double date, introducing Pace to Gloria's Polk City friend Lois Bridges. Pace had been dating a lot of girls, including a jazz pianist and a married woman. He and Lois hit it off well and started seeing each other regularly.

A trip to Tallahassee with Pace should have shown me that what I really needed was to get *away* from Auburndale and Polk County. If you're afraid of ghosts, you should get out of the haunted house. In Tallahassee there was a music man who was well known in his hometown of Auburndale. Big John Taylor was four years older than me and was finishing a business degree at Florida State University. John had some regional hits in Central Florida in the late 1950s as an instrumentalist and owned one of the very first portable delay, or echo, units in the world. He used it with his Fender electric guitar and the effect was rockin' and riveting. After doing an international tour with Tampa's local rockabilly star Benny Joy, John enrolled at FSU, where he eventually put together an excellent band that played fraternity parties, nearby military bases, and, in the summertime, Panama City Beach. He wanted me to come up and hear "Big John and the Untouchables" at a frat party and sit in. So I got Pace to go with me.

Pace and I had our usual good time and, of course, did things we definitely should *not* have done, such as me driving blindfolded on Highway 27. Picture this crazy blindfolded guy behind the wheel and this big, pointy-headed guy with a little pointy nose and eyes like an owl, sitting real close so he could grab the wheel if necessary, saying, "Okay, just *barely* to the right . . . now just a *leeeetle* bit to the left here . . . Okay, hold it steady."

We stopped at a roadside stand, and I bought an iguana for Gloria. That night Pace and I got drunk at the frat party. For the entire weekend there was no anxiety, depression, aches, or pains, only a mild hangover.

Gloria liked her baby iguana and named it "Iggy." Within a few months it would mysteriously disappear from its cage. Gloria suspected that her father let it out. Years later there would be stories about fruit pickers refusing to work in some orange grove because they had seen a big "dragon" there.

In November, after I'd lost an insurance job that lasted all of one week, Dad talked to someone and managed to get me a job at the Florida Citrus Commission in Lakeland, a state agency whose purpose was to promote Florida citrus. It was seasonal and would last until March. My job was to box up colorful posters and displays and ship them to supermarkets all over America. One more job. Just a job. I had made up my mind that I was either going to go to college or to Nashville. Someday.

One day I left work early with pains in my arms and chest. I went to Lakeland's tallest building, the ten-story Marble Arcade Building, to the office of Dr. Edwin Fuller, the physician our family used whenever there was an ailment too complex for Auburndale's two doctors. Dr. Fuller gave me a shot to relax me, then picked up the phone to call my father.

"Mr. Braddock, Edwin Fuller here. I just gave Bobby a shot and don't think he should drive, so maybe you folks could come by my office and pick him up. He's fine. I don't think he's had a heart attack, heh-heh."

Dad had been experiencing significant hearing loss and misunderstood Dr. Fuller, who talked in a quick, low monotone. Dad immediately called Mom, who was having her hair done at Amanda's Beauty Parlor.

"Honey, come ho-o-ome quickly," he said with solemn urgency. "We have to go to Lakeland riiight awaaaaay. Bobby's had a heart attack."

Mom ran out of Amanda's, crying, "Bobby's had a heart attack!"

Within twenty-four hours, it was all over Auburndale that I had *died* of a heart attack. One guy called Kersey Funeral Home and asked if they had my body there. For some reason, Mr. Kersey's assistant said, "Yes, we do." People were calling the house to offer their condolences, many of them gasping when I answered the phone. I took more than a little gratification, however, in what I heard about Mary Lou Dunlop, my high school crush—the girl whose appearance at the Auburn Theater door made me lose control of my dad's '56 Ford and hit a garbage can on the sidewalk. When informed of my death, Mary Lou broke down and cried right in the middle of Publix supermarket.

Don Pace came a lot closer to dying than I did. I'm not sure how it happened, maybe someone finally called his bluff, but he got worked over by a bunch of guys in the parking lot of a bar on the outskirts of Lakeland. One of the thugs was using brass knuckles, and Pace's jawbone was badly broken.

When Don and Lois's wedding day rolled around about three weeks after the attack, his teeth were still wired firmly together. As he was making the wedding vows, some of the things he was saying sounded like *other* things. I was his best man but not a good enough man to keep from laughing. When I *did* laugh, everyone else in the Polk City Baptist Church, including the bride, started laughing too.

On the night of December 29, 1961, I made a tape recording of a small family celebration for my father's seventy-ninth birthday. When I discovered this long-lost tape four decades later, it was a shocking revelation. I'm not sure how I've lost so much of the corn pone in my voice over the years. I would have a non-Southern-speaking girlfriend in the early 1990s who kidded me so much about the way I

pronounced *on* that I started rhyming it with *John* instead of *stone,*
the way I had been raised to say it. Listening to this recording from
1961 made me realize that I used to be a very lazy Southern speaker.

"Daddy, uh, uh, tell us 'bout when you were mayor," I mumbled,
à la pre-Hollywood Elvis.

"I was persuaded by my good friennnnds to enter the race for
mayor," he said in his deep resonant voice, almost formally, as if he
were making a political speech. "After that, I was to beee appointed
city manage-uh and municipal judge, and various and sundry othah
jobs that I had to doooo-o-o in connection with liquidation of the
city debt." When asked about life lessons, he said, "The man worth-
whiiile is the man who can smiiile when everything else goes dead
wron-n-ng."

"Do you remember what our theme song was?" Mom chirped and
drawled.

"Our theeeeme song?"

"Uh-huh."

"Was it 'Let Me Call You Sweet-haawwt?' " he asked.

When Mom reminded him that it was the song he used to tip the
orchestra to play at a Spanish restaurant in Tampa, he immediately
went into a rendition of "(I'll Be Loving You) Always." Mom joined
in, singing the harmony. After listening to the recording many, many
times, I still get a lump in my throat when I hear it.

Dad rented what we called the garage apartment to Don and Lois
Pace. My parents had lived there when they were first married and
when my brother was a baby. It was nestled in a small orange grove,
overlooking the shores of the big lake, Ariana. The Paces invited Gloria and me there to a small party to celebrate the arrival of 1962.

Don had a friend from Lakeland named Lucas Jones, a big, loud,
good ol' boy who was married to his total opposite, Charlotte, who
was my age. Intelligent and witty, Charlotte was what Vivien Leigh
as Scarlett O'Hara would have looked like with Bette Davis's big eyes.
Lucas called her "sonofabitch" as though it were her name, like, "Hey,
Sonofabitch, hand me a beer." At the New Year's party, I couldn't
keep my eyes off Sonofabitch. I still had strong feelings for Gloria,

but I had finally started to show interest in other girls. Gloria and I still saw each other but not as often. And when we *were* together, we didn't go to the orange groves as much.

In my Gulf Fertilizer Desk Diary and Almanac for 1962, I made this strange little entry one day in January: "Gloria wants me to date so she won't take me for granted."

When Gloria started dating other people, the first girl I approached was Jan Moore, a very cute brunette who worked at the Top Hat drive-in restaurant. She went to Auburndale High, but having been raised in Miami, she seemed a lot more sophisticated than most of the girls in town. She said sure, she'd like to go out with me. Gloria was very much aware of who Jan was and was jealous. Good, I thought.

Jan was intelligent and well-read. She said she was interested in psychiatry and might pursue that as a career. I decided to quote Sigmund Freud. President Harry Truman once said, "When you're the best-read boy in Lamar, Missouri, you mispronounce a lot of words." I had *never* heard anyone *talk* about Freud, I had only *read* about him.

"*Frude* once said . . . " I began.

"Oh," she said as she rolled her eyes, "do you mean *Froid*?"

This is about the time that I started attending Florida Southern College in Lakeland on Tuesday and Wednesday nights. Another entry in my Gulf Fertilizer Desk Diary (actually it's more of a date book than a diary) tells me that I took Fundamentals of Speech and History of Civilization, and was really excited about it all. I did well on my tests and was applying myself, not just getting by as I had done in high school.

I look back on these little diaries in amazement. I kept a record of every penny I spent. A movie was ninety cents, a newspaper was five cents; it was thirty cents for a pack of cigarettes. There are words in there that are no longer in my vocabulary. If my friends and I were talking, we were *shooting the breeze* (sometimes *shooting the bull*); if we were out barhopping, we were *messing around*; if I was feeling a little sick, I was *feeling punk*. I have *no* idea what "*Poosh!*" meant. But I *do* remember what *cock* meant: in the South, it referred to the *female* anatomy. Yes, that's right, and it definitely *did* cause confusion in conversations between Southerners and Northerners. I haven't heard *cock* used that way for probably thirty years, even by men of that generation. There was even a name for a guy who got a lot of sex: *cocksman.*

Old memories flood back as I read in the diary about making the final payment on Gloria's ring . . . or about a group of us standing on the loading dock at the Florida Citrus Commission building, pointing to a tiny silver light in the sky as John Glenn, the first man in space, flew overhead.

I have strong memories of something else I saw in the sky. I was beginning to conquer the Polk City Road panic attacks and had started driving to Gloria's house by myself again. On my way up there one late winter day, as I approached the one-mile stretch that borders Lake Juliana on the left and a swamp on the right, I noticed that the sky was as black as ink and so was the lake, but suspended there between sky and water was a white funnel. I slammed on the brakes and watched it get bigger and bigger. I sat there as transfixed and paralyzed as a rabbit in the headlights. As a fierce wind blew in off the water, the tops of the trees that lined the lake, just a few feet away from me, came off in one big slice, as though there were an invisible man with a chainsaw cutting through the wood. I looked up as the whirling mass of white clouds passed over me. The twister was a baby one—perhaps a waterspout—and it hadn't quite touched the ground. But I was shaking so badly that my foot was jumping up and down on the brake.

I drove as fast as I could to the Gelder house. David, Gloria's handsome, mild-mannered, twenty-seven-year-old brother, was coming out the front door as I ran up through the yard. I went on and on about what I had just seen.

"And . . . and . . . this big white funnel came across the lake and took off the tops of the trees like a big *chainsaw,* and it passed overhead, just *whirlin'* around . . . "

David's deep-set blue eyes twinkled, and he smiled as he softly drawled, "Well, Bobby, you think maybe it was a tornado?"

Gloria had two siblings who were past thirty: Glen, then living in

Kentucky, who reminded me of Humphrey Bogart and who had gotten into quite a bit of trouble when he was a teenager; and Nora, who was a school teacher in Orlando. But David was the beloved one. He had gone through a bad marriage and a lot of other bad things, but he was always calm and kind. David was close to all of the family but especially to his younger brother Rodney.

Rodney was the clever one. He was bright, cynical, and had a crackling dry sense of humor. He had a knack for seeing the irony in life, yet he was confounded by it. Despite his beakish nose, he had a nicely chiseled face and wore his dark blond hair in a flattop. He resembled his Germanic father, whom he adored, but he was embarrassed by his mother's rough country ways. Rodney loved jazz and was a bit different from the rest of his family and from the rest of us, but his company was sort of like a glass of bubbly champagne—that is, until he fell in love with Madeline Watts.

Madeline lived in Lakeland. Though she was married, she and her husband were separated when Rodney came home from the army. They met one fall night and Rodney fell instantly and madly in love. Madeline was pretty and extremely sweet-natured, but she looked all of her thirty-six years, fourteen years older than Rodney. One night Rodney and Madeline were at the Paces' garage apartment. Stanley Cox, Red Cannon, and I were also there. After Rodney and Madeline left, I wisecracked, "Well, it sure was nice of Rodney to bring his mother." Everybody guffawed.

Rodney was a fan of Brother Dave Gardner, who was a comedy sensation in 1962. Gardner was a hip and jazzy white Tennessean with prematurely white hair who appealed to young Southerners, especially those in college, who were not nearly as racist as their parents but loved Brother Dave's black jive-talkin' delivery. His commentary on the space race between the United States and Russia was about the scientists: "Hey man, it's Germans on both sides playin' rocket ship!" Gardner was performing in Tampa one Saturday night, so Rodney suggested that we get a group together and go see him.

When Pace, Stanley, Red, and I picked Rodney up at his apartment in Lakeland, we were amused to see that he was wearing the button tab on his collar *across* the tie, rather than under it. He said he liked it that way. Before the show, we went to a busy restaurant in downtown Tampa that had very slow service. Rodney betrayed just a hint of a smile as he rocked his head back and forth, left to right, left to right, and told the waitress, "Well, if you *don't* (head left) bring my *dinner* (head right) then I'll *just* (head left) *drink* my dinner (head right)."

Two days later, Evelyn Sinsky, a girl who Stanley Cox occasionally dated, called Stanley and told him that Rodney was acting very strange. She said Madeline had gone back to her husband and Rodney was so distraught that he had quit his job and was saying he was going to commit suicide. Stan and I were concerned, so we went to Rodney's apartment in Lakeland. He seemed a little woozy but was friendly enough and invited us in. When I commented on his Jacqueline Kennedy calendar, he grinned and rocked his head from left to right as he told me he was just doing his patriotic duty. Then he took a swig of vodka straight from the bottle.

"Uh, Rodney," Stan said in his slow, measured drawl, "we *sure* don't want to be stickin' our noses into your business, but we just wanted to make sure you were okay."

"S-s-somebody told us you were saying you were gonna kill yourself," I told him.

With a "that's ridiculous" look on his face, Rodney looked down and rocked his head and said, "If I ever decide to commit suicide, I won't be going around talking about it. You'll read about it in the paper."

"In other words," Stanley said with a grin, "you don't want us runnin' over here checkin' on you."

"Not based on what Evelyn Sinsky tells you," he said. He knew Evelyn had called Stanley, because he had run into her the night before.

"Should we come over if your mother calls us?" Stan asked. A few weeks before, Rodney had been missing for two or three days, and Mrs. Gelder had begged us to find him, which we did.

"Don't pay any attention to her."

"How about your dad?" Stanley continued.

"Not even if *he* calls."

"How about David?" I asked, knowing how close he was to his older brother.

Rodney paused and smiled and gave it some thought. Then he finally said, "No, not even if *David* calls you."

So we left because even though he was being cordial, it was obvious that Rodney wanted to be alone with his vodka. He just looked really bad . . . and scary.

Although Charlotte Jones had told me that she found Rodney, with his sharp mind and dry wit, sexy and attractive, I couldn't recall him dating in high school. It seemed as if he had been saving all his love, all these years, for this older woman. This mad love or sexual addiction had consumed him, and when Madeline dropped him, it was as though she had opened a gaping hole in him that exposed a thousand stirring hornets. A couple of days worth of vodka had blunted some of what was screaming inside him, but you could see that it was there. As Stanley and I walked down the apartment steps to my car, I thought that Rodney seemed only slightly embarrassed that we had seen him at his most vulnerable and unpredictable.

The next day, a Tuesday, was coolish for late March in Central Florida. The bright blue sky was adorned with puffy little clouds scattered about. I put on a sweater before leaving the house with Stanley to go across town to see Jody Anderson, the man who owned the little record company. I was going to produce two sides, both of them songs I had written, on a friend named Billy Joe Chambers, to be released on Jody's label, DJ Records. We stayed there for about an hour, then headed back to my house. As we turned into the long dirt driveway by the key lime tree, I could see a strange car in the backyard. When we were about a hundred feet from the house, there in the middle of the road stood Larry Brown, a cousin of Gloria and Rodney's. When I stopped the car, he ran up to my window, and I remember wondering for about two or three seconds: just what horrible thing is he about to tell us?

"Rodney shot David," he said breathlessly, "then he shot Madeline," the words were coming out in spurts, "then he shot himself."

"*No!*" I yelled.

"David and Madeline are dead and Rodney's in critical condition at the Lakeland hospital."

"*What happened?*" I demanded, shaking all over.

"Rodney kidnapped Madeline and her mama and brought 'em to the Gelders' house."

"Where's *Gloria?* Was she there? *Is Gloria okay?*" I shouted at the top of my voice.

"She was at school. Somebody went and got her."

He explained that Rodney had taken Madeline and her mother at gunpoint to the Gelder house in the late morning. It was Mrs. Gelder's fiftieth birthday, and she was frying chicken because David, who was foreman of a crew that was working in a nearby grove, had promised that he would drop by at noon and share a birthday meal with her. Rodney introduced the two women to Mrs. Gelder, who thought both of them were acting very nervous. In an unusual display of affection, Rodney hugged his mother and wished her a happy birthday. When David came in through the front door, Rodney had just taken Madeline into the living room. Apparently David saw that his younger brother was holding a pistol on Madeline, and he either tried to talk Rodney out of the gun or tried to take it away from him. There was a shot, and David took a bullet through the heart. Madeline ran out the front door and onto the clay road, down by the little lake. Rodney chased her down, shot her in the head, then fired a bullet into his own head. David died with the telephone receiver in his hand, a recording playing over and over, "*The number you have reached is not in service.*" The paramedics found Rodney lying on the road next to Madeline, moaning, "Oh, baby, baby."

Stanley felt that in this very personal family nightmare, he shouldn't go with me to the Gelder's, that I should go alone. I took the curves fast around Lake Ariana, stopping to run up the stairs to the Paces' garage apartment. Pace had just gotten home from work and was sitting on the couch. I breathlessly blurted out the horrible news. He just sat there, silently stunned. He had been closer to Rodney than any of us. "Damn," he muttered.

I hit the floorboard as I headed north on Polk City Road. I hadn't even called the Gelder house—I had to get there in person. In a time of terrible tragedy, everything becomes a part of it; the sky, the citrus groves, the swamp fox running alongside the road; they all become props and players in a heartbreaking epoch.

When I got to the Gelder house, Gloria ran out to the front yard where we stood locked in a long embrace. She clung tightly and spoke of how unfair the tragedy was, and then commented that Rodney was so intelligent that he saw both sides of things, and she wondered if that made him go crazy. She kept talking about how sweet and kind David was and how she knew that Rodney really loved David a lot, how close they were. Gloria had no problem opening up and expressing herself, unlike Mr. and Mrs. Gelder, who seemed at a loss for words, both of them just standing around in a daze.

The next night I went with Gloria and her family to Kersey Funeral Home to see David's body. Mrs. Gelder broke her silence when she started crying and said, "Look at that sweet face. He never done anything bad to nobody." That's when everyone lost it.

I stayed with Rodney at the hospital throughout the next day as family members came and went. The neurosurgeon said he had a fifty-fifty chance of surviving, and if he lived, he would most likely be blind. They had radically lowered his body temperature by packing him in ice. A middle-aged nurse kept going to his bed and saying in her soothing country voice, "Rodney, why did you do it, son, why?" Once, his eyes popped open really wide while his mouth was opening and closing at a rapid pace, like a ventriloquist's dummy. That night, Gloria and I went to a Lakeland funeral home to for Madeline's visitation.

David's funeral was the next day, and it was one sad affair. The man was truly loved by a lot of people. One of his closest friends commented that wherever David was, he wasn't mad at Rodney, because David knew Rodney wasn't himself that day. At the Gelder's house after the services, Mrs. Gelder answered the telephone, listened for a few seconds, then dropped the receiver, and ran screaming through the house, "Oh, God, I cain't take no more. Rodney's dead! Rodney's dead!"

At Rodney's funeral, those of us who were pallbearers, Pace, Stanley, Red, and me, and a couple of Polk City boys, were standing in front of the little Baptist Church. The minister approached Stan and asked him to please put out his cigarette. "I'm standing here trying to keep from bawlin' and that guy's worried about my cigarette," Stanley drawled.

At the end of the service, before they closed the casket, we walked by for a last look at Rodney. Despite the big elastic bandages that helmeted his head, he looked nice and much more at peace than the rest of us. Stanley reached down into the casket and unbuttoned Rodney's collar tab, then put it *across* the tie, the way he had worn it in Tampa a few nights before.

All this tragedy brought Gloria and me closer for a while. I seldom left her side the next couple of weeks. The incident took place on a Tuesday, so I missed two nights at Florida Southern College and didn't have the spirit or energy to catch up in the next couple of weeks. Although I had been making really good grades, that was the end of my formal education as it fell victim to tragedy's ripple effect.

After a few weeks, my temporary job at the Florida Citrus Commission ended. I bought a used piano amplifier and played around Central Florida for several weeks with a good rock 'n' roll band called Ron and the Starfires. I joined them on a demo session, backing up a sixteen-year-old rich kid from Winter Haven named Gram Parsons who would die eleven years later in California of a drug overdose and eventually be heralded as "the father of country rock."

I was listening to pop radio stations for cool music like Bruce Channel's "Hey Baby" and to country radio stations for totally believable music like George Jones's "She Thinks I Still Care." I knew who wrote all the songs. I knew Dickey Lee wrote the George Jones hit, and I wanted to be in Nashville doing the same thing. I just didn't quite know how to get there.Gloria and I saw the legendary honkytonk singer, Grand Ole Opry star Ernest Tubb, when he and his Texas Troubadours appeared at Club 92. Gloria got him to autograph an 8 by 10 glossy for her mother, who was a fan. Mr. Gelder found the picture and accused Mrs. Gelder of having an affair with Ernest Tubb.

In the late spring of 1962, again I used a strange choice of words to write in my diary: "It should be added that I love Gloria and I feel that she loves me. Let no one think that the either of us is a fool. Jesus Christ is the son of God." But she was starting to drift away from me again, and I was about to drift up to Tallahassee, then back down to Orlando.

Big John Taylor, who had the great frat band at FSU, asked me if I wanted to play at an Orlando nightclub for a few weeks in the summer. I said yes. I went up to Tallahassee to rehearse and went out a couple of times with Big John's pretty twenty-six-year-old neighbor. I stayed with my Uncle Junior who had retired from the marines and was attending FSU himself, majoring in library science.

The band was made up of guitar genius Big John, who never became a big name in the world of music but could have and should have; singer Ken Ashburn, a likable, good-looking, Deep Southern, lazy-talking, lounge-lizard sort of guy who could sing like just about anybody and could hop into bed with just about anybody; electric bassist and singer Gene Watson (not the future country star), who had been a Polk County rock 'n' roll celebrity when he was in high school in the late fifties, and at this time was working on an engineering degree at FSU; and another FSU student, a criminology major who was the drummer I had played the New York gig with in 1960 (and later recommended to Big John), Ash Bodden from Miami. The five of us moved into a motel in Orlando.

Our gig was at the El Patio, which is like saying our gig was at *the* The Patio, but "the El Patio" is what everybody said. It was a large but rundown-looking club on South Orange Blossom Trail. Within a few nights the place was jumpin' because "Big John and the Untouchables" were a great live jukebox. I never heard the term *cover band* back then, but that's what we were. We sounded a lot like the records, whether it was current material like "Hey Baby" and "I Can't Stop Loving You" or older ones like "Daddy's Home" and "Baby Let's Play House." John worked us to death at rehearsals because we had to sound like the records. It was a first-rate rock 'n' roll band, and there were production numbers and choreography. On top of that, Ken pulled in the women and Big John was Mister Politician, working the room at break time like he was campaigning for votes. The band was an instant hit, but it was nothing compared to what it would become.

Gloria and I were both dating other people. She was now out of high school and had an office job in Lakeland. Every weekend, though, she drove up to Orlando to the club, usually as my guest, but sometimes with a girlfriend and even once on a date with some guy. A couple of times she came up with Charlotte Jones, the Vivien-Leigh-with-Bette-Davis-eyes girl. I had eyes for her and whenever I mentioned her name in my diary, I underlined it.

The six weeks at the El Patio helped me a lot. I was feeling saner. I wasn't cured but I was definitely much better. I still had strong feelings for Gloria, but I no longer felt that I *had* to have her in my life. She was doing okay, had a good office job, and was making enough money to buy a red English sports car. She went out with other people, more than I did. I read a lot of books, like William Shirer's huge definitive story of Nazi Germany, *The Rise and Fall of the Third Reich.* I was starting to write a lot of songs, nothing great, but the first decent ones in two and a half years. If I was losing Gloria, I wasn't sitting around crying about it.

The Cuban Missile Crisis drove Gloria back into my arms and also into the arms of Jesus. I chronicled the gathering storm day by day in my journal. It really looked as though there might be a nuclear war between the United States and the Soviet Union. I titled my entry "A Turning of History," giving an account of Kennedy appearing on TV and what Russia's reaction seemed to be. Then I wrote: "War seems unavoidable, inevitable. Gloria's heart acted up tonight."

I had come to realize how obnoxious I had been about religion and decided to quit being an evangelist, but I guess all my preaching to Gloria the previous year had finally kicked in. We had been attending Lake Wire Church of Christ in Lakeland from time to time. She so badly wanted to make sure she was in good stead with the Lord in case nuclear war came that she wasn't going to risk waiting until the next Sunday. She wouldn't even wait until "prayer meeting" on

Wednesday night. It looked like doomsday could happen any mo-ment. The missile crisis began on Monday, October 22, 1962; on the very next day, Gloria asked me to call up Brother Butler and see if he would meet us at the Lake Wire church and baptize her right then and there. I drove as fast as I could so we could get Gloria into the water before the Russians could get a bomb into her backyard.

Dad's backwoods Florida Cracker tractor driver, Rosco Wig-gins, had his own take on the Cuban missile crisis. Mispronouncing Khrushchev and having no idea what to call the Cubans, he said, "I seen whur ol' Crowshit done gone and stirred up them Woptalians or Greektalians or whatever they aire."

It was about this time that Mom—because of her involvement in Woman's Club, Garden Club, and the Auburndale Library Commit-tee—was named Auburndale's Woman of the Year. She could just as easily have been named Manipulator of the Year. It was a sweet and loving manipulation, reminiscent of twenty years earlier when she started putting *syrup of ipecac* in my father's liquor, resulting in him getting on the wagon because "I just can't keep that stuff on my stomach any-mo-o-ore." In 1962, the problem was Dad's driving. His spells of not knowing what he was doing, caused by pressure on the brain from the car wreck he had been in long before I was born, were becoming more and more frequent. One day he was headed for his groves and ended up in Bartow and couldn't figure out how he got there. Mom was afraid he would have one of his seizures and wreck the car, or run over some kids as he passed through a school zone, so she informed the Florida Highway Patrol that his driving was a public safety hazard. They informed Dad that there had been nega-tive reports about his driving and that they would suspend his license unless he was able to pass the driving test. Now, there's one for liber-tarians to contemplate! Anyway, Mom felt certain he would fail the test because he had never gotten the hang of parallel parking. Dad blamed everyone from the local police to the governor of Florida but apparently never suspected that Mom had anything to do with it. He passed the written test with flying colors because he had memorized the Florida Drivers Handbook, but he was never able to pass the driving examination, even though they gave him several chances. I felt sorry for him; just before all of this happened, he had traded in his Ford for a new white Corvair, to be his grove car. For the remainder of 1962, my primary job was being P. E. Braddock's chauffer.

Pushing eighty, my father had adult-onset diabetes and could no longer enjoy my mother's sweet things. (He especially missed her pecan pie.) He got his seventh (it was Mom's second) grandchild, Paul Edward Braddock III, in November 1962. Rather than his fifty-five-year-old wife making him seem younger, I thought it was the other way around, that Dad made *her* seem *older*. Mom's closest friends were in their sixties and seventies.

Both parents were proud of whatever talent I had and were always asking me to play something on the piano for visitors—"Make it something nii-ice and pretty," Dad would suggest—but I don't think they believed I would ever make a decent living at music.

Through the Andersons, who had the little local record label, I was able to get some songs published by Grand Ole Opry star Jimmy C. Newman. He and Dot Anderson's uncle, Jimmy Key, jointly owned Newkeys Music in Nashville. Newman, a great Cajun singer from the bayous of Louisiana, took the time to write me a nice letter. I also made a new friend at a jam session, a classical and jazz guitar player whose parents ran a dry-cleaning business between Auburndale and Winter Haven. I never dreamed he would someday become a recording star and comedian with his own network TV show. On November 13, 1962, I wrote about him in my diary: ". . . Jim Stafford, 18 yrs. old. FABULOUS guitarist, great potential musician. Far better than me."

I had high hopes for music and for life in general as 1963 approached. Gloria and I celebrated New Year's at the home of Lucas and Charlotte Jones in Lakeland. Crude Lucas and sophisticated Charlotte with the beautiful slightly freckled face and the Bette Davis eyes. We flirted and danced. After we left their house, I told Gloria I was worried about Charlotte. She insisted that we call to make sure Charlotte was all right. In my diary, I wrote in a code I had devised: "Lucas insanely jealous, called Charlotte a whore (she is *not*). I hope I'm not falling in love with her."

If it sounds as though I was about to jump into an affair with

Charlotte, well, that didn't quite happen, not then anyway. I was taking off the shackles and stretching my legs; it was a good feeling. The fog had started lifting a few months earlier, probably when I went to Orlando with Big John's Untouchables, but I think of this as the time that I fully realized I was okay. It was almost as if I had gone to a wedding up in Georgia almost three years earlier and had been abducted by aliens who brought me back in 1963. After three mostly bad and sad years, I was ready to get back to the business of living.

I don't deny that I loosened my grip on religious fundamentalism as I regained mental clarity, but I don't mean to dismiss my religious beliefs as a part of the craziness. The Church of Christ remained my religion for several more years. It was a part of my spiritual search and growth. If I have held several points of view at different times in my life, how can I say at which point I was right or at which point I was wrong? And I certainly don't renounce the part that Gloria played in my life or blame her for anything she did. I was a nut case almost from the beginning of our relationship, when she was little more than a child. She was a sweet girl with a good spirit. There's an Eagles song called "The Best of My Love." I think I gave Gloria the *worst* of my love.

I feared that reliving those years by writing about them might be the emotional equivalent of eating a barrel of live slugs and washing them down with a bucket of bile. Actually, it was more like several thousand dollars worth of therapy.

CHAPTER TEN

Rockin' in Orlando (and Birmingham)

EL PATIO CLUB

presents

BIG JOHN'S UNTOUCHABLES

THE ROCKINGEST
GROUP IN
THE SOUTH

**Located on
SOUTH ORANGE
BLOSSOM TRAIL**

PICTURE A GRIZZLED OLD cattleman standing on his front porch, on a cool, crisp day in Central Florida, talking with a stranger who was wanting to buy his land, all forty acres of it. Over the next two or three years, other strangers would approach other owners of grazing land, orange groves, piney woods, big swamps, and little lakes in the vicinity. Word would go around about a mysterious company secretly buying up property in the area, one piece at a time. It would eventually come to a total of 27,000 acres. The mysterious company was, of course, Walt Disney Productions.

Disney World would dramatically alter the face of Central Florida, for better or for worse. The closest city to that 27,000 acres was the rough cowboy town of Kissimmee, in Osceola County; the population of that county would increase from 19,000 in 1960 to 250,000 today. The gargantuan theme park(s) would transform the nearby pleasant little city of Orlando into the most important tourist city in America, with a present-day greater metropolitan area population of more than 2 million. The Disney-driven growth would spill down into Polk County, changing it from *old* Florida to bustling *new* Florida by the twenty-first century.

On this cool, crisp, pre-Disney, *old* Florida day, while some buyer and cattleman may have talked about land up toward Orlando, opportunity was knocking on *my* door down in Orbundale. Big John Taylor was talking me into becoming a full-time member of Big John's Untouchables and a resident of Orlando.

"They want us to be the permanent band at the El Patio," he said. "You'll be gettin' $150 a week."

That would be nearly $1,000 in today's money. I made up my mind and said I would do it about a half a second after he asked me.

John Wilkie Taylor was a big guy, very tall, not fat by any means, though well fed, with a slightly round but handsome face. He had curly brown hair, bright blue eyes, and nice white teeth—long before the days of dental bleaching—on display, clenched together when he smiled, which was often—when he was listening, which he was good at—and while he was playing guitar, which was constantly.

He had come to Auburndale as a little boy, the youngest child of a large, hard-working family from the hills of Tennessee. About four years older than me, Big John had had a taste of celebrity back in the 1950s when he got hooked up with music business bigwig Buck Ram (who managed the famous Platters), got a record deal, and did a worldwide tour. But this outgoing country boy, whose personality brought to mind Sheriff Andy Taylor of Mayberry, wanted the security of a college degree (in business administration), so he quit touring and worked his way through college by putting together the best rock 'n' roll band on campus. Now that his pursuit of a higher education was behind him, he was ready to go into the band business full time.

"*Lord* have mercy," boomed the big man with the big enthusiasm, "we're gonna have us the best band in Orlando."

So I tied up some loose ends, played on another demo session for Gram Parsons, and within a few days I was on my way to Tallahassee, where Big John was still living. A week of serious rehearsals awaited. Dot Taylor, John's wife of one year who had been his high school sweetheart, supplied delicious down-home cooking while we put in about twelve grueling hours a day, going over the entire band repertoire. There were a lot of songs to learn in a short period of time. I collapsed on the couch at my Uncle Junior's house every night, with songs and more songs pounding in my head.

When one worked for Big John, there was never any doubt about who was in charge. He ran his band with an iron fist and knew what he was doing. He had a genius for listening to a record and picking out the parts that were being sung and played. I was not only learning piano licks but also background vocal harmonies.

The lead singer in the old Untouchables FSU fraternity party band was not some Joe College, but a twenty-six-year-old Tallahassee used-car salesman named Ken Ashburn. He had been working with John for four years and was one hell of a mimic. Part of understanding Ken Ashburn is understanding his hometown. By the twenty-first century, Ken's native Tallahassee would be big and cosmopolitan like Florida itself, but in the 1930s, when he was born, the little capital city—sitting up next to the Georgia line in the middle of cotton and tobacco country—was as Southern as Jackson, Mississippi, or Montgomery, Alabama, only much smaller. So Ken was a true son of the Deep South. Think of a dark and handsome young man, with all the slickness and naiveté of Ted Baxter on the Mary Tyler Moore Show and an accent as thick as molasses, and you've got Ken. His good looks, good nature, and good voice made him a magnet to women like no one I've ever seen that didn't have superstar status. And his fractured syntax was legendary.

The guys in Big John's old band liked to tell the story of the night they were booked to play an officers club at Ft. Rucker, an army base up in Alabama. It seems that their mode of transportation was an old hearse that Ken was driving. When the MP at the checkpoint asked them what business they had on the base, Ken poked his head out the window and announced, "We the band what belong to play h'yuh tonight."

Over the next couple of years, I would have my own favorite Kenisms to recount. For instance, one night, he had just seen one of the low-budget Japanese "Godzilla" science fiction movies, this particular one titled *King Kong Versus Godzilla*. When we asked him what he had seen, he said, "King Kong Visits Gonzales!"

Big John and Ken were the only holdovers from the old band. The new recruits included a drummer named Denny Hogan, a twenty-four-year-old flattopped little guy from Savannah, Georgia, who had a very high-pitched voice, and electric bass man Lew Widger, approximately the same age as John and Ken, a gentle laid-back fellow from upstate New York who had been living in Orlando.

We worked up hard rockin' blues songs like "Annie Get Your Yo-Yo" and "Candy Man," which featured Big John playing great blues harp. We did several Ray Charles songs, with Ken doing a convincing impersonation of the Genius. We turned novelty songs of the Coasters, "Little Egypt" and "Along Came Jones," into production numbers, using costumes and props. And there were the slow instrumental dance songs that were essential to bands in those days, such as Big John's version of "Sleep Walk" and my rendering of "Last Date."

But John was convinced that we were missing one essential ingredient: an organ. He said if I had an organ, not only would I be featured on songs like "Green Onions," but I could also play the string parts and horn parts that were on the records we were copping. He felt certain he could equalize it on our sound board, to make it sound less like an organ on those particular numbers. (Big John was his own sound engineer.) So we went to Orlando a couple of days earlier than originally planned. With some help from P. E. Braddock, I bought a Hammond B-12 organ and a slightly used spinet piano that we sort of forged together into one instrument, a clumsy forerunner of today's multisound keyboards.

There was an adage, "the farther south you go in Florida, the farther north you get," but I think this applied more to the coastal regions. The interior of Florida was still pretty strongly Southern culture clear down to the Everglades, but it was less so in Orlando, which sits about thirty-five miles northeast of the geographical center of the state. I would guess that in 1963 at least one out of every three people in Orlando had been born in the North. With a population of 90,000, Orlando was more than twice the size of Lakeland. Martin Marietta Corporation was the city's biggest employer, and a lot of people were coming to the area to retire. Part of the appeal was Orange County's one thousand lakes, with some of the lakes in the city featuring floating fountains that lit up at night. A lot of the allure was a result of the town's green thumb, which inspired the nickname "The City Beautiful." The 1939 WPA Guide to Florida described "landscaped parkways shaded by live oaks, camphor trees and a profusion of native and imported palms" and "subtropical shrubs, citrus trees and winter-blooming flowers in contrast (with) the dull red of brick-paved streets and the sparkling blue of lakes." That's the way Orlando still looked in 1963.

It was forty-five miles from my parents' house to the El Patio, and, taking the new interstate, the trip took me forty-five minutes or less. The traffic around Orlando wasn't at all bad in those days. The El Patio was on South Orange Blossom Trail, which would many years later become a high-crime area identified with urban prostitution and drugs, but in 1963 it was quietly suburban. (Not too far down the road, it became downright rural, heading south to the cowboy town of Kissimmee.) Surrounded by palm trees, the club, with its large parking area, sat back off the road next to a lake and a small orange grove. The building was big enough to cram in a few hundred people and had a large patio on the lake side that had once been used for outdoor dancing. Sometimes after a heavy rain, the snaky lake would flood the patio, leaving dead fish and wriggling reptiles at the club's side exit.

The owner was the nice but sad-faced Eleanor West, a hard-drinking middle-aged woman originally from Polk County. The club manager was her live-in boyfriend, a short, muscular guy from West Virginia named Monk. They stayed there at the club, and at some of our rehearsals we would hear the sound of angry voices and crashing furniture from their living area. Sometimes Monk would get kicked out, both as boyfriend *and* club manager. His departures would always be speedy and his absences short-lived.

We got rooms at a place called Burdsall Motel, where I was given a little kitchen that had been converted into a sleeping room.

Big John worked us relentlessly; we rehearsed every afternoon and performed every night. The addition of my organ meant we would cover some records that had big arrangements—like "Rockin' Robin," the big pop hit "Go Away Little Girl," and even the lavish movie song "Theme from Picnic."

There was one problem: Denny, the drummer. He was a nice enough guy and surely didn't mean to be annoying, but he was. Before long, he started getting on Big John's nerves. At rehearsal, instead of just making a comment, he would step up to John, clear his throat, and ask, in his high-pitched voice, "Can I say something?" The third or fourth time this happened, John's eyes got big as he clenched his teeth and nodded impatiently and coaxed, "Goodness gracious, man, just say it. Don't *ask* me if you can say it, just *say it.*"

Not long after we arrived in Orlando, Denny and I almost came to blows at a rehearsal. After that, I tended to hang out with Lew, the bass player, and Big John hung out with Ken—that is, when Ken wasn't with a girl. Poor Denny hung out with Denny. Not that Denny didn't get girls. A *mummy* could get girls if he played in a popular rock 'n' roll band.

By the first weekend, we were rockin' and sounding pretty good. The place was almost full. Gloria came up to Orlando to hear the band and brought along Charlotte Jones, the Scarlett-O'Hara-with-Bette-Davis-eyes girl, the *married* one. I was sitting with them during our breaks, and though I wasn't a very good dancer (typical of musicians), I wanted to be alone with Charlotte so I could ask her out, so as soon as the jukebox played a slow song, I asked Charlotte to dance.

"We have Sunday nights off," I said quietly in her cute little ear as we shuffled lazily around the floor. "Gloria and I are doin' something tomorrow night, but why don't you and I get together the next Sunday night? Would you . . . do that? Would you meet me somewhere?"

"Well, *well,*" she softly exclaimed, smilingly giving me a what-a-naughty-boy look. She continued to hold her head back as we danced, still smiling as she looked right at me with her big blue eyes. It seemed like forever before she said, "We have out-of-town company next Sunday but I can meet you the Sunday after that. Will you be available?"

"Yeah," I nodded, smiling all over. "Where shall we meet?"

"I'll have to figure that out," she said in her naturally sultry, sexy voice. "You know, I don't typically do this sort of thing."

"I know," I assured her.

"I really *don't,*" she reiterated. "You can't call me at work and you *certainly* can't call me at home. You need to give me your phone number."

"Mmmm," I said in frustration, "there's not a phone in my room. *Hey,* I've got a book of matches from Burdsall Motel, the address is on there. Just write me there, but make sure you give me really good directions."

She gave me a tight squeeze and abandoned all playfulness as she spoke in a stage whisper, "Oh, Bobby, I've waited so long for this."

When the band quit playing at 3:30 a.m. Sunday morning, I took the girls to eat, then they followed me to my room where I grabbed some clothes and my shaving bag. We headed for Polk County in a two-car caravan. A few miles from the Auburndale-Polk City exit, Gloria pulled up beside me as Charlotte shouted, "Pull over, I need a *light*."

I had forgotten to give her the matchbook. As we pulled over on the shoulder of the interstate, I jumped out and ran up to Gloria's car and lit Charlotte's cigarette through the window, then handed her the matchbook with the motel's address. "Here keep these," I told her, "My car lighter's working."

The three of us sat on the trunk of my 1960 Ford and watched the sun come up. Gloria was so busy babbling about the guy she was dating that she didn't notice there was something in the air between Charlotte and me. I was just Gloria's *buddy* now.

The next afternoon, I saw Gloria's red sports car pull into my parent's driveway. When I walked outside, I realized it was Charlotte behind the wheel. She had the top down and the motor was running.

"Gloria didn't feel like driving me to Lakeland last night, so she let me take her car. I was afraid Lucas would give me a hard time if I'd stayed over at her house. Anyway, I'm returning her car and having her drive me home. I just thought I'd drop by and say *hi*, Mister Braddock."

"You look like Elizabeth Taylor in *Butterfield 8*," I observed.

"You know just what to say, don't you," she said as she smiled coyly and turned the car around and headed out. She sped away down the dirt road driveway, her long dark hair blowing in the wind.

"Who was *that*?" Mom asked from the breezeway door.

"Oh, her name's Charlotte, uh, friend of Gloria's."

"Looks kinda like a *beatnik*, doesn't she?" commented Mom with a smiley face.

Toward the end of the next week, I got a letter from Charlotte, written in the small, orderly script of highly aesthetic and intelligent people. She wrote about Lucas calling her *sonofabitch* as though it were her name, about his philandering, and about him getting her pregnant in her senior year in high school (at a drive-in movie) and them having to get married. Then she gave me directions to a girlfriend's house where we would meet. "See you Sunday after next," she wrote. I got a rush. I didn't know if I was falling for her, but I knew I was wildly attracted. She was smart, fun, intriguing . . . and sexy without even trying.

That weekend, I went home. I jammed with Jim Stafford on Sunday afternoon and that night I took Gloria to a drive-in movie to see a great film, the original *Manchurian Candidate* starring Frank Sinatra. Gloria went on and on about the guy she was dating, said she still loved me but, "I think I love Eddie more."

The next Friday, I was surprised to see Gloria at the El Patio, sitting toward the back by herself. As I sat down with her on my break, she immediately asked me, "Will you go to church with me in Auburndale Sunday night?"

I started stammering, but before I had a chance to say much of anything, she continued, "Because if you say 'no,' then I'll know that you're planning to meet Charlotte that night."

My mom had done it again. The super snoop had gone through my things the prior weekend and found my letter from Charlotte, then reported it to Gloria.

"Well, you have a new boyfriend, what do *you* care?" I asked her.

"It's just not right, Bobby," she said firmly, her face frozen with barely contained anger. "She's supposed to be my friend. And she's *married*. Are you going to go to church with me or not?"

I called Charlotte the next day. She told me she couldn't really talk, that Lucas was in the next room. I told her she didn't need to talk, that I just wanted her to know I couldn't meet her, that we'd been found out. "How can you *do* this to me?" she demanded in a loud whisper. She told me I was chicken. I told her she was right. On Sunday night I went to church with Gloria.

There were plenty of girls at the El Patio. I was glad to get Ken's rejects. One night I left with a tall, gorgeous nineteen-year-old who had also been out with Ken, a violation of a band rule that monogamous John had made for Ken's benefit. Ken would normally have said something to Big John about me going out with someone he had dated, but on this particular night he was too focused on a half-French, half-Spanish beauty who I thought was the most stunning girl I had ever seen. Not only did these ladies not know that Ken had a wife and little kids up in Tallahassee, he was in fact telling some of them that he was single.

John and Ken each made twice as much as Lew or Denny or me, which was fair enough, but Ken was definitely John's guy. Whenever there was a dispute about anything, Ken always automatically came down on John's side. But disputes were irrelevant, because it was John's band. Normally very protective of Ken, John allowed us to have a little fun with him occasionally on a Monday or Tuesday night, generally our slowest nights. We would kick a song off in the wrong key—as far as we could get from the key he usually sang it in—and watch Ken panic as he'd sing it high, then drop his voice an octave, searching for the right notes and trying to figure out what was going on. When he realized what was happening, he'd say, "You sons of bitches," and we'd all die laughing.

Lew and I got a kick out of John's stinginess. Big John Taylor was perhaps the biggest penny-pincher I had ever met. Sometimes he would go from restaurant to restaurant, saying, "I just wanna see the menu, please." He would price the food, like he was shopping for a car, finally eating at the cheapest place. He eventually found us the most reasonably priced eateries in the area, a place called the Sundown for supper and the nearby Florida Diner for after-work breakfast.

Walgreen's drugstores typically had a food service section, with a lunch counter and booths. There was a Walgreen's at a strip mall (we called them shopping centers) on Orange Blossom Trail. One day I went there for lunch. We never got up until early afternoon, so by the time I went for lunch, the place was empty except for one man who was seated about two or three booths down from me. He and I were directly facing each other. The guy was about thirty and had a flattop haircut.

"You wanna eat a hot dog?" he asked, a big smile on his face.

"Uh, no," I replied and smiled back at him, "guess I'll have me a steak sandwich."

The guy gave me a dirty look. I wondered, what's with this guy? About half a minute passed, and he started in again.

"Yeah, nice big *hot dog*, that's what you're gonna get."

"No, heh heh," I said awkwardly, "I'll stick with my steak sandwich."

He glared at me. Why in the world would *he* care what *I* ate? I didn't know this man. Was he the local distributor for Armour hot dogs? Was he coming on to me, the wiener being a phallic symbol?

As the waitress approached his booth, he shouted, "*Hot dog.* You wanna *hot dog?*"

Before I had the chance to ask him if he'd lost his mind, I suddenly saw little arms waving in front of the guy. "Yeah, I want *hot dog,* Daddy, I want *hot dog!*"

As I felt my face turning red, I just wanted to crawl out of there. I was hoping the waitress hadn't seen this little episode. I remembered her from when I had eaten there a few times the summer before. She had a doll face: button nose, big brown eyes, and short dark hair. She was very tall and leggy in her green Walgreen outfit, maybe a bit too skinny and sticklike, but I thought she was adorable. And always friendly.

"I think I'll have a steak sandwich," I said, transfixed on her eyes.

"And I bet you want that steak rare, don't you?" She had a sensual mouth that was always a bit open, whether she was smiling or not.

"Y-you sure have a good memory. I haven't eaten here in five months."

She soon brought me my steak sandwich. In those days, I was a red-meat-eating carnivore; I wanted to see the blood and she didn't disappoint me. "It's got your name on it."

"You don't even *know* my name," I laughed. She did, she remembered that too. We kept a running conversation and when her shift ended she sat down at my booth and we chatted. Her name was Billie Swift, and she was from Arcadia, a cattle town about seventy miles south of Auburndale. She was twenty, and had two kids, ages one and two. Her husband was a staff sergeant at nearby McCoy Air Force Base. I told her to come see us at the El Patio sometime, and she promised that she would.

Within a couple of nights, she was at the club with a girlfriend. Billie was down to earth, open, easy to talk to. I felt comfortable around her. I started eating lunch at Walgreen's often. Sometimes in conversation she would suddenly stop talking and just stare at me with big brown eyes, mouth half open. There was a little crackling of electricity whenever our eyes met.

There was a dance, I can't remember what it was called, in which all the participants hopped around the dance floor. It wasn't the Bunny Hop—I'm not *that* old. But I thought it was pretty goofy. I decided, as I watched the dancers from the stage, that only someone I was *really* attracted to could do that dance without looking ridiculous. Whenever Billie did it, I thought she looked totally cool.

One Tuesday night, the club was not quite half full, so she was easy to spot. I wasn't expecting her; it was a nice surprise. As soon as we took our break, I headed for her and she headed for me. We met in the middle of the aisle between the side tables and the dance floor. She looked like she had something to tell me. I was thinking: is it good, is it bad? What?

"Frank and I had a spat, and he told me not to come home tonight."

"Well, what are you gonna do?" I asked.

She didn't speak a word, but her eyes told me she wanted to hang out with me.

After I finished the last set, we had breakfast, then went to my place . . . and talked . . . and talked. Something serious would have happened if either one of us had pushed it, but the time didn't seem right yet. This wasn't just some girl I had picked up at the club.

"You're the first man I've kissed or gone out with since I got married," she told me. I kissed her again. "You know, right now I love you," she said.

I took her to her car. She left her sweater at my place, so I returned it to her at Walgreen's the next day. Later that afternoon, she drove up to the front of the El Patio as I was coming out of rehearsal;

she beckoned me to her car window and kissed me, in front of her babies, which put a few extra pounds on my already weighted-down Church of Christ conscience.

I adored her mannerisms and the way she said things, like "This is pretty scary, huh?"

Then Frank came with her to the club, and I liked him a lot. He seemed like a really good guy. If I had met him sooner, it might have stopped me, I'm not sure. But over the next few weeks, Frank became a regular at the club, which meant he became buddies with Big John. Sometimes I'd sit with Billie and Frank, and she would grab my hand underneath the table.

"You'd better watch it, Bob," Big John warned me.

We watched it all right. We got together every chance we had. That kind of infatuation is crazy and reckless, and that's exactly what we were. Both of us felt guilty but not guilty enough to quit.

Gloria, noticing a major shift in the level of attention she was getting from me, suddenly developed feelings for me again. She had Mrs. Burdsall call me to the office phone one morning so she could talk to me about a house and marriage. That touched me, but it didn't affect the raging fire that was burning for Billie. Often I would go to Billie's house on my way to play at the El Patio, after she had gotten her kids to sleep. It was a little rented house in the middle of a big yard that was more like a ball field, so it was okay to park anywhere. I pulled up tight against the back of the house where the car wouldn't be visible from the road. Frank's duty at the air base was until midnight, so we thought we were pretty safe. One night she gasped, "Oh, my God, it's Frank," as headlights shone through the cracks in the blinds into her unlit living room. As she would soon learn, he had come home to get some kind of wrench to take back to the base. "Oh, no; oh, *no*," she whispered frantically. As Frank came through the front door, I was running out the back door with my Untouchables suit and patent leather shoes in my hands. I don't know if it was some reprieve sent down from Heaven or *what*, but Frank Swift never saw my car parked out back, didn't notice my engine starting up as he turned the light on in the living room, and didn't seem to become suspicious when he saw that Billie was taking a nap on the couch without her clothes, which were piled on the floor. I turned onto South Orange Blossom Trail in the cool February night and drove to the El Patio in the nude.

At this point I should probably pause and be a bit introspective, and try to figure out why a twenty-two-year-old guy, with access to so many single girls, was getting involved with a married one. I was probably too wild and crazy to give much thought to how risky it was, but I certainly did think it was very, very wrong. Was it my way of rebelling against strict parents? Was it my way of distancing myself from the past three pitiful years of being an emotional cripple? Maybe. Who knows? But of one thing I'm certain—when I climb into my time machine and find myself back in Orlando in 1963, I can once again feel the magic that was in the air. I had never felt it before that time, except for Mary Lou Dunlop back in high school, but with Billie, it was the first time I had felt it and had it reciprocated. It was a terrible thing for me to do, no doubt, but if I were to say that I look back on it with no pleasant memories, I'd be lying.

We were packing them in at the El Patio. Friends of mine were coming up regularly: Pace, Stanley, Charlotte, Jim Stafford, people I went to school with, my brother and his wife, and their friends. My parents even came up one night—P. E. Braddock at a rock 'n' roll club!

I got a Wurlitzer electric piano and now had *three* instruments made into one. I stood up and gyrated on the piano songs and sat down for the organ numbers; often I played piano with one hand and organ with the other.

I had a microphone for singing background harmonies. Sometimes Lew, the bass player, sang harmony in my mic, and sometimes he worked on the "front line" with John and Ken. The three of them did choreographed steps on a lot of the rockin' songs.

It was my job to decide which song we would play, then call out the title to the rest of the band. While the drummer counted the song off, John would grab some knobs on the sound board and then have his hands free in time to hit his guitar on the first note. There were two giant speakers on opposite ends of the stage, which also served as our sound monitors.

One of our most requested numbers was the Ray Stevens novelty hit, "Ahab the Arab," in which I played the part of Ahab's girlfriend Fatima.

John was excited because the guys from his old college band were going to be at the club one Saturday night to hear the Untouchables in their new incarnation. They were coming on the same day that I attempted to become my own piano tuner. I had been told more than once that a piano, which has notes that are both much lower and much higher than the other instruments, would not sound right if it were tuned like a guitar or bass, that it had to be modified to the *equal-temperament* musical scale in order to be in tune with itself. I didn't believe it. I thought either something was in tune or it wasn't. I told John that I should tune my piano myself, instead of hiring a piano tuner every week. John had an electric Strobe Tuner, which most musicians use for tuning now but was relatively unheard of back then. I went to a music store and bought one of my own, and I chose this important day to conduct my little experiment. Well, I tuned it perfectly, according to the Strobe, but it sounded like shit. It just sounded horribly out of tune, and it made the band sound awful. So here we were, the house was packed, and the old band was there to see if we were really as good as John had built us up to be, and we never sounded so bad. In fact, it was probably the only time we *ever* sounded bad. I saw Big John get drunk only twice in the nearly two years I worked for him, and both times were because of something I had done. This was one of those times.

"Fawwwwwk!" Big John squawked like an angry old hen. He just sat there in a chair in the El Patio kitchen by himself, mouth gaping, staring into space, saying "Fawwwwwk!" I felt very guilty about ruining his night. The first thing Monday morning, I returned the Strobe Tuner to the music store.

Although Big John was very fond of Gloria, he admitted that Billie and I were a great match, and he understood the attraction. Nevertheless, he was worried.

"Bob, I'm afraid you're gonna get in trouble. Man, you really need to be careful. Billie's a married woman."

"Well, Ken's a married man."

"Yeah, and jealous husbands are more dangerous than jealous wives. Besides, Ken's wife lives 260 miles from here and Billie's husband lives just down the street. And Ken never falls in *love* with anybody."

One night Ken asked me, "Whut's it feel like havin' those long legs wrapped 'round you?" I immediately went to Big John and told him I wasn't going to listen to Ken talk disrespectfully about Billie. John told Ken to apologize to me and he did.

Gloria was getting in the habit of coming to Orlando every weekend, staying with her sister and brother-in-law and coming out to the club. Whenever Billie was there by herself, I would sit with *her* on my breaks. I told Gloria that Billie and I were just good friends. Finally, Gloria told me my mom had informed her that I was having an affair with a married woman. She said Mom was really upset about it. I would come to find it was the other way around; Gloria had told my mother. I guess she had put two and two together after seeing me hanging out with Billie so much, and had started nosing around the club and asking questions. So I no longer tried to hide it from Gloria.

"What's the matter, honey, do you feel bad?" Gloria asked one night, as I put my head down on the table while the band was on break.

"I was thinking about *Billie*," I snapped at her.

On another night I got terribly drunk, and Gloria came to my room the next day, giving me Alka-Seltzer and wiping my brow with a cold washcloth as I lay miserably in bed. "What can I do for you, honeybun?" she asked me sweetly.

"Will you go to Walgreen's and tell Billie I said hi?" I asked. She did it without hesitation.

I realize now how cruel that was. Maybe I was a little resentful that Gloria had not wanted me—indeed, had been flaunting her new boyfriend until she realized that my heart was somewhere else—and then all of a sudden she wanted me back. And even though I was crazy about Billie, Gloria was pulling me back in, just a little.

I took her with me one Sunday to see a Grand Ole Opry show in Tampa so I could talk with singer Jimmy C. Newman, who had published some of my songs.

"Honey, can we exit up here and find some woods where I can hold you and kiss you for a little while?" she softly suggested. I couldn't resist. She had just turned nineteen and was looking better than ever.

Not long after that, in the middle of the week, I was in a bar with Billie up near Colonial Drive in Orlando, and from out of nowhere appeared Gloria, playing private detective. When she saw Billie and me wrapped up in each other, she let out a little scream and ran out the door. I ran after her. She said she was going to go kill herself. I wouldn't let her get in her car and told her she needed to ride around with me until she had calmed down.

"You *need* to look *after her*," Billie said.

I persuaded Gloria to ride with me, but she kept trying to jump out of the car, opening the door as I held tightly to her wrist, screaming that she wanted to die. Finally, by the time we got to Burdsall Motel, she had calmed down. I told her I wouldn't see Billie anymore. I didn't mean a word of it.

Billie was at the El Patio that night. We hung out together after the band stopped playing and had our usual wonderful time. The next morning she was banging on the door of my room.

Her face was bruised. "Frank beat me up last night," she blurted out.

"Damn him for that! Does he know about us?"

"I don't think so, it was because I came home so late. He suspects something but he doesn't know it's you."

"That doesn't give him the right to beat you."

"Honey, I don't think we should see each other anymore as long as I'm married." There were tears in her big brown eyes.

"Baby, I don't want to lose you, but I know you're right." I was thinking about her and her family, about Gloria, about my mom.

We had a sweet and tearful good-bye. She said she hoped we could really be together someday and not have to sneak around.

Saying good-bye is one thing, staying apart is another. Two nights later, I was in Billie's backyard, waiting for her to get her kids to sleep so she could come outside and play with me.

So it went throughout the spring as Florida nights went from cold to cool to mild, and Florida days went from cool to mild to hot. Billie and I saw an ending but continued to put off the inevitable. I understood when she remarked, "I'd rather be unhappy and miserable than to do anything to hurt my kids."

Despite the long hours spent at the keyboard rehearsing and performing, and all the emotional turmoil I was experiencing because of the affair with Billie, there were other things going on in my life. The occasional songs I was writing then were heartfelt, but none of them would ever be recorded. I had become a big fan of modern jazz, especially the Dave Brubeck Quartet. I had also become interested in classical music, my favorite composer being Johann Sebastian Bach; oddly, I didn't perform Bach songs but had the *style* down pretty well—I made up my own Bach-like songs that a lot of people *thought* were actual Bach fugues—and I became a fan of a the Swingle Singers, who did hip, jazzy versions of Bach.

There were movies whenever time allowed; sometimes with the guys in the band, sometimes with Gloria, a couple of times with Billie. I saw Gregory Peck in *To Kill a Mockingbird* and thought it was at least as good as Harper Lee's great book. Books were constant companions, a favorite being MacKinlay Kantor's Pulitzer Prize–winning novel of the Civil War, *Andersonville*. And politics had become more than just a passing interest.

I was developing a political philosophy and ideology, and it was pretty much centered around Republican senator Barry Goldwater from Arizona. Goldwater is generally considered to be the father of the modern conservative movement in America. He was solidly anti-communist and pro-military, and he was passionately opposed to a strong central government. Although Goldwater wasn't a racist, he appealed to a lot of Southern racists because of his stand for states rights as opposed to an authoritarian federal government. Years later, many conservatives felt that he had become more liberal because of his pro-abortion stand, and especially so toward the end of his life, when he voiced support for gays in the military. He would respond that he was being the same old anti-big government Goldwater, that the government had no right to tell a woman what to do with her body or a soldier what to do with his sex life. But in 1963, abortion, and gays in the military had not yet become issues, and the conservative movement wasn't yet tied to the evangelicals. Once again I became a proselytizer, this time for a political cause instead of a religion. Within a few months I had everyone in the Untouchables on the Goldwater For President bandwagon, although the election was a year and a half away.

It was May, Billie had turned twenty-one, and Central Florida had turned hot. My room at the Burdsall Motel was like an oven. I decided to pay a little more and took an air-conditioned room at the Court Cadillac Motel, which had a decent weekly rate and a swimming pool. There were occasional one-nighters with other girls. I didn't pursue Charlotte Jones because she was someone I could have become very interested in, and I had room for only one love interest, Billie.

But there was one thing that *did* get my attention, and it happened around the middle of May. Big John and I had gone to a party at someone's house after we knocked off at the El Patio, and by the time we made our way back to the parking lot at the club, I was seriously buzzing. It was in the early morning hours, probably close to daybreak but still dark. Suddenly the eastern sky lit up and for just a second everything was almost as bright as day. I wasn't sure if it was a nuclear bomb or the return of Jesus, but I went from considerably drunk to totally sober in a matter of seconds.

"*Good Lord*," John exclaimed. "They're launching that space flight from the Cape. Goodness gracious, Bob, you look like you've seen a *ghost!*" he said with a hearty laugh.

A couple of days later, John told us that he had us booked at a place in Birmingham, Alabama, called Pappy's Club. He'd heard about it from other musicians who had played there. It wouldn't pay quite as much as the El Patio, but the proprietor also owned the Rebel Courts motel next door, and we could stay there for free. My love life was volatile and turmoil filled in Orlando, so it seemed like a good time for fate to intervene.

On our farewell night at the El Patio, the crowd was overflowing, as was their affection. Before I left for Birmingham, I drove Billie down to her hometown. We held hands and neither of us said much. Though we talked about seeing each other when I got back from Birmingham, I don't know if either one of us believed it.

Birmingham liked to call itself "the youngest of the world's great cities." Actually, Miami is younger. Nonetheless, there was no Birmingham during the Civil War. It came into being in the 1870s, so there is nothing antebellum about the place. The economy there was not based on cotton or banking but on minerals. This was a steel city, the "Pittsburgh of the South." In 1920, it was considered a viable rival of Atlanta for being the predominant city of the region. By the early 1960s, it was known as the most violently racist of America's big cities. Some theorized that this was because Birmingham was the only highly industrialized big city in the Deep South, and the blue-collar whites saw blacks as a threat to their jobs. The steel barons were known as the Big Mules. They, the supposition goes, did nothing to promote racial tolerance because they actually *wanted* the poor people to be divided along racial lines. In other words, better that the poor whites hate the poor blacks than to hate the rich folks who were keeping *all* the poor people down.

The upper- and upper-middle-class white people of Birmingham, long accused of being indifferent and insulated in their nice homes "over the mountain," grew tired of Birmingham's superracist image and joined with black voters in electing a more moderate city government in April of 1963. But in early May, just four weeks before the notorious Bull Connor's reign as police commissioner would come to an end, three thousand young African Americans gathered at Kelly Ingram Park to demonstrate their opposition to discrimination in Birmingham. The world looked on in horror as the network TV news showed Connor's police unleashing dogs on the demonstrators. Even Southern segregationists wrestled with their consciences when they saw firemen turning high-powered hoses on the youngsters, many of them children, knocking them down and shredding their clothes with what Paul Hemphill described in his book *Leaving Birmingham* as "special water cannons capable of tearing bark from a tree at one hundred yards." America began to think it was time to *do something.* President Kennedy remarked that the civil rights movement "should thank God for Bull Connor. He's helped it as much as Abraham Lincoln."

So this was the city of "Bombingham," rich in iron but poor in human relations. It was ugly if you drove through the slums and smoke-clogged valleys beneath the big blast furnaces that belched fire and fumes twenty-four hours a day. It was beautifully magnificent if you drove across Red Mountain after dark and looked down at the lights of the city or up at the flaming torch in the mighty hand of the cast-iron statue of Vulcan, the Roman god of fire. By the twenty-first century, steel would be long gone, and Birmingham would be a health care and banking center that had not had a white mayor for decades. But when the Untouchables came to town, it was the capital of the New Confederacy and one could almost hear the drums of war.

Pappy's Club was located on Highway 78, Forestdale Boulevard, northwest of the city, practically out in the country. Pappy's was an okay place with a restaurant in front, but our free rooms at the Rebel Courts, located across a gravel parking lot from the nightclub, were a disgrace. It was almost as though the concrete had been poured on the hillside without a foundation; the rooms rose and fell with the lay of the land. I could drop my car keys on the floor next to the lumpy bed, and they would slide downhill across the room. The only thing that made it bearable was my roommate Lew, someone to laugh about it with. Ash Bodden, from Big John's old college band, came up from Miami to replace Denny on the drums. Ash refused to stay at Rebel Courts and paid for a room at a better motel down the highway.

Ash was a Miamian of British Bahamian parents. He had one year left to get his degree in criminology and decided to give the band a shot for the summer and see what happened. He was a great drummer, and we were all very happy to get him. Ash was tall and skinny, with black hair, dark eyes, and a gaunt, sunken face. Destined to become a Miami detective, he was introverted and hard to get to know, but funny as hell once you did. Though Big John encouraged us to politick, to sit and talk with the customers on our breaks, Ash told me "I didn't come up here to win any popularity contest." Not being much of a Southerner, coming from Miami, he had been amused while attending Florida State University to learn that Southern-talking North Florida boys used "cock" as a female-related rather than a male-related word, and sometimes in the middle of a rockin' number he would yell out from behind his drum set, "Eat that cock!" He referred to elderly customers as *slow cats*. If you scored on a date, it was *long doggin'* but a date with no sex was *short doggin'*; hence his question, "Long doggin' or short doggin'?" Once he said to me, "Hey, we're in Alabama, let's go out and look at the grit trees." *"Thaaaaas* right," which would become my trademark expression, I stole from Ash.

Most of Pappy's clientele were steel workers and their women, as well as assorted rock 'n' roll fans from the area. They were a good rowdy crowd, and the band went over great.

When I got to Birmingham, there was a letter from my mother awaiting me at Pappy's Club. In several guilt-inducing pages, she said, among other things, that my father had suffered a supposed heart attack upon hearing about my affair. She urged that I clear my brain of alcohol long enough to find a Church of Christ minister and confess my sins and tell of the horrible affair I had had with that "married woman." By the last screaming page, her handwriting was large and shaky, with half of the words underlined, every sentence punctuated with several exclamation points. I replied thusly:

Birmingham
Thurs. June 16, 1963
4:10 AM

Dear Mom:
Got your letter today & thought I would straighten out a thing or two.
I am very sorry that I have done anything to bring sorrow or strife to anyone. I am especially sorry to upset you or Dad.

You seem to be under the impression that I am some kind of alcoholic. In Orlando, I drank occasionally—maybe to excess a couple of times, but overall in moderation, probably no more than when I was home. I have always held that moderate drinking is not wrong. I argued that with Brother Lee, remember? We've made an agreement in the band to not <u>drink on the job</u>—not even one beer (beer is the only alcohol served at Pappy's).

Mom, you know so much about me and "the married woman," it's time you heard about it from me. I met this girl last summer in Orlando, she was a waitress where I ate (this old married woman was 20 years old). I came to know her pretty well before she even knew there was an El Patio Club. I never "went out" with her until 3 or 4 months ago when she had an argument with her husband about her working. He told her not to come back—so she went to the El Patio with a couple of girlfriends and she and I got together and talked, but that's all we did. Being a nice girl, she felt bad about even that. Eventually, I would eat with her at the restaurant and would meet her once in awhile—meet her, <u>that's all.</u> There was nothing dirty about it, you've got to believe that. Wrong, yes, because she's married. I fell for her, she fell for me—actually before I even went with her, before she ever went to the El Patio. I felt bad about it because of so many people being hurt. She felt bad about it because of her two small children, a little boy and girl. You don't really have much to worry about as far as her giving up her home to marry me. She said she had to put her children before and above everything else & she would rather be miserable for the rest of her life than have her children brought up in a broken home. And I wouldn't want to break up a home either.

We both know we made a mistake. The only thing that was wrong was the fact that she was married. If she were single—even divorced—I would have probably married her, but being the one who breaks up a home is another matter.

Regardless of what you think, she is a nice girl, a very nice girl, a very likable girl, I don't know of anyone who doesn't like her.

That is my "big sin," Mother. It could happen to anyone & you know it. It would have happened if I were an insurance agent in Orlando.

Being a musician had nothing to do with it. A pleasant, cute girl who had a personality that complemented mine, before we knew it, it had hap-

pened. It's over now. I think it's more sad than it is sinful, but I <u>know</u> it was wrong.

Will you make me <u>regret</u> being open with you? Please don't discuss this with anyone, except maybe Daddy. If you were to go to this girl or anyone else, I don't think I'd ever come home again. She has been through more "hell" than anyone else. She stayed upset half the time.

As far as church is concerned, the main wrong I've done is quit going. I plan to try to go here in Birmingham.

I have told you the truth. Please try to understand. I love you & Dad both very much. I'm sorry I hurt you. Gloria is a wonderful girl, I'm sorry I hurt her.

The affair has ended, don't worry about me. Give all my love to Dad, I'll write you both soon.

Love,
Bobby

In some places, the letter seems to try to leave the false impression that my relationship with Billie was platonic ("I would meet her, *that's all*"), and I wasn't *exactly* being honest when I told Mom it was over between us, because it wasn't *official,* but in my heart I felt that we were really through.

In early July, I finally got a letter from Billie. She said she was just finding out how many people she had hurt. She didn't say it was over, but I think she wanted to give *me* the opportunity to say so. I felt a combination of grief and happiness when I read: "When I think about you, I still get a little weak. Guess we had it pretty bad, huh?"

I wrote her at the post office box I had rented for her in Orlando. I told her that our relationship was the most wonderful thing that had ever happened to me, that it had been like magic and that I would always have strong feelings for her, but I had come to realize how wrong it was and that it was tearing her family apart. I told her I thought she wanted to try to make her marriage work and I urged her to do so. She never wrote me back.

It was about this time that I got my notice from Uncle Sam. Though I had registered for the draft in Florida, as a temporary resident of Alabama I was ordered to go to the induction center at Montgomery. My mother had sent a letter from Dr. Izard, the psychiatrist I had seen in Tampa, stating that he did not think I was psychologically fit for military service. I was reluctant to take it along because even though I wasn't crazy about going into the military, I also dreaded the humiliation of being turned down for psychiatric reasons. John definitely wanted me to take the letter. "There's not any *war* goin' on. They don't need you," he said.

After a night of playing at Pappy's Club and with zero hours of sleep, I boarded an army bus in Birmingham and headed for Montgomery. I learned two things while standing around naked at the induction center. I learned that it is entirely possible to go to sleep while standing up, and I learned that African American males were definitely more phallically blessed than their white counterparts.

The army doctor was a major, a tall, gruff man. When I presented him with the letter from Dr. Izard, he read it, then handed it back to me and growled, "We sure won't be needing *you*." And it was almost as simple as that.

And so began the feelings of guilt that would follow me for a very long time. By the time my two years in the service would have been over, America would be in a major war in Vietnam. In 1965, I would favor the war but feel that I had no right to. In 1969, I would oppose the war but feel that I had no right to. Only when most Americans would come to consider the war a mistake so many years later, would I be able to feel at all okay about not having gone to Vietnam.

In the summer of '63 I spent a lot of spare time at Birmingham's downtown library and reading in my sloping room. There were girls now and then, none of whom I ever took to the Rebel Courts. I always went to some other motel or to the girl's place or to the woods.

I went out a few times with a really nice-looking blonde who had been out once with Ken. It seemed as though all Ken had to do was sing "Baby Let's Play House" and throw out a little wink from the stage to get whatever girl he wanted. Even though he was through with the blonde, when he found out I was dating her, he tattled to Big John. John, the judge and jury of the band, told me there was a rule that prohibited me from dating a girl who had been with another

Untouchable. I didn't like the rule but didn't think dating the girl was worth the friction it would cause, so I quit seeing her.

I got a letter from Gloria, asking if she could ride a Greyhound up to Birmingham to visit me. I called her and told her to come on. It seemed like a good idea. My mother was bankrolling the trip. After seeing me involved with a couple of married girls, Gloria was looking pretty good to her. I had been looking forward to seeing her, but when she got there it just didn't feel right, and I couldn't quite figure out why. I think I was still grieving over Billie. I put Gloria up in a nice motel but never went to the room with her. A couple of days later when I put her on a southbound bus, we were both pretty depressed.

I started going out with a cute brunette, about a year younger than me, named Linda Fay Lowden. Linda Fay worked for Continental Can Company ("I'm proud of muh job") and insisted on picking up the tab when I took her out to eat because she didn't know that musicians got paid to perform. She was a sweet girl who spoke the truth when she said she had never been able to enjoy sex. When I finally had the opportunity to find that out for myself, Linda Fay gave me a pretty good idea of what necrophilia is like, though it's doubtful that dead people say, "are yuh through yet?"

Between our first hello and our cold copulation there was a span of a few weeks. She thought she was in love with me, and I thought I would be the first man to bring out the hot, wild beast in this cute girl from the hills of North Alabama. Wrong. She was absolutely the most frigid woman I've ever known, but during that wait I learned some important life lessons that make more sense to me now than they did back then.

There were and are many kinds of racism. Linda Fay didn't hate black people, but she was afraid of them; her prejudice was based on fear, and her fear was based on ignorance. She thought there were more blacks in America than whites. When I told her that African Americans made up only about 12 percent of the total population of America, she didn't believe me. Knowing that Alabama was a little under 30 percent black, I asked her what she thought the percentage was.

"Oh, I reckon about 80 percent," she said. She was mistaken

in thinking that African Americans were so plentiful, and she was wrong in thinking that she should be afraid of them in the first place, no matter how many there were.

Linda Fay's excuse for racial prejudice was ignorance, but *I* had *no* excuse. In 1963, I would have told you in all sincerity that I was not a racist. I was kind to black people and cherished the friendships that I had had with them: drinking beer with Texas Ray; co-conspiring with my father's grove worker Wilson; always being just as eager to stop and lend a helping hand to a black person in trouble as I would be to help a white person. But I loved the history and traditions of the South, and felt that change had to come about voluntarily. I believed that the Constitution gave the individual states the right to make their own laws. The fact that most Southerners felt that way does not absolve me. There were not a lot of forward-thinking Southern white visionaries in those days, but there were *some,* and I was not one of them. I don't have to think very hard to know what it was like to be one of the "good" Germans who didn't hate Jews but stood by and let Hitler do his evil. Martin Luther King said, "History will have to record that the greatest tragedy of this period of social transition was not the strident clamor of the bad people, but the appalling silence of the good people." If only I could, I would march backwards in time and into the Southern streets with Martin Luther King, singing "We Shall Overcome."

If I was one of the "good" Southerners who wore blinders, and if Linda Fay was one of the "ignorant" Southerners who didn't know any better, then Rose Faircloth was the worst of the worst. Rose was a very good-looking young woman, articulate—she wasn't a redneck—but she was one of the most virulent haters I ever met. She belonged to the National States Rights Party, essentially an American Nazi group, and often quoted the party newspaper, the *Thunderbolt.* Rose was obsessed with her hatred of blacks and Jews.

One night, one of the suds-sipping steelworkers at Pappy's Club told a Southern racist joke that was making the rounds.

"I like niggers," the man said. "I think *everybody* oughta own one."

"Well, *I* don't like niggers," Rose shouted. "Not for *any* reason."

"Goddam, Rose, it's just a joke," the steelworker said with a frown.

"Niggers are no joke," she sneered, glowering, looking at nobody. Rose was a racist that less extreme racists could point a finger at to try to prove that they weren't racists themselves.

How would one describe Birmingham in the late summer of 1963? Unrest? Powder keg? Time bomb? On August 20, the home of black attorney Arthur Shores was bombed. On September 2, Governor George Wallace held a segregationist rally at Ensley Park and the next day sent state troopers to Birmingham's Graymont Elementary School to block the registration of two little African American boys. On September 8, the home of Birmingham's leading black businessman, A. G. Gaston, was bombed.

Then on Sunday, September 15, the Ku Klux Klan perpetrated a tragedy that more than any single event would bring about the complete integration of the South. That certainly wasn't their intention when they blew up the 16th Street Baptist Church and murdered four innocent little girls. If we wear masks to typify our sentiments, then on that day, the white South wore the mask of shame. Even Linda Fay Lowden said it was a bad thing. I don't know what Rose Faircloth said; she probably said that the blacks had done it themselves to gain sympathy. The rest of America wore the mask of outrage. The little girls would be martyred for all time, and the Klan, ironically, did the very *last* thing they ever intended to do: they played a major role in the eventual passage of America's first real civil rights bill. Birmingham was placed under curfew and there were highway patrol cars on practically every street corner. George Wallace's state troopers, anticipating black violence, were wearing battle helmets. I thought of a war zone, of Europe twenty or twenty-five years earlier.

In my mind, the soundtrack for my few months in "America's Most Segregated City," was abstract and surreal and had absolutely nothing to do with what was going on around us. I had been tuned in to local pop radio and the songs that I still associate with that time and place are "It's My Party (I'll Cry If I Want To)," featuring teeny bopper Lesley Gore, "Easier Said Than Done," by the Essex, a black group who wouldn't have been allowed to eat in any of Birmingham's nicer restaurants, and "Sukiyaki," a song sung entirely in Japanese. And how did the Untouchables fit into Birmingham's summer struggle? Not a one of us had any interest in the civil rights movement. I thought we were so cool, playing "Green Onions," me showing off my organ-playing. But we weren't the cool ones; that would be Booker T. and the MGs, the interracial Southern band who *recorded* "Green Onions." They were ahead of their time; we were troglodytes.

During our last week at Pappy's Club, I woke up one morning to the sight of a little green snake awkwardly wriggling across my inclined floor at Rebel Courts. I promptly moved in with Ash Bodden at the motel down the highway. I was ready to get back to Florida, but there were plenty of bizarre Birmingham incidents that would ever be etched in my memory. Like the night we rode up Red Mountain, overlooking downtown, and I drunkenly tried to climb up the giant statue of Vulcan, as Big John yelled for me to come down. Or the time I sat amazed in a restaurant as I watched, with about a hundred other people, a man break his own record by eating twenty-one hard-boiled eggs in one minute. Or the night I watched two attractive young women rolling around in the gravel of Pappy's parking lot, punching and kicking and biting each other over our singer, Ken.

On an unseasonably warm fall day, we packed our things and walked out into the late afternoon smoke and dust—from the steel mills or from the bombs or whatever—bidding "The Magic City" adieu.

We got back to Florida just in time for Big John to take his wife Dot to the maternity ward for the birth of their first child. Ken lost a roommate when John moved his little family from Auburndale to Orlando. Within a few days we were back playing at the El Patio. Lew's girlfriend, who was now his fiancée, wanted him to quit the band. Big John didn't have to look far to find a replacement. Our biggest competition in Orlando had been a group called Sue and the Dynamics. On their weekly night off, Sue's electric bass player, Tony Purvis, and drummer, Robert Nix (who later became a part of the famous pop group Atlanta Rhythm Section) always came to the El

Patio because they were big fans of the Untouchables. Sue and the Dynamics had just broken up, so we got Tony.

Tony Purvis was nineteen and from Jacksonville. He was a good-natured, lively guy, whom Ash immediately nicknamed "Howdy Doody" because there *was* a little resemblance. Howdy Doody with glasses. He already knew most of our repertoire and could sing "Big Boss Man" just like Jimmy Reed, the blues cat who made the record. Tony would never sing more than a couple of songs, so Ken never considered him a usurper and welcomed the relief. We lost a good man but we gained one. Tony usually wore a big smile and was fun to work with. I was no longer the baby of the band.

Upon going back into the El Patio I learned some bad news. Billie's little sister Betsy told me that Frank had found the letter I sent to Billie when I was in Birmingham. We were totally busted. Frank had never suspected anything about Billie and me until he read the letter.

"You really need to be careful," Betsy warned me. "He said he was going to kill you."

A couple of nights later, it was a Monday or a Tuesday, we were taking a break, and I walked out under the entrance canopy in front of the club to get some fresh October night air along with my cigarette (an oxymoron, for sure). There were no more than twenty cars parked in the lot. I immediately recognized the one that pulled up and parked about a hundred feet away. Frank turned off the lights, got out of the car and started walking toward me. Slowly but surely. It was like a Western movie, but this was no gunfight because I didn't have a weapon. And I wasn't going to run. I stood there as he got closer and closer, looking right at me. Frank was a little shorter than Billie, but he was a good-looking guy with curly light brown hair. We were looking each other square in the eye as he got closer and closer. When we were face to face, he stopped. He offered me his hand. I shook it.

"You know people get killed for doing what you did," he said, not with anger.

"Frank, I wouldn't *blame* you if you killed me," I said, meaning every word of it.

"I think I *would* have if I'd seen you when I first read that letter. But you know what? She was seeing somebody else while you were in Birmingham. So you were only the first. If it hadn't been you, it still would have happened, sooner or later."

When he told me who the guy was, I felt jealousy and anger. It was a guy who had been after her for a long time. His family had money, but I thought the guy was piggish and crude. I was disappointed in Billie.

"But she can have you or him or whoever she wants, because I'm getting a divorce."

"Frank, *Billie* doesn't want a divorce, does she?"

"No, but it doesn't matter."

"*Please* give her a chance, for the sake of the kids." I pleaded. "She always told me she didn't want the kids to be brought up in a broken home."

"Well, I don't think I could ever take her back. I dunno. I've got a lot of thinking to do."

"Frank, it was so wrong, and I'm so sorry."

"Thanks, Bob," he said, as he shook my hand again, then turned and walked away.

My attitude was, *whew*, that was a close one, and *boy*, glad to still have Gloria. But, I didn't. One year earlier, after almost three years of craziness, Gloria hadn't wanted me and I didn't blame her. Then, when I was having an affair with Billie, she *did* want me but couldn't have me. When I turned up free again and was open to having her in my life, she was interested in someone else. It was the guy her mama had run off with the baseball bat.

So I went about my business of making music and going out with girls now and then. One October night, by the time I started to look around the club for female companionship, it was almost quittin' time and the ranks had thinned out because of heavy rain. So when we finished our last set, I decided to check out the bar and see if I could strike up a quick acquaintanceship. I ran across a young woman who was not at all bad looking until she smiled and displayed a mouthful of crickets, so to speak. We went to the motel where I had recently moved, the El Ranchito, a couple of miles south of the club on South Orange Blossom Trail. A hard rain was coming down as we ran to my room.

After we had undressed, she said, "You know this is gonna *cost* you, don't you?"

Somewhere in my convoluted moral code, I, who would commit adultery in a heartbeat, felt it was a terrible thing to pay for sex. Almost any kind of sex was fine under any circumstances, but to pay for it was, well, sinful.

"I'm sorry," I replied, as I shook my head, "that would just be against my principles."

"Well, okay," she shrugged, and started putting her clothes back on.

The thunder was getting louder, sometimes exploding only a split second after the lightning sizzled and popped in the air just overhead. The rains were torrential, and the wind had started blowing with gale force. I looked out my window and could see that the parking lot looked like a lake.

"I don't think we should drive in this stuff, do you?" I asked.

"Naw," she sighed, as she lit a cigarette, "I guess we oughta wait awhile." She was really attractive when she didn't open her mouth.

I sat there watching her make smoke rings as my bedside lamp flickered off and on and the wind howled outside.

"You know," I spoke softly, saying her now long-forgotten name, "since we're not goin' anywhere—we're gonna be here for awhile anyway—don't you think we might as well go ahead and *do* it?"

She looked down and softly laughed, "Oh, hell, I guess we might as well."

We did. There was a correlation between us and the weather. We lay there smoking cigarettes as a quieter, softer rain came down. We got out of bed and put our clothes back on. As we headed for the door, she stopped and took hold of my arm and looked at me intensely.

"Look," she said with great earnestness, "don't you tell anybody about this, okay?"

"Uh, w-well, okay," I stammered. "I won't. But how come?"

"Because my fiancé told me if he ever heard of me giving it away for free, he'd kill me!"

In the wee hours of an autumn morning, Ash and I were at our favorite after-hours breakfast place, the Florida Diner, sitting at the counter in our green-gray Untouchables suits. I was having my regular, a "Texas breakfast," which was steak and eggs with hash browns. A bespectacled woman, well into her fifties, was sitting at a nearby table. I recognized her from the club; most of the El Patio customers were younger than her.

"Ain't you the Braddick boy?" she drawled, smiling an unfriendly smile.

"Yeah, I am," I said with surprise, "how did you know that?"

"I heard you was playin' here and you look like yer daddy. I was raised down in Orburndale."

"Well, hey there, Auburndale. Good to see you. What's . . . "

Before I could ask her name, she said, "I bet you didn't know your mama and daddy was livin' t'gether before they got married, did you?"

The whole place went silent. I think I sat there looking at her with my mouth open for a few seconds before I shouted, "That's a lie. Go to hell, you old bitch! You're a *liar!*"

"Well, I know you don't like t' hear it, but it's th' truth," she intoned in her whiny voice, as she got up and walked out of the diner with her axe that apparently needed a good grinding.

Ash, who often said "*thaaaaas* right," looked a bit embarrassed as he said quietly, "*Thaaaaas* wrong."

A man seated next to me at the counter growled, "I don't blame you. I'd have cussed her out too."

"It's a damned lie," I muttered, as I violently slapped an ejaculation of too much Heinz ketchup onto my hash browns.

In late November, I noticed that President Kennedy was going to be in Tampa. I had planned to drive there and stand alongside the street with a big sign that read: "REMEMBER THE BAY OF PIGS." Here was this man who, halfway through his term, had been confronted with the most dangerous conundrum in the history of the world, the Cuban Missile Crisis, and he stood up to Russia and did it in a way that averted the destruction of our planet—and there I was, wanting to protest something that had happened in the opening days of his presidency. Thankfully, for some reason, I didn't do it. JFK's next stop after Tampa was Texas.

On the morning of November 22, I was getting into my car at the El Ranchito motel to go to a band rehearsal at the club. The proprietress of the motel was a late middle-aged, frumpy, blonde New Yorker. Her live-in boyfriend was a tobacco-chewing old guy from Georgia. As I climbed into the car, the lady yelled from the office door, "Kennedy's been shot in Texas, and they shot Governor Connally, too. Johnson had a heart attack."

"I'm glad they shot the nigger-lovin' sonofabitch," the old man said.

I was in such a state of shock that I didn't even say anything back to them. I turned on my car radio and headed for the El Patio. The first thing I heard was that Kennedy had been taken to Parkland Hospital in Dallas in critical condition. Lyndon Johnson had not had a heart attack. Nobody knew who the shooter was. By the time I made the three- or four-minute drive to the El Patio, it was announced that the president was dead.

Later, I called Gloria from a phone booth. She was very upset. It was almost as though she was daring me to not be sad about it. She needn't have; I was stunned, saddened, and depressed. I was also afraid that the assassin was a right-winger who would bring great discredit and damage to the conservative movement. That night, even though it was a Friday night, the crowd was small at the El Patio. Everyone seemed in a daze. The dancers seemed to be moving around the floor in slow motion. We went home early.

On the following Monday I left my parents' house to the sound of hoof beats, carriage wheels, and muffled drums on TV. It followed me in my car radio, it was on a television set in a jewelry store where

I picked up a watch, and it continued to accompany me as I got on the interstate back to Orlando. No one who heard the sad sounds of President Kennedy's funeral procession would ever forget it.

The event, like Pearl Harbor before it and 9/11 after, would change the country, the world, and the course of history. I remember it as a sad time, and also as a time when there was nobody in my life except my band mates and an occasional young lady I would take to breakfast and bed. I heard that Billie was pregnant. I was still sad about her; she had made a major impact on my life. One night, after driving a girl from my motel room to her car, I went back to my place and got out a notebook and started writing a song that began, "Tonight I almost got happy for just a little while . . . "

Big John and I had been invited to a Christmas party on a Sunday night when I had stayed in Orlando, rather than going home to Auburndale. I had just gotten a 1962 Oldsmobile, apparently formerly owned by a cop because it had a spotlight on the side. I went by John's rented house in Orlando to pick him up in my new wheels. When we went through the door into the home of the Untouchables fans who were having the party, I looked across the crowded room and there stood Billie. She stared right at me with those big brown eyes, mouth half open. I was transfixed on her eyes and headed right toward her.

"*Lord,* have mercy, Bob, are you *crazy?*" John quietly yelled. "Come on, I'm gettin' you *outta* here." He took me by the arm, opened the door, and gently pushed me outside. We got into my car, and I took him home.

"Now where are you goin'?" he asked me.

"Auburndale."

"Good boy," he said.

I never saw Billie again. Not long after that, I heard that Frank had gotten transferred and that they had moved to Georgia. I wonder if they stayed together for many decades or for just another year or two. I wonder if Billie climbed up the socioeconomic ladder and is tonight a slender woman who looks young for her age, drinking a good pinot noir in an expensive restaurant. Or is she a fat and funny granny, the delight of everyone in her neighborhood? Or did she leave us early, falling victim to one of those unpredictable phantoms always lurking in the shadows along life's highway? Whatever became of her, here's to Billie for that shared magic that doesn't come along very often in one lifetime.

I saw 1964 come in at the El Patio Club. The place looked like Polk County. There must have been thirty people who were friends or classmates or relatives. I was hanging out with a large group that kept getting smaller and smaller until finally there was nobody left but me and pretty Charlotte Jones and her big Bette Davis eyes. I was supposed to take her immediately home to Lakeland but we got sidetracked and ended up in my room at the El Ranchito. It wasn't innocent, but there was no actual adultery committed.

"I guess you'd better deliver me to my car at the Royal Castle in Lakeland," she whispered in the dark.

Before making it to the little fast-food place near her house, we pulled into an orange grove on the outskirts of town and kissed some more. When I finally pulled up next to her car, there was Lucas Jones, one giant of a mean country boy.

"Bobby, what *is* this shit?" he demanded.

I don't know what I said, but I said it fast and furiously, and it must have been pretty good.

"Well, I'm prob'ly a dumbshit for believin' you, but okay," he sighed.

"I have too much respect for you and Charlotte to do anything like that, Lucas."

"Well, come on sonofabitch," he told her, "get yer ass in the car." The mismatch of all time. I didn't feel very guilty.

I decided to go to my folks' house to get some sleep before heading back to Orlando. As I drove past the swamps on Highway 92 between Lakeland and Auburndale, I could see a faint coat of gold and pink spreading out above the partly cloudy horizon up ahead, the first sign of the sun rolling in from the ocean onto the chilly green peninsula. Hovering in the sky above, I could almost make out "1964." No matter what kind of year 1964 turned out to be, I thought, it couldn't possibly be as eventful as the one we'd just had.

I thought of the past year, tumultuous though it had been, and felt that on balance things had gotten much better for me personally. I felt saner and stronger, shamelessly (or shamefully) sexual, smarter (sometimes), and stupider (*so many times*). There had been a whole lot of sweetness and a whole lot of sadness, much of which I would forget about until I sat down decades later to write a book about it.

I was listening to a country music station, traveling through downtown Auburndale as Buck Owens sang "Love's Gonna Live Here Again." I drove around little Lake Stella, turned left at the key lime tree and went down the dirt road to the red-roofed white stucco house. There was a light on in the kitchen. I could see my dad in his bathrobe, putting on his early morning coffee. For some reason I didn't have a spare key with me, probably because I didn't typically come to Auburndale in the middle of the week. I rapped on the jalousie door of the breezeway until Dad started walking toward me, looking cautiously through the kitchen windows.

"Happy New Year," I shouted.

The frail figure moved through the breezeway. He squinted his eyes as he peered through the glass louvers, looking every one of his eighty-one years.

"It's *me*, Dad, *Bobby*."

The feeble, puzzled gape turned into a big bright smile as he grabbed the lock and said, "Well-l-l, look whooo's heaahh!"

CHAPTER ELEVEN

The Road to Nashville

I F I WERE GIVEN ANOTHER shot at directing *Bobby's Love Life*, I'm sure I could do it much, much better, but I don't think I would want to replace a single one of the players. Even in what would turn out to be the very hardest relationship I was ever in, I know it was worth every bit of the misery that we visited on each other when I consider what was born of this union.

In early 1964, when I met the mother of my future children, I thought she was someone I would really like to get to know. Sadly, I never did. Major events in her past would remain under lock and key, not only throughout our courtship but for our entire marriage. Not until many years after we were divorced did I have information that would help me put the pieces together and better understand the woman I lived with for so long, but never really knew.

When Big John's Untouchables had been booked into Pappy's Club in Birmingham, Ash was dating a lady named Ella, who was several years older than us and wore her black hair in a tall beehive. After we moved back to Orlando, Ella came down every few weekends to be with Ash. In late January 1964, Ash told me that Ella was bringing a girlfriend down with her. While we were rehearsing on a Friday afternoon, the two girls walked into the El Patio and sat at a table by the door. I could see that Ella's friend was a very cute little thing with big blonde hair.

"Bobby, this is *Sue,* Sue this is Bobby," Ash said, after we had finished rehearsing. I smiled and took her hand in mine. Tony, who had already hurried over to the table and introduced himself, stood by grinning a little uncomfortably as he realized it was Ash's intentions to fix *me* up with Sue.

Nancy Sue Rhodes was nineteen, stood not much taller than five feet, and weighed not much more than ninety pounds. She giggled effervescently and joked flirtatiously. When she laughed, which was often, her Technicolor blue eyes crinkled and sparkled. She was vivacious, engaging, and obviously smart.

She told me she was a night student at Birmingham Southern College and worked as an information operator for Southern Bell telephone company. I amused her with my goofy gallery of voices, imitating various information-seeking telephone customers. She had an endearing little mannerism; after a round of laughter she would rapidly brush downward on the tip of her nose, three times in succession, with the side of her index finger.

We spent almost every minute of that extended weekend together. I took her down South Orange Blossom Trail toward Kissimmee to a zoo called Gatorland. On my Sunday night off, she said she would like to meet my parents.

"Let's go to AW-bun-dale," she drawled in a Scarlett O'Hara Deep South plantation accent. Girls brought up in the blue-collar neighborhoods of Birmingham's steel mill suburbs didn't speak in such a genteel manner, but Sue was on a roll and wasn't about to let reality get in her way. She had me believing that she not only *worked* for Southern Bell but *was* one. So we went to Auburndale, and Sue charmed my parents just as she had charmed me.

"When your father came out into the living room, he looked like *royalty*, with his beautiful white hair and his long silk bathrobe," she cooed, as we climbed into my car and headed out around Lake Stella.

I had enjoyed our time together. When she left, I was hoping we would stay in touch, and she didn't disappoint me. Almost daily I received a lengthy, laudatory letter from Birmingham, extolling the many virtues of Bobby Braddock. When a good-looking girl starts telling a guy that he's the smartest, the handsomest, and the most talented man in the world, well, fools are susceptible to flattery, and every joker likes to think of himself as a king.

Sue was getting home from work in the late afternoons about the time our band was getting through with the almost daily rehearsals, so I got in the habit of giving her a call from the phone booth in the El Patio bar. She oozed sweetness and kindness—that is, until one day when it appeared pretty obvious that she had fibbed to me about a couple of things. I felt that if we were getting at all serious, then it was certainly something worth discussing. Sue immediately left the phone, and another person, also named Sue Rhodes, who lived at the same address in Birmingham, began talking. This Sue Rhodes was defensively ice cold, then belligerently red hot, a completely different person from the one I knew. A couple of days later I got an Air Mail Special Delivery letter from the *sweet* Sue Rhodes; it was lengthy and laudatory, extolling the many virtues of Bobby Braddock. I continued to call her from the telephone booth after band rehearsals.

The band constantly rehearsed, polishing old songs and learning new ones. If a song was a current hit, then it was a good candidate for our repertoire. In the early part of 1964, it seemed that half of the hits on the radio were by the same new act, the Beatles. This was music like none that I had ever heard. My first reaction to "I Want to Hold Your Hand" was, "Oh boy, rock 'n' roll with a lot of chord changes!" We donned Beatles wigs and sounded as much like the Beatles as we could.

There was one huge hit that was unusual for the rock 'n' roll era. It was the Broadway musical title song, "Hello, Dolly," sung by the sixty-three-year-old king of New Orleans jazz, Louis Armstrong. I had been an Armstrong fan since I was in junior high school and did a pretty good impersonation of his gravelly voice, so Big John insisted that we work it up and I sing it. I would get a trumpet-shaped kazoo to emulate Louis' horn-playing and hold a big white handkerchief so I could do his trademark mopping of the brow.

On a crowded Saturday night, I stepped up to the mic with my "trumpet" and handkerchief. The room broke out into loud cheers as I sang *Hello, Dolly, this is Louis, Dolly.* When I started to mop my brow with the handkerchief, it slid down my forehead like a snow sled whizzing down a mountainside. What I hadn't realized was that one of the guys, who suffered from a chronic sinus condition, had a handkerchief that he hawked into sometimes between songs, and he had left it on a chair by my piano. I had grabbed *his* hanky instead of mine! I quickly grabbed *my* handkerchief and wiped off the slime as best I could.

There was an ironclad rule in Big John's band: we were there for every set and absolutely did not leave the stage until the end of the set (even the time we all had the flu and a high fever). We were on forty minutes and off twenty. I had sung "Hello, Dolly" at the beginning of the set; consequently, there was a long wait before I could exit the stage and wash my face. As soon as we took our break, I ran to the kitchen. The only thing I could find to clean up with was powdered dishwashing detergent. I wet my face and scrubbed it vigorously with the detergent and a dish rag until it was bloody red.

The El Patio closed down for a few days in February for repairs. I decided to take that time to go to Nashville and kick around for a couple of days and try to play my songs for some music publishers. I drove up through Alabama, which was the preferred route to Nashville before I-75 opened up through Florida and Georgia. This would give me the opportunity to stop off in Birmingham and see Sue Rhodes.

Darkness had just fallen on Alabama as I rolled into America's most segregated city on a bitterly cold night. I drove around beneath the red Birmingham sky until I found the apartment building where Sue lived. It was a decent enough place, resembling on old brick school building. She seemed overjoyed to see me but didn't want us to stay there. It was never quite clear to me whether she had a roommate or not. There was a lot of mystery about her, but I didn't really care; she was a good-looking girl who acted like she was crazy about me. We went to a motel about twenty-five miles to the south, in the little town of Calera, and spent the night.

I drove into Nashville on Highway 31, which became Franklin Road. An inveterate map reader, I knew about the streets in the area and thought there was something charming and enchanting in their names: Granny White Pike, Harding Place, Old Hickory Boulevard. As the road approached the city, I admired the beautiful, stately homes. On the edge of town, I felt like I was in Hillbilly Heaven when I saw the fabled Acuff-Rose Publishing Company. Not far ahead was the York Motel, where I stopped for the night.

The next day, I wandered aimlessly up and down Music Row, which consisted of three streets of old houses that had been converted into record labels, recording studios, publishing companies, and management offices. I wanted to play some songs for Jimmy Key, a partner in Newkeys, the company that had published a few of my songs the year before, but he was tied up and couldn't get with me. I had come into town with no plan and was unable to see anyone of importance. I vowed I would return, figure out what I was supposed to do, then do it. I had an affinity for this city as though it were my own hometown. To many, it was the Athens of the South because of the many colleges and universities as well as the Parthenon replica in Centennial Park. To some it was the Wall Street of the South, a center of investment banking and big insurance companies. To others, it was the buckle of the Bible Belt, a Protestant Rome and a great center of religious publishing where more Bibles and Sunday School books were printed than anywhere else in the world. But to me it was Music City, U.S.A., and as I headed back to Florida, I knew I would someday live in Nashville.

The letters from Sue became even more serious and ever more flowery, with phrases like "my darling" and "our precious love." Despite occasional appearances by the other Sue Rhodes, the one with the icicles in her voice who would almost but not quite come to the point of yelling at me, I found her attractive and sweet, but I didn't experience the magic that I had felt with Billie Swift, and I had become too strong and self-sufficient to feel a needy kind of love like I had felt for Gloria. Though I thought Sue was special, I also thought she was secretive and perhaps a bit disingenuous. But she had definitely become my steady girlfriend. This "love" tide just seemed to have carried me on out to sea, whether I wanted it to or not. What was love anyway? My mother had asked me if I was falling in love with Sue, and I said I thought so, probably thinking that would please her because she liked Sue. Sue often told me that she loved me, so I just chimed right in and told her I felt that way, too. I didn't think I was lying to her, but neither was I certain that I was telling the truth. Back then I guess love was something you said. A pattern had been established, and I had become a part of it.

On one warm spring weekend when Sue was in town, we were on our second or third tour of Gatorland because we both enjoyed watching the animals (especially the monkeys). As we got in the car and began the drive back to my room at Bolton's Motel, she started saying things that absolutely astonished me. It was as though she had picked up the wrong script, a script for another play rather than the one we were in. She was talking about our *wedding*.

"Darling, have you made up your mind about who your best man is going to be?" she asked me.

"Uh . . . uh . . . my *best man?*" I gulped.

"Y'know, Gordean is probably my best friend and I was thinking about asking her to be my maid of honor. But my sister Pat is *really* like a best friend, *too*. Which one do you think I should ask, precious?"

"Uh, well . . . I . . . I don't know."

She went on and on about the wedding, as though it were a topic we had actually been discussing. I had *definitely* not asked this girl to marry me. I wanted to tell her so, but how, without crushing her? *She honestly thinks I've proposed to her,* I thought. *Somehow, I said something that she totally misconstrued and misunderstood.* It never crossed my mind at the time that she might be manipulating me.

The talk was incessant. It went on into the night and picked right back up the next day. Each word of it frightened me more—I was scared of getting married but *horrified* of breaking Sue's heart. So I just went with the flow and tried to rationalize it. Everyone gets married at some point, and I was twenty-three, so it was probably time for me to marry. My parents liked Sue, and I wanted to please them, especially my mother, after having put her through so much anguish over my affair with a married girl. Sue was pretty and sweet and adoring almost to the point of being worshipful.

But if she honestly thought I had proposed to her, didn't she think it was odd that she had received no ring? So that was my next step, the ring, which I bought for her that week. This is the true story of how I became, for the second time in my young life, a fiancé. But this wouldn't be a long, drawn-out tentative engagement like it had been with Gloria.

"Darling, we really *must* set a date, don't you agree?" This girl had no intention of letting me get away.

Big John thought it would be a good idea for everyone to take a few days off so I could get married. He said he had some business he needed to take care of anyway. So Sue and I set the date for July 20 at the church she had attended as a child, Wilkes Baptist Church in the Birmingham steel-mill suburb of Bessemer, Alabama. The only one in the band who made plans to attend my wedding was Ash. I told Don Pace and Stanley Cox they could toss a coin and see which one would be my best man; they did, and Pace won the honors.

I had been harassing Big John for some time about us becoming a recording band or going to Nashville or doing *anything* to keep from playing in nightclubs for the rest of our lives. I think to placate me, he told the rest of the band that I had some good songs and they should all pitch in and help me record some demos to send to Benny Joy in Nashville.

Benny Joy had been a local rockabilly hero in Tampa in 1957 and 1958. He and Big John had recorded together, then toured Europe together. Benny had since gone on to Nashville and made several unsuccessful records for Decca but by 1964 was having some success as a country songwriter. Another reason John wanted to help me demo my songs was that he and Benny had been talking about starting a publishing company. Benny had come to see us play two or three times. He was friendly but somewhat overbearing. Though only in his late twenties, he was such a nervous wreck that his entire *head* trembled. He was tall and thin, his skin was pale, and his features were batlike—big dark eyes, large ears, and a little pointy nose.

The Untouchables weren't quite as proficient as a recording band as they were live, but they worked hard, spending an entire day backing up my vocals, helping me cut some pretty good demos. One of the songs, "I'm Still In Love With Us," I had written a few months before, and I don't remember if it was about Billie or Gloria. Another one, "I Knew Her When" was about a pretty girl who drove down to the river and committed suicide.

I sent the demos to Benny. He wrote a long letter, informing me that my melodies were "fairly good" but my lyrics were bad and needed a lot of work. He said he would have to rewrite them and become a collaborator before they would be presentable. I wrote him back and thanked him but didn't take him up on his offer to fix my broken songs.

Time marched on and the days turned over as I went about my business, growing more and more apprehensive as the wedding day drew closer.

And the band rocked on. We played "Sugar Shack," a big hit by Jimmy Gilmer and the Fireballs, the same Jimmy Gilmer who would become my friend in Nashville ten years later. We played Chubby Checker's "Limbo Rock" and watched the dancers contort and punish their bodies out on the floor. We played the new Beatles hit "A Hard Day's Night," with Big John playing in real time George Harrison's mechanically sped-up guitar solo.

About two months before the wedding date, I got an Air Mail Special Delivery letter from Sue. It read, in part: "I miss you darling. I need you with me. You are no longer a luxury to me but a necessity. I can not do without you and wouldn't even want to try. I love you so much. Less than two months and I'll be with you all the time. Won't that be wonderful?"

Actually, it made me very nervous. A couple of weeks later, during Sue's last visit to Orlando before the wedding, I suggested that we might give ourselves a little more time. She didn't seem to hear me. When I was a child, I had seen a movie titled "When Worlds Collide," an end-of-time tale about a rogue planet on a collision course with Earth. The threatening planet hung there ominously in the sky, each day growing a little bigger than the day before. That was my wedding day.

But life went on. One day, Ash, Ken, and I had been to a movie and were having a late-afternoon meal at the Florida Diner. Ash looked out the window and yelled, "Hey, Bob, there's a guy out there going through your car." People weren't as apt to lock their vehicles in those days. As we ran toward my car, the burglar bolted, dropping a handful of items he had gotten from my glove compartment. He was a tall guy, about twenty, had a reddish-orange flattop. We set out after him on foot in hot pursuit. After a block we started gaining on him, and Ash finally grabbed his arm, slowing him down enough for Ken and me to tackle him. Ken started beating him unmercifully.

"Hey, Ken," said Ash, the future Miami detective, "no need to *kill* the guy, let's just take him to a phone booth and call the cops."

A typical Central Florida early summer thunderstorm was about to unleash its fury, and I wasn't in the mood to hang around, so we let the guy go. Besides, no judge would have sentenced him to anything as bad as what we had already put him through.   As I climbed into my Oldsmobile, there were violent flashes of white hot lightning with the sound of big booming thunder all around, then hissing torrents of rain, the kind of rain that makes you sit in your car a few minutes before turning on the ignition.

When the sky cleared, I could almost see the planet Marriage looming larger than ever in the sky. I thought, *Shouldn't I know my bride as well as I know Gloria?* I asked myself, *Shouldn't I be as crazy about my bride as I was about Billie?*

"Mom, I'm really having some serious doubts about marrying Sue," I confessed in a reflective conversation.

"Well, honey, if you're having doubts, you'd better speak up soon," she said.

I had talked to Gloria on the phone. She was now twenty and had matured considerably. As though she had not already endured enough family tragedy, fate came back around and did it again. Her father had recently died of a heart attack, then her only remaining brother, Glen, the one who reminded me of Humphrey Bogart, was killed in a car wreck on his way from Kentucky to Florida for the funeral. Of the seven Gelders, only three remained; Gloria, Mrs. Gelder, and Gloria's sister Nora. When I had driven down to Polk City for Mr. Gelder's funeral, Gloria asked me to please call her, so I did.

I told her I was on the fence, trying to decide whether or not to back out of the wedding. I got the feeling that Gloria didn't want me to get married, and she even talked about the possibility of us having a reconciliation, but she wasn't begging me *not* to get married either. I was under the impression that she was seriously involved with Jeff Richards, the guy her mother had chased with a baseball bat. I felt that if I decided to call off the marriage to Sue, Gloria would then have to decide between Jeff and me, and I could end up without Sue *or* Gloria in my life. I didn't know *what* to do, and Gloria wasn't much help. As June gave way to July, there was a fear that I could actually feel in the pit of my stomach.

More than eight hundred miles to the north, men much older and wiser than I had been struggling with problems that were much more serious and important than the minutia that Bobby Braddock was agonizing over in Orlando, Florida. The land of the free hadn't really been that, not for *all* Americans, but that was about to change. On July 2, President Lyndon B. Johnson signed into law the Civil Rights Act of 1964. There were two major factors that had brought about this day of justice. The Birmingham church bombing that killed four little black girls had so enraged all African Americans and most white Americans that President Kennedy, after dragging his feet on civil rights legislation during the earlier part of his term, had fully committed himself to the cause. Then, after Kennedy's assassination, LBJ picked up the battle flag and cried, "Let us continue," using his legislative skills and the reservoir of sympathy for JFK to overcome Southern opposition to the bill.

Overnight, the old theory that the government couldn't force people to do the right thing was proven wrong. The old myths had been dispelled. In the Florida Panhandle, black travelers no longer had to relieve themselves in the piney woods; they could use a filling station restroom; *it was the law.* In movie houses throughout Florida and the rest of the South, blacks no longer had to sit upstairs in the balcony looking down at the screen because now they could sit anywhere they wanted to; *it was the law.* In Orlando, the Sundown restaurant, where we ate our supper almost every evening, could no longer refuse to serve black customers; *it was the law.*

When an ebony-skinned teenager integrated the public beach on Lake Ariana in Auburndale, a Ku Klux Klansman drove by and shot him, seriously wounding him in the shoulder and arm. White teenage swimmers pulled the young man from the water, carried him to a car, and rushed him to the Winter Haven Hospital. Bob Dylan could have been marching through the middle of Auburndale singing his just-released "The Times They Are A-Changin.' "

Just a few days before the date that had been printed on the wedding invitations and in the Birmingham and Polk County newspapers, I called up Gloria and we agreed to meet not very far from the Gelder house. It was a pleasantly warm afternoon, not unbearably hot and humid, as it usually was in Florida in July. Gloria looked very pretty, her once frizzy hair glamorously styled, her slender body well tanned and attractively freckled, her nice green eyes misty as she smiled and touched me gently. We went hand in hand from her car through some piney woods and walked into a clearing. We held each other tighter than we had ever held each other before, and it got very emotional. I had made my decision, but it brought me no relief. As she got into her car and I got into mine, and we drove away from each other, I was hurting very badly and would for a long time.

The first time I ever met any of my future in-laws was the day before the wedding. Sue's widowed mother Louise was a pleasant but shy lady with hair dyed jet black. Louise's side of the family, mountain folk from the northeastern corner of Alabama, were sparsely represented at the matrimonial brouhaha. The paternal side, the Rhodes family, were what you might call middle-class, cleaned-up blue-collar people, raised around the Birmingham area. Two of Sue's uncles worked in the steel mills—I think one was a foreman—and a third uncle, her favorite, was a school teacher and perennial student. Her grandmother, Mama Rhodes, whom Sue disliked "because of the way she treated my mother," was the glad-to-be matriarch of the clan— my mother would years later recall hearing Mama Rhodes say on that day, "I sure hope Sue makes Bobby a good wife," and wonder why she said that. Sue's pretty brunette sister Pat was the maid of honor. Pat's four-year-old daughter Cheryl, was the flower girl and disliked me because I was taking her Aunt Sue away from her.

No one from the band was at the wedding; Ash had sent his regrets, asking me if I was ever going to get organized and ribbing me about how sorry he felt for Sue. Don Pace was my best man. My ushers were my brother, my half-brother-in-law, plus a couple of friends of Sue's family whom I had never seen before and haven't seen since. Mom was smiling her biggest smile and Dad seemed a bit confused, definitely being the oldest of the white dinner-jacket brigade.

When a very bad organist attempted the wedding march, Pace got me back for laughing at *his* wedding. The minister who read our vows was one of the most cheerless, long-faced men I'd ever met. What do you say of brides, that they're beautiful and radiant? Sue was all of that. Approximately six months after first meeting and after spending a total of perhaps five weekends together, Sue and I were united in marriage.

We left Birmingham for Orlando the next morning. Don and Lois Pace, who had ridden up to Birmingham with me, were driving Sue's black Volkswagen back to Florida. The first argument of our marriage occurred five minutes after I'd started the car, and it was over some criticism she had made of Don and Lois. The second argument happened about twenty minutes later when I pulled up in front of a café and she informed me that her daddy had always told her to never set foot inside a restaurant that had an Alabama State Liquor License in the window. The third argument took place at a filling station in North Florida because I wanted to buy a caged baby wildcat that was for sale. We had our fourth argument when we arrived at the little house I had rented for us on West Kaley Avenue in Orlando; she didn't like Big John leaving some of his music equipment in the living room. And the final argument of the day was about the house itself; although I had sent her an envelope full of pictures, she said it was smaller than she had realized and she didn't want to live there. Other than that, we'd had a damned good day.

There was a larger, more expensive rental house a few doors down, so the next day I inquired about it. The elderly owner was happy to have us as tenants. He said it was his policy to rent only to Southerners. The Civil Rights Act protected African Americans, but I'm not sure if there was anything written into the bill about discrimination against Yankees.

We had a couple of days to "honeymoon" so we went to Daytona Beach, which was an hour's drive from Orlando. We checked into an oceanfront cottage in the late afternoon. The next morning, something amazing happened. If Sue had not been with me to witness it, I might have thought that I had dreamed it. We were sitting in front of the cottages where we were staying, relaxing in lounge chairs next to the wooden steps that led down to the beach, enjoying surf, sun, and seagulls. My eyes had been closed, and when I opened them up I was looking straight ahead at the ocean. The tide was high, so the water's edge was no more than 120 feet away. I did a double take, scarcely believing what I was seeing.

"Oh, my God, it's Gloria," I muttered. What were the odds of Gloria and me being at this exact spot at the same time? But there she was, at the edge of the water. Then she saw me and let out a muffled cry. The young man with her was probably Jeff Richards—I couldn't tell because the one time I had met him, we had been outdoors at night. Gloria was visibly upset and appeared to be crying. The guy seemed to be trying to comfort her. Sue recognized her from pictures she had seen. I immediately got up to go back to the cottage. We followed the little sidewalk as the sea breeze rustled the palm fronds and blew gently on our backs.

"What kind of a stupid little dramatic act was *that?*" scoffed Sue. I was wondering the same thing. But Gloria stayed on my mind the rest of that day and haunted me that night as I lay awake listening to the sad moaning and sighing of the ocean that had been there long before I was born and would be there long after I was gone. I missed Gloria a lot and was very unhappy.

The Untouchables started back up at the El Patio, and Sue was able to get a job transfer with Southern Bell, from Birmingham to Orlando, so we were both working. We were getting along okay until the night she went with me to the El Patio. Band wives were allowed to come to the El Patio only on designated nights, usually a Saturday. Big John had undoubtedly made this rule for Ken's benefit, since

John didn't run around on his wife, I was newly married, and Ash and Tony were single. So Sue sat with John's wife Dot, and when we got home, she began raising hell. Sometime during the course of the night, someone had told her that Gloria was still wearing the engagement ring I had given her four years before. Sue insisted that I call her up and tell her she had to give it back to me. The more I tried to talk her out of it, the more determined she was that I call Gloria, from our house, with her listening in on the extension. I hated it, but I did it.

I tried to be nice enough that I didn't hurt Gloria's feelings but not so nice that I made Sue angry at me. Gloria was polite but firm in refusing to give the ring back. Every day for three days, Sue insisted that I call, and I did, but to no avail.

"Bobby, precious, I've got you a nice cold grape juice, darling," Sue cooed over the extension for Gloria's benefit, apparently trying to rub in the married bliss. Gloria said she didn't really believe that *I* was the one who wanted her to give the ring back. Sue got huffy and said, "He *most* certainly *does* want you to give the ring back! *Don't* you, precious!?"

I mumbled a *yeah*, but I think both of them knew better.

Sue continued to give me a hard time for several days, and I finally agreed to call Gloria once more, with the same result, she wasn't budging. Then at the beginning of the next week, there was a knock on our door. It was Gloria and her brother-in-law Dean Haywood (Nora's husband), a tall Texan air force master sergeant, stationed at McCoy Air Base. I was sympathetic to Gloria, but I thought Dean's attitude was condescending and arrogant.

"First of all, the phone calls need to be terminated," he said, as though he were issuing orders to recently recruited airmen. Sue was already huffing and puffing, like the bull spotting the matador's red cape.

Gloria pulled out a letter. "The main reason I'm here is because I just got something in the mail that I think you should see," she said, looking first at Sue and then at me.

She had written Ann Landers, the syndicated advice columnist, and had received a reply. Ann Landers had said, essentially, that the ring was a gift from me to Gloria and she didn't have to give it back if she didn't want to.

"See there," Gloria said, showing Sue the letter, "Ann Landers says . . ."

Suddenly, Sue let out a loud piercing shriek as she lunged forward onto the porch and kicked Gloria between the legs. Gloria screamed in pain, as Dean and I restrained Sue, who was still in full attack mode. I held a struggling, kicking Sue's arms behind her as Dean led a sobbing Gloria away to his car. He looked back at me and said, "You've got a serious emotional problem on your hands there."

"Gloria, why did you have to come here like this?" I yelled after her.

I got in my car and drove until I found a phone booth. When I thought Dean and Gloria had had enough time to get back to the Haywood house, which was a few miles outside the city, I called and asked to speak to Gloria. I apologized effusively and asked if she was all right. She said she thought so and told me she wasn't mad at me. I told her I wasn't mad at her, and also told her I was miserable with Sue.

"Oh, Bobby, I really hoped you would be happy," she said, with almost convincing sincerity.

That night, when I got home from the El Patio, I was drunk. It was like Mr. Flame walking in to see Mrs. Dynamite. I told Sue what a horrible thing I thought she had done to Gloria. She yelled words at me that she didn't learn at Wilkes Baptist Church in Bessemer, Alabama. The previous Friday, while she was at work, I had stumbled across a couple of her old high school annuals, in which she was pictured as a brunette. I certainly didn't mind the black hair, but I didn't like the deceit. So after a few minutes of her verbal tirade, I said, "Shut up, you black-haired bitch." She slapped me so hard that I saw sparks and flashes. I was so enraged that I kicked out the living room window; glass flew everywhere. I then left the house to cool off. Even in my intoxicated condition, I knew that Sue and I were sitting on top of a nuclear arsenal and something had to be done. What kind of a *failure* would I consider myself to be if my marriage didn't even last a month? And this marriage was just about at the point of being over, there was no doubt about that. I walked up and down West Kaley Avenue until I felt certain she was asleep, then I went home and slept a couple of hours on the couch.

The first thing the next morning, I went out and found someone to replace the glass in the window. Then after a little more sleep, I took a shower and waited around until Sue got home from work. She wouldn't even look at me, much less talk to me.

"Do you want to move to Nashville?" I asked her.

It was as though I had asked her, "Do you want a million dollars and a new Jaguar?" I probably could have asked, "Do you want to move to Kansas City?" or "Do you want to move to Houston?" and gotten the same reaction. She wanted us to get away from Gloria. No discussion of the ring was needed, no rehashing of the incident or the fight was necessary. The other Sue walked out the door and the sweet Sue walked in and stood in her place. We sat down on the couch together.

"Just give me a few days, and I'll give Big John my notice," I said, "when we go to Cocoa Beach." John had us booked into an ocean-front club called the Vanguard, near the Kennedy Space Center. We were closing out at the El Patio the coming weekend and would start at the Vanguard two days after that. I didn't want to hit John with this news until we were situated at the beach.

"Okay, darling," she said softly, as she smiled at me.

"It's only fair that I promise to stay with the band until he has a good replacement and I'll have to help him break the guy in."

Her smile disappeared, "How long do you think that'll take?"

"I can't say, but I'll start the process as soon as we go to Cocoa. I'm promising you that we're going to move to Nashville, okay? I've always wanted to do this. The folks gave us a thousand dollars for a wedding present. And I know I can get a job playing piano *somewhere* up there. Please just be patient. I promise you, we're going."

She took my hand and said, "I just know you're going to do so good in Nashville."

Sue wanted to go to Oz to get a brand-new start. I wanted the wizard to give me a golden pen. A bond was formed, and the war was over.

In 1950, as the government was in the process of setting up a rocket-testing site on Cape Canaveral, the population of Brevard County, Florida, was 23,653. Many of the people made their living directly or indirectly from citrus and vegetable farming; the beaches were nice but largely undeveloped and undiscovered. By 1964, the population had increased sevenfold to around 160,000, a dramatic growth rate rarely seen at any time in any place. The business of space exploration and the technology that accompanied it had brought legions of workers, white collar and blue collar, from all over the South and other parts of America as well. Many aeronautic-industry people from California had relocated there. Some of the best scientific minds in the world had moved to the cape. Cocoa Beach, where our new band venue was located, had the springing-up-overnight feel of what Miami must have been like six decades earlier, or some of the boom towns in the Old West; you could see it building up around you. The sound of jackhammers and electric saws was everywhere, and little buildings-in-progress dotted the landscape.

The Vanguard was a pretty decent oceanfront motel, named for the early space vehicles that had been launched from the cape. Big John had us booked into the lounge, a big room that opened out onto the beach; it was a very popular night spot in the area. He had an arrangement with Eleanor at the El Patio. She would hire bands at her club for only four-week stints; that way the Untouchables would have the option of either renewing at the Vanguard or going back to Orlando to play. It was time for me to tell John that I had plans to leave. He wasn't happy, but he tried to be philosophical.

"Well, man, I hate it, but I can't blame you. I know you've always wanted to go to Nashville. But this is really going to put us in a bind, y'know."

"L-like I say, John, I won't leave until you've found a replacement you're totally happy with."

"I know, Bob, and I appreciate it, buddy, but it's gonna be rough," he half-laughed, with white teeth clenched and blue eyes open wide.

We had what Atlanta Rhythm Section's Robert Nix would tell me many years later was the best band of its kind he had ever heard. Our business was to sound as much like the records as possible. Some of the songs, after we'd played them a long time, would go through a metamorphosis and start rocking a lot harder and be better for dancing, especially the Jimmy Reed blues numbers. After several incarnations, the Untouchables had finally become the sound machine Big John wanted.

Big John was a great guitarist (and harmonica player and background singer, and he was even a good fiddler). John could have become world-famous as a musician or highly successful as a record producer had he ever been willing to be a small fish in a big pond, instead of a big fish in a small pond, long enough to make that trip to the top, which requires equal parts faith and patience.

Ash was as solid and reliable a drummer as I've ever seen; there were no surprises with Ash, and he was perfect for our sound. Same with Tony, solid on the bass, never tentative, and a first-rate singer as well. I won't say I was good, but I had the equipment, and I had a lot of parts to perform and I knew them all. Finally, Ken Ashburn, who was a great mimic, could sing like practically anybody, and he was a handsome guy whose easygoing manner on stage was an essential part of us being so popular. Ken, John, and Tony *never* looked corny doing their choreography on stage—they looked like they were just rockin' and having a great time, which they were. John even had me doing it when I was standing up and playing. We were the perfect band Big John had dreamed of having, and I was about to screw it up.

It was at least an hour's drive from Orlando almost due east to the coast and Cocoa Beach. Since this was just a four-week gig and Sue had her job with Southern Bell in Orlando, she needed to stay there. I didn't want her to be there alone, so I elected to do the long nightly commute.

It wasn't certain that we would be able to open at the Vanguard on schedule. Hurricane Dora was churning around out in the Atlantic and was expected to hit land around the cape and travel across the peninsula right into Orlando. I went to a hardware store and bought a hurricane lamp for our home on West Kaley Avenue. I was getting that little hurricane rush and experiencing fond Lake Stella memories, recalling my brother and me making a hut from the big glider cushions that we had to bring inside the house as the giant winds howled outside, remembering the sting of the horizontal rain with Gloria as we witnessed Hurricane Donna's awesome performance from the screened porch. Dora, however, moved on up the coast and made landfall around Jacksonville, missing the central part of the state. So we opened as planned, and the band was an immediate hit.

But there was another storm in the making around Cocoa Beach. John had auditioned a couple of keyboard players who were working in the area but was dissatisfied with them both. A bitterness seemed to have set in. I had my agenda, and John had his. His agenda was the band. I was leaving the band, and he was becoming angry with me. Ken, always taking his cue from John, had become angry with me, too.

The biggest music event on the Space Coast was the Sunday afternoon jam session at the Vanguard. Being the house band, we were the featured group, but other area bands would play during our breaks. The lounge was packed solid, and with the big glass doors slid back, we could see a huge crowd on the beach, dancing to the music that was piped through the outside speakers.

Because I was leaving the band, John had turned my song selection duties over to Ken. It was now Ken's job to choose each song we would do and call it out to the band. A hostile Ken turned to me to announce the next number.

"Balixmmpphss," he mumbled in a low voice. I couldn't possibly have known that the song was "Baby Let's Play House."

"Ken, I can't hear you," I said.

"BALIXMMPPHSS," he yelled.

"Ken, all you're doing in *mumbling louder*. What's the song?"

He glared at me. "Boy, when we through playin' this afternoon, I'm gonna *whip yo ass!*" he jeered hatefully.

Ash had already counted the song off when I flew into Ken. We hit the floor together and disconnected Big John's guitar cord from his amplifier. John was hitting the guitar strings but no sound was coming out, Ken and I were rolling around on the floor, and Ash was laughing, banging the snare louder than ever, yelling, "Hey, Bob, hit him once for me!" I was told that Big John's white teeth were clenched together and his big wide-open blue eyes were filled with terror.

"It's all a part of the show, folks," John yelled unconvincingly into the mic.

The crowd was gathered around the stage, some of them cheering us on and some of them standing with their mouths open in disbelief. The club owner, the bouncers, and Big John pulled us apart.

As I mentioned earlier, I saw Big John get drunk only twice; the first time was the night I untuned my piano and made the band sound terrible. This was the second time. He got so drunk that he tore the door off his motel room. Ken sported a black eye for the rest of the week and wouldn't speak to me.

The Untouchables had split into factions, Big John and Ken versus Ash and me, with Tony playing the role I had once played, the guy who got along with everybody. Four decades later, Tony recalled the big onstage fight and said, "Man, I was so embarrassed I just wanted to crawl through the floor."

Because of some dispute John was having with the club owner, we weren't going to play the full four weeks, only three. After the big fight, John told the other guys that the group would temporarily disband when we finished our Vanguard stint, until he found a good keyboard player. I think John and Ken were too angry to even work with me until a replacement could be found. One more week, and that would be it.

The day after the fight, I took Sue to a doctor in Orlando. When I picked her up, she got into the car wearing a big smile and said, "Hi *Daddy.*"

Sue was having morning sickness and had just quit her job with

Southern Bell. There was a customer at the Vanguard who had told me he owned some new rental units in Cocoa Beach and would gladly rent me one, short term. I called the man and told him that if it was okay, we would occupy the apartment immediately. At the end of the week, I would get a trailer and load up my keyboard equipment, then go to Orlando, where we would pack up everything from our rental house.

So we settled into a unit in the three-story aqua-blue concrete block apartment building. Sue was sick most of the time we were there. I was not much of a cook, but luckily the only thing she had an appetite for was cornbread, so I got pretty good at fixing instant cornbread. She didn't venture out very much. Big John saw her once and was not very friendly; I think he thought that she had talked me into leaving the band and going to Nashville.

The apartment building was about three hundred feet from the ocean, and the only thing separating us from the beach was grass and scrub, palmettos and sea oats. One day Sue was feeling a little better and said she felt up to going down to the beach. When we were out in the water, I thought I'd play a little joke on her.

"I love my wedding ring," I said as I held the gold band up in front of me, standing in water up to my chest.

"I'm glad you do, darling, but please be careful that you don't drop it."

My plan was to let a big wave knock me over and come back up sputtering that I had lost the ring, all the while wearing it on one of my toes, held securely in place by tightly flexing the two neighbor toes. The wave came along and I let it knock me over, popping back up, shouting, "Oh no, I *lost* it!" with the band safely and snugly ensconced on my index toe. Before she had time to react, another bigger wave came along and hit me by surprise, this time *really* throwing me to the ocean floor and knocking the ring off my toe. We spent two hours diving and combing the ocean floor but never found it.

On a warm sunny day in mid-September, we pulled out of Cocoa Beach with a U-Haul trailer hitched to my Oldsmobile. Ash and Tony had helped me load up my equipment. Big John and Ken were nice enough to shake my hand and wish me good luck, but the band was breaking up because of my departure, and I was not leaving on good terms. If I had known then just how quickly the hard feelings would dissipate, I would have been driving away a much happier man. Big John had taught me things that would help me for the rest of my life and had brought out things in me musically that I didn't even know were there. I hated there being any hard feelings.

For just a few moments, let's leave undisturbed this tranquil Florida scene from September of '64—an Oldsmobile zipping along with a U-Haul trailer in tow, I behind the wheel and lost in my thoughts, a napping Sue curled up beside me, the Brahma bulls and piney woods and cypress marshes flying by the window. Let's take a quantum leap to Auburndale over three decades later, on a pleasantly cool day in early February 1995. I walked up to Big John Taylor's homey white stucco house, overlooking Ariana Boulevard and the big Lake Ariana. This is where John and Dot had been living most of their married life—all those years after the band breakup, all those years that John had served as Assistant City Manager of Auburndale—and where they had anchored a close-knit family.

The Untouchables never regrouped after I left. Ken and Tony put a band in at the El Patio for a while. John continued doing the music part-time for a few years, some of it with Tony around Polk County. Then, after leaving the music alone for a very long time, John took it up again after he became a born-again Christian and organized a band at his church.

I was at John's house on February 5, 1995, to attend the Untouchables reunion that I had *thought* about putting together for years but had never gotten around to until this day. Time was no longer on our side. John, who had struggled with diabetes and heart disease for several years, had recently been diagnosed with advanced terminal cancer. The big, highly energized man had become, at fifty-eight, gaunt and pale, which, along with his gray hair and glasses, made him look all of his years. He sat on the couch in pajamas and a robe, and though he was weak and tired, he seemed happy, happy to see all of us.

Tony couldn't make it because his father was seriously ill in a Jacksonville hospital, so that meant I was once again the baby of the band, two months younger than Ash, both of us fifty-four. Ash's usual dry sense of humor was intact ("Are you still trying to get organized? Thaaaas right!"), and he had been living with a transplanted heart for several years, finally retiring from the Miami Police Department just a few months earlier. Skinny Ash had become extremely obese and had less than two years left to live. Ken was looking good, had grown a mustache, and was all smiles. We had a big laugh about our infamous fight on the stage at the Vanguard.

There were also a couple of guys from the original Untouchables. Gene Watson, who was in the group when I first played the El Patio in the summer of 1962, was a professor in California and had a flask of whiskey in his briefcase. John York, the original piano player, had spent his adult life working for the railroad.

Big John was so tired that he had to go back to bed for a while. Dot brought out a delicious lunch. She said she had faith that God would heal John's cancer. Their son and three daughters, ranging from mid-twenties to early thirties, were all upbeat and positive. Before we left, John came back out. His son, Jay, a good-looking and personable young attorney, was carrying a stack of plaques that John had gotten for us. Of all the many awards on my "ego walls," none means more to me than the one that reads:

BIG JOHN'S UNTOUCHABLES
BOBBY BRADDOCK
IN APPRECIATION FOR THE MANY
HITS PERFORMED DURING THE
GRAND OLE ROCK & ROLL YEARS.
FEBRUARY 5, 1995

A few weeks later, I talked with John on the phone for the last time. His voice was very weak, and he said he was ready to do whatever God wanted him to do. I mentioned the El Patio and he said those were some great times.

When I was growing up in Auburndale, guys might have kissed their daddies or their granddaddies on the mouth, but they didn't hug their male buddies, and they didn't tell other guys that they loved them. I picked that up in Nashville in the music business, but I don't think people of my generation who live in small Southern towns generally do that sort of thing. And John in particular was not a touchy-feely type person. But when I closed the conversation, I said, "Well, I love you."

"I love you, too," he said in a weak voice.

The Brahma bulls and the piney woods and the cypress marshes were flying by the windows as Sue woke up from her nap.

"Are you feelin' okay?" I asked her.

"Of course I am, we're goin' to *Nashul*," she said, assigning Nashville one of her silly little names that she liked to bestow on people and places. Any regrets I had, any other girls I had been missing or longing for, all of that was history. This woman was carrying my child.

In Orlando, we loaded the car and trailer with all our possessions, then went to Auburndale to spend the night with my parents before going to the new land, the new world.

"Bobby, you're going to beee a lo-o-ong way from home," Dad said the next morning, as we stood around in the Braddock backyard saying our good-byes.

"Now, don't expect us to come visiting you in the *winter*," Mom joked.

"Oh, we'll be down *here* in the winter," Sue laughed. Sue was probably the only person in the world, besides me, who thought I should be pursuing a music career in Nashville.

As I headed the car and trailer out the long dirt driveway, we turned around to wave one more good-bye.

Dad stood there, a bit humped over and frail, waving good-bye with the tops of his fingers, like a little boy. Though he would soon become an invalid, his breathing body would be around for another seven years.

I looked at the house where I had spent most of my life, this fine old odd-shaped one-of-a-kind stucco house. It would fall victim to a tornado in nine years.

Mom was wearing a teary smile, raising the intensity of her smile and her tears as she waved a vigorous good-bye and blew us a kiss. She would be around for another thirty-three years.

We were on our way to Music City at last. We turned left at the key lime tree and headed toward the big lake. We drove around Lake Ariana to the Polk City Road, where we breezed along for miles past orange and grapefruit groves, heading north past Polk City and through the desolate cattle country and the Green Swamp in the northern part of the county.

Good-bye, Polk County! I would never live there again. I look back from another century at a place and a time that are long gone. To the old Orburndale and Polk County prejudices and racist attitudes that were so much a part of me then, I say, "Good riddance." Much of that has disappeared around there, not only with the influx of so many Northerners, but in the changed attitude of white Southerners as well. But I mourn the loss of the rural and small-town neighborliness of 1964, the orange groves and cattle ranges that are being replaced by condos, housing developments, and shopping malls. I miss the slow pace and the light traffic.

We drove up through Lake County, which would become Orlando's suburbs by the twenty-first century. But on that day in early autumn of 1964, we looked out at the great expanse of grove-covered hills and little blue lakes that touched the horizon in every direction. We continued northward, up through the horse country Ocala, then into the flatlands and tobacco country of North Florida and South Georgia, talking all the way about our hopes and dreams, occasionally listening to country music on the radio. When I turned left on Highway 84, heading west toward Alabama and U.S. 31, Sue slid down into her seat a little. Even with sunglasses, the sun was a bit hard on the eyes. We both became quiet. I turned off the radio.

We were getting along well, both enthusiastic about our great adventure, our exciting journey into the unknown. The child she would give birth to was a boy and would live only eight weeks before succumbing to Sudden Infant Death Syndrome. Sue and I, away from our familiar environs in a world full of strangers, would become quite close before becoming totally estranged, and she would give me a gift that would ever be my greatest blessing, a wonderful daughter. As we drove through the Georgia afternoon, we didn't know, just as none of us ever know for sure, about the future. At the moment, everything seemed in harmony. As the motor softly hummed and as we glided into the Georgia sun, a railroad track paralleled the highway, and a long train rolled along beside us, slowly leaving us behind. The train, the Georgia sun, made me think of another trip, long, long before.

I was a very small boy, looking across the aisle and out the window of a train, at an egg yolk of a sun levitating above the Georgia horizon as we headed north. A tall young man in an army uniform, one of the many young men on the train on their way to and from the battles in foreign lands and seas, had just offered my father a drink of whiskey.

"No-o-o, thanks, soldier, I just can't keep that stuff on my stomach anymooore," he said, then telling the GI how he had bought a lot of war bonds and had encouraged everyone he knew to do the same.

We were taking a train trip to visit my mother's sister who lived in North Georgia. Gas rationing in World War II made it necessary to be very selective about car travel. I was sitting in a coach next to my mother, with Daddy and Paulie in the seats behind us. We had just purchased sandwiches from a porter who said he would bring around some pillows in an hour or so.

"Are those mountains?" I asked, pointing out the window.

"No, honey," Mother said with a big smile, "those are just pine trees on a hill. We'll see mountains at Aunt Ruth's. We can climb the mountains around their house. They live up real close to Tennessee."

I didn't hear the place as Tennes-see, I heard it as Tennes-sea. "Are there. . . are there ten *oceans* there?" I asked.

Daddy laughed big from behind me and reached around the back of my seat to hug me. "No-o-o, darling, there aren't any *oceans* in Tennessee. But there are big *mountains* theah. Aunt Ruth and Uncle Dick will drive us up to a place called Lookout Mountainnnn."

When the porter brought our pillows, I cozied up to mine, listening to the clickity-clacking rumble of the train, thinking about what an exciting time I was going to have. I could hardly wait to climb those mountains.

"We're gonna live in Tennessee, Daddy," Sue said, breaking the silence. Since finding out she was pregnant, she had started calling me *Daddy*. The sun was sliding down into the horizon up ahead.

"Mom said she was gonna start calling us her little hillbillies," I laughed.

"Well, maybe the *Beverly* Hillbillies. You're gonna make us a lotta *money*, Daddy," she said confidently.

"I don't know about a *lot* of money," I shrugged. "And it won't be easy. It'll be like an obstacle course up there. But I'm sure ready to give it a try."

Sue eased back down in her seat. As the sun set on the road to Nashville, I smiled, feeling good about the journey we had decided to take. I could hardly wait to climb those mountains.